ABSTRACTS OF THE COUNCIL OF SAFETY MINUTES

STATE OF
NEW JERSEY

1777-1778

Richard S. Hutchinson

HERITAGE BOOKS
2009

HERITAGE BOOKS
AN IMPRINT OF HERITAGE BOOKS, INC.

Books, CDs, and more—Worldwide

For our listing of thousands of titles see our website
at
www.HeritageBooks.com

Published 2009 by
HERITAGE BOOKS, INC.
Publishing Division
100 Railroad Ave. #104
Westminster, Maryland 21157

Copyright © 2005 Richard S. Hutchinson

Other books by the author:
Abstracts of the Council of Safety Minutes, State of New Jersey, 1777-1778
Burlington County, New Jersey Deed Abstracts: Books A, B and C
Middlesex County, New Jersey Deed Abstracts: Book 1
Monmouth County, New Jersey Deeds: Books A, B, C and D
Abstracts of the Deaths and Marriages in the Hightstown Gazette *[New Jersey], 18 April 1861–28 December 1871*
Abstracts of the Deaths and Marriages in the Hightstown Gazette *[New Jersey], 4 January 1872–27 December 1877*
Abstracts of the Deaths and Marriages in the Hightstown Gazette *[New Jersey], 3 January 1878–29 December 1881*
Abstracts of the Deaths and Marriages in the Hightstown Gazette *[New Jersey], 5 January 1882–31 December 1885*
Abstracts of the Deaths and Marriages in the Hightstown Gazette *[New Jersey], 7 January 1886–26 December 1889*
The Mercer County Genealogical Quarterly [New Jersey], Volumes 1-6
CD: The Mercer County Genealogical Quarterly [New Jersey], Volumes 1-6

All rights reserved. No part of this book may be reproduced or transmitted in any form or by any means, electronic or mechanical, including photocopying, recording or by any information storage and retrieval system without written permission from the author, except for the inclusion of brief quotations in a review.

International Standard Book Numbers
Paperbound: 978-0-7884-2505-9
Clothbound: 978-0-7884-8145-1

Introduction

Abstracts of the Council of Safety Minutes, State of New Jersey 1777-1778

In the 1760s when the British crown was in need of funds, they looked toward the American colonies as a source of revenue. In 1763, the British Parliament began considering a method of procuring this needed revenue from the colonies by proposing a Stamp Act. This proposal would raise revenue by taxing the imports from Britain to the colonies and also limit the trade between the colonies and other nations. After years of consideration, the British Parliament finally passed the Stamp Act in March 1765.

With the imposition of these taxes being universally opposed throughout the American colonies, and with the opposition to them continuing to grow, including the boycott of British goods which impacted businesses in England, the British Parliament in 1766 repealed the Stamp Act. However, whatever good resulted in the repeal of the Stamp Act, it mattered little in the colonies. The damage had already been done and the American colonies began their march toward independence and revolution.

The Assemblies of the colonies had become aroused, as had the general population. Massachusetts advocated the individual colonies come together by each colony forming a "committee of correspondence," along with other committees within the towns in order that all of the colonies could "readily" communicate with each other on any major issues.

In 1775, the Provincial Congress of New Jersey set about organizing a militia whose members would be required to sign their allegiance to defend the colony, and any neighboring colony, while obeying its officers under orders either from the Continental Congress, the Provincial Congress, or the "Committee of Safety." They also directed that each county organize a "Committee of Observation" to carry on and direct the business of the county and a "Committee of Correspondence" to maintain communications with the other counties and colonies. In October, they also appointed from within their own ranks, a "Committee of Safety." From time to time, all of these "committees" had their membership reconstituted.

The question is what was the "Committee of Safety" and what did it actually do?" They received their power from the Council and the General Assembly of the State of New Jersey, under an "Act for investing the Governor and a Council consisting of twelve, with certain powers ... for a limited Time." It was appointed to deal with matters concerning the defense of the country when the Provincial Congress was in recess. A Committee of Safety, which later became known as the "Council of Safety," was also being organized in the other colonies. In 1775, the New Jersey Provincial Congress appointed eleven members to be a "Committee of Safety"- Joseph Borden, Azariah

Dunham, Hendrick Fisher, Frederick Frelinghuysen, John Hart, Enos Kelsey, Isaac Pearson, Peter Schenck, Jonathan D. Sergeant, John Shurman and Samuel Tucker. In March of 1777, the state reorganized the "Committee of Safety" to become the "Council of Safety," which now consisted of twelve members, including "His Excellency the Governor, William Livingston," who acted as the "President" of the council.

In general, the function of the Council of Safety, which received their funding from the state treasury, was to protect the State of New Jersey from the enemy while providing the militia with whatever they needed in order to fight. They subpoenaed suspected disloyal persons, known as "disaffected persons" before them, called witnesses against them, questioned and examined them under oath, and transcribed their testimony. Depending upon the person's answers, they were either dismissed, required to obtain a surety and post a bond for their appearance before a court of law, or were simply sent to prison. In some cases, they were given a "choice" of either joining the new "Navy" or being sent directly to prison. All who appeared before the Council of Safety were required to either subscribe to certain Oaths to the State, or to Affirmations with the same effect in the case of Quakers. If the persons did so after being brought before them, they were released while those who refused the Oaths were sent to the Gaol. Those "disaffected persons" could be brought before the Council based upon the information of a neighbor or any suspicious activity, their having crossed into and/or come from the enemy lines, the selling of commodities for prices higher than that allowed by law, or charging more for an item than was allowed by law. The simple act of talking to another person and expressing your views in a negative fashion upon any subject could land you in front of the Council.

The Council was also charged with outfitting the New Jersey militia with clothing, food, flints, powder and ball, and bounty pay. From time to time, they paid for the care of wounded soldiers and helped with monetary aid to those women who were in distress and/or those made widows by the deaths of their husbands during battles. They developed and paid for the construction and the manning of warning "beacons" on the mountains in New Jersey, which were to be used to signal the enemy's movements. They had the power to execute the exchange of their Loyalist prisoners for their own men taken prisoner by the British raiding parties with the highest ranking members of the British Command.

All in all, the New Jersey Council of Safety wielded a tremendous amount of power and played an important role in the American Revolution. Due to this power and the powerful members of the State of New Jersey who sat on this Council, the members were always fearful of capture by the enemy. They moved from place to place secreting their lead, powder, flints and hard money and other commodities with various trusted people around the state. They traveled under armed guard while bringing with them by horse and wagon their papers and prisoners. They met seven days a week in patriot's homes, taverns, and many other places around the state.

Today, not all of the Council of Safety's records survive nor were all of their activities fully recorded. However, almost one hundred years later, the State of New

Jersey passed an Act on April 6, 1871, calling "for the better preservation of the early records of the State of New Jersey." In 1872, the state preserved the limited written record of the Council of Safety of 1777-1778. These records were printed in book form, by printer John H. Lyon of Jersey City, but told nothing about the Council of Safety nor contained an index of the names recorded in their record for those years.

Today, the researcher knows little of the New Jersey Council of Safety or the role that it played during the American Revolution. Although having been established in previous years, written minutes of the Council's meetings covering from March 18th, 1777 through October 8th, 1778, can be found recorded in five volumes numbered 1 through 5. However, this record ceases with no explanation on this later date and it would appear that the Council of Safety was apparently eliminated in October 1778.

This present work is an "abstraction" of the important proceedings found in the above mentioned five volumes of the records of the Council of Safety and has a complete index of all the individual names as were written therein. It should be noted that depending upon the "recording secretary" for the Council of Safety on any day, the names of persons recorded in these records were spelled phonetically in many different ways even though the records were referring to the same person. The indexed names in this work include the members of the Council attending a session, those individuals appearing before them, their sureties, their prisoners, the names of those imprisoned and/or who voluntarily went over to the "Enemy" in New York City, or who were forcibly removed from New Jersey and moved into the enemy's lines, including the names of their wives and children, when so indicated. It names those sent by the Council of Safety to General Washington for his decision upon their fate and also gives us the names of those persons securing the warning beacons, the lead, the flints, those making the bullets, the names of the millers, the coopers, and those of other professions. It includes the names of those paid for guarding the Council, some of the wounded soldiers and their doctors and/or wives and other care-givers when they are named.

The importance of this work is preservation of the names of those people who had the fortune or misfortune to appear before the Council of Safety. Those that had their names recorded in the record are now known. It is an untapped source for the genealogist working on New Jersey families, or on those persons who were New Jersey Loyalists or suspected of being Loyalists, and on those persons "banished" from New Jersey to New York. The record of the New Jersey Council of Safety is a little known but an important source for New Jersey history during the American Revolution.

Council of Safety, State of New Jersey

Volume 1

Members - John Cleves Symmes, William Paterson, Nathaniel Scudder, Theophilus Elmer, Silas Condict, John Hart, John Mehelm, Samuel Dick, John Combs, Caleb Camp, Edmund Wetherby, Benjamin Manning.

18 March 1777 – [Tuesday]. "Pursuant to the Power and Authority given, in and by an Act of the Council and General Assembly of the State of New Jersey, entitled 'An Act for investing the Governor and a Council consisting of twelve, with certain powers therein mentioned for a limited time,' The Governor and Council of Safety met;" Present: His Excellency the Governor, Mr. Symmes, Mr. Paterson, Mr. Scudder, Mr. Hart, Mr. Mehelm, Mr. Dick, Mr. Combs, Mr. Camp, Mr. Manning. The Board was informed that Captain Walton brought six prisoners from Monmouth and it appeared that the six were taken in a boat from Philadelphia to New York...they were examined and it appeared that they belong to Pennsylvania. Walton was ordered to take them to Philadelphia and deliver them to the Council of Safety of Pennsylvania with the evidence to be examined. Board adjourned till 9 o'clock the next day.

19 March 1777 – [Wednesday]. Governor and Council of Safety met. Present - Governor, Symmes, Scudder, Hart, Dick, and Camp. The Board examined the prisoners sent to Haddonfield some time since by General Putnam. Prisoners Abraham Briton, Jonathan Forman and Robert Barns were examined, took and subscribed the Oaths of Abjuration and Allegiance...and were discharged, as were Jacob Rotor and Joseph Hornor. Anthony Woodward, son of William, being a Quaker, took Affirmations to the effect of the Oaths above mentioned, went into recognizance with David Hurley in 300 pounds each, for appearance in the court of Oyer and Terminer, County of Monmouth, to be of good behavior, and was dismissed. Moses Ivins acknowledged he gave 500 pounds previously for his good behavior, entered into recognizance with Abraham Britton in 300 pounds each, and was dismissed. Board adjourned till 3 o'clock.

Met pursuant to adjournment. Isaac Rogers, Abner Rogers, John Coperthwaite, William Emley Junr., Samuel Emley, Bickley Steward, and Richard Huntley of Upper Freehold, and George Brewer of Shrewsbury were examined and they declared they were Quakers, adverse to bearing arms but they were willing to take the Affirmations to the State, which they did and were discharged. Ordered that prisoners lately brought from Frederick Town, Maryland, and lodged in the Gaol of Salem County, be brought under guard to Bordentown, to be there as soon as possible, and that Coll. Dick to detach as many of the Militia of his Battalion to carry out the order. Captain Elisha Walton was paid for a guard and six prisoners belonging to Pennsylvania, which were taken from Haddonfield to Philadelphia, on the 18th and 19th. Board adjourned until the 26th instant to meet at Bordentown.

26 March 1777 – [Wednesday]. Bordentown - The Board met. Present - Governor, Symmes, Hart, and Manning. There not being a quorum, they adjourned till tomorrow.

27 March 1777 – [Thursday]. The Board met. Present - Governor, Symmes, Scudder, Hart, Manning. There not being a quorum, they adjourned till tomorrow.

28 March 1777 – [Friday]. The Board met. Present - Governor, Symmes, Scudder, Hart, Dick, Manning. Governor gave a letter from Israel Shreeve, Esqr., Colonel of the Second Battalion of Continental Troops, of New Jersey, by which Charles Axford, appointed Quarter Master, on February 4th last, has not joined and supposes that he declined...that on his arrival at Princeton, Benajah Osmun was appointed and pray that he may be continued. Board appointed Osmun as Quarter Master to the Second Battalion. Board adjourned till 9 o'clock tomorrow morning.

29 March 1777 – [Saturday]. The Board met. Present as before. They examined Thomas Groom, Morgan John, Joseph Groom and John Ashton, prisoners apprehended and suspected as being disaffected to the State and brought by Gen. Putnam. Adjourned till 3 o'clock this afternoon.

PM - The Board met. Morgan John and John Ashton were discharged after taking the Oaths of Abjuration & Allegiance. The Board examined Major Seabrook in reference to three prisoners, Benjamin Wilson, William Valentine, and John Jones, who were sent last March to Frederic, Maryland, but now returned to New Jersey. It appeared they went on board a vessel of the enemy in distress and without orders and without intent to assist the enemy or harm the State. They took the Oaths and were discharged. Mr. Paterson took his seat. Resolved that the Governor draw from the Treasurer, 300 pounds, in part of the sum of 1,000 pounds, which he is authorized to draw by the Act instituting the Council of Safety. The Board adjourned till Monday at 9 o'clock.

31 March 1777 – [Monday]. The Board met. Present- Governor, Symmes, Scudder, Paterson, Dick, Manning. Ordered that Thomas Watson, Esqr. be examined respecting his having taken protection from the enemy. Watson attended and was examined. Ordered that Capt. Arnold be directed to send two of his Light Horse to attend the Council of Safety. Ordered that John Pope and William Newbolt be subpoenaed as witnesses against Thomas Watson. The Board adjourned till 3 o'clock.

The Board met. Present as before. Ordered that John Lawrence, Esq., of Burlington, be desired to attend the Board. The witnesses against the prisoners didn't arrive and the Board adjourned till tomorrow.

1 April 1777 – [Tuesday]. The Board met. Present as before. John Butler was examined as a witness against Thomas Watson and his affidavit taken in writing. John Cox, Junr. examined in like manner. The Board adjourned till the afternoon.

The Board met. Present as before. William Newbolt and John Pope attended and were examined as witnesses against Thomas Watson. The Board adjourned till tomorrow.

2 April 1777 – [Wednesday]. The Board met. Present as before. Mr. Randolph and Mr. Savage were examined as witnesses against Joseph Salter. Ordered that Isaac Potter and Daniel Giggle be subpoenaed as witnesses against Joseph Salter. John Lawrence Esqr. Attended the Council and was examined and the Board adjourned till the afternoon.

The Board met. Present as before. The Governor presented a resolution of Congress, of January 14th, in reference to the payment and subsistence of the Continental Troops stationed in the State. The Board administered Oaths to the State. [No names mentioned.] Adjourned till tomorrow.

3 April 1777 – [Thursday]. The Board met. Present as before. The Governor presented to Council, a memorial from John Van Anglin setting forth that he is a Lt. in the 1st New Jersey Regiment during the War; that two junior officers in the regiment have been placed over his head, and asks that his case be heard and that his rank properly adjusted. Ordered that it be referred to the Council and Assembly in a joint meeting. Ordered that subpoenas be issued to Thomas Phar and Joseph Lawrence, Esqr. to appear before Council on Saturday next to bear testimony against John Lawrence, Jr. of Burlington. Ordered that subpoenas be issued to Abraham Hendricks, Peter Imlay and Mary Davison to appear before Council on Saturday next to bear testimony against John Lawrence, Sr. Testimonials from Gen. Dickinson and Gen. Heard certified that Doctor Hendry had served as Surgeon to a brigade of militia and acted as Director and Superintendent of a hospital, and recommended that he be compensated for his services. Read and referred to Congress. Adjourned till afternoon.

Met according to adjournment. A letter was read from General Heard in reference to the Battalion of Col. Beavers, in Hunterdon, and such persons as had taken Protections and refused to deliver them; and also certain disaffected persons in Sussex, who were enlisting men for the enemy. Agreed, that the Governor write to Col. Beavers and desire him to convene the companies of the Battalion to elect officers. Agreed, that such Magistrates in Somerset, who live nearest Gen. Heard be written to and asked to convene before them such persons who have taken Protections and to give them the Oaths of abjuration and allegiance. Agreed, that Gen. Heard be directed to detach a file of men to apprehend the persons referred to in his letter and to take them, to consult certain persons in Sussex County, who will give the necessary aid and assistance. Garrat Covenhoven, Thomas Wolley, Charles Lucas, John Davidson and Zachariah Sickles, of Monmouth County, and apprehended by Col. Forman by an Order from Gen. Washington, appeared before the Council & took the Oaths to government as established by an Act of the Legislature, and were then discharged. Adjourned till tomorrow.

4 April 1777- [Friday]. Council met. Present as before. A petition from the Field and of the officers in the county of Monmouth showing that certain persons acted as Commissioners under Lord and General How, and granted Protections and Administered the Oath of Allegiance to the King of Great Britain, and pray the such persons be dealt with according to the law. Hezekiah Wood of Bordentown appeared and took the Oaths of Government; Jacob Lawrie of Bordentown appeared and delivered his Protection and being a Quaker took the Affirmations to Government. It was Ordered that the following persons be brought before the Council-Samuel Burling, Thomas P. Hewlings, Colin Campbell, John Taylor, John Wardell, John Laurence, Sr., James Grover,

Joseph Saltar, Edmund Williams, Robert Hartshorn, Ezek Hartshorn, Daniel Hendrickson, Middletown, Henry Waddelle, Joseph Leonard, Doctre. John Laurence, Robert Cooke, William Guisbertson & Thomas Thompson. Ordered that Richard Waln and Daniel Ellis be summoned to take the Oaths to Government. Adjourned till 3PM.

Met according to adjournment. Ordered subpoenas be issued to Gilbert Barton and William Laurence to appear and give evidence against John Lawrence Senr. The rest of the afternoon taken by hearing disaffected persons from Monmouth County. Adjourned till tomorrow 9 o'clock.

5 April 1777 – [Saturday]. The Council met. Present as before. Benjamin Baird, Esqr., first Major, Second Battalion, Foot Militia, Somerset County, having deceased and Enos Kelsey, Esqr., Second Major in same Battalion resigned his position after being appointed D.Q. Master and Commissary, the Council appointed Peter D. Vroom, 1st Major and William Verbryck, 2nd Major, in the aforesaid Battalion. Thomas Farr appeared and gave evidence against John Laurence, of Burlington, which was written down; Joseph Laurence, Esqr. gave evidence against John Laurence of Burlington; Mr. Peter Imlay gave evidence against John Laurence Senr. of Monmouth. Agreed that Justice Symmes be directed to take recognizance of Jos. Laurence and Peter Imlay, etc. Mr. William Laurence by subpoena appeared and gave evidence against John Laurence, Sr., put to writing. Adjourned till 3 PM.

Met according to adjournment. Mary Davison was examined. Abraham Hendricks and Gilbert Barton were examined under Oath respecting John Laurence, Sr., and it was written down. Adjourned till Monday 9 o'clock.

7 April 1777 – [Monday]. Met pursuant to adjournment. Present - Governor, Symmes, Paterson, Dick, Manning. No quorum and adjourned to 3 PM.

Present - Governor, Symmes, Scudder, Paterson, Dick, Manning. Isaac Potter and Daniel Griggs examined under Oath respecting Joseph Saltar and it was written down. John Jones, Samuel Heath, Ephraim Drake Harris, John Harris who were apprehended and sent to Philadelphia by Gen. Putnam, appeared and were examined and they took the Oaths and were discharged. Adjourned till tomorrow 9 o'clock.

8 April 1777 – [Tuesday] - Council met. Present as before. Joseph Saltar was called before the Board and informed of the charge against him under Oath; being heard was order to withdraw. Ordered that Joseph Saltar be committed to the Keeper of the Gaol of Burlington. Samuel Burling & Thomas P. Hewlings were called before the Board and informed of the charge against them and them being heard, it was deferred till the afternoon. Adjourned till 3 PM.

Met according to adjournment. Samuel Burling, Thomas P. Hewlings, Colin Campbell, Daniel Ellis appeared and refusing to take the Oaths to the State, but they being willing to be bound with Sureties for their appearance at next Court of Sessions, of the Peace, Burlington County, the Board gave them until Friday to obtain the sureties. William Harley, Thomas Pollock, John Mee and John Lee, apprehended persons and sent to Philadelphia, appeared and took the Oaths and were discharged. The Petition of William and Matthew Paterson was read setting forth that they were natives of Ireland and had considerable Freehold estates and that they have signed the Association and had been in Captain Green's Company of Militia, and would gladly defend the State provided it would not put their property in jeopardy or subject to forfeiture, asked the Board for Relief in the Premises. Order that the petition be tabled. Nathaniel Lewis appeared and was examined on the charge against Thomas Watson and his Recognizance was taken for his appearance as a witness at the next Court of General Gaol Delivery for Burlington County. Adjourned till tomorrow 9 o'clock.

9 April 1777 – [Wednesday]-The council met. Present - Governor, Symmes, Scudder, Paterson, Dick, Manning, Combes. A petition from various resident of New Ark, County of Essex was read stating that the most inveterate Tories remained after the enemy fled, had been arrested and sent to Head Quarters but now had been discharged, and on their return threatened those who had arrested them, some fled with the enemy leaving their families and estates, which are now being carried away by those who had been released, all due to the want of proper authority to arrest them, and that many person have refused to comply with General Washington's Proclamation to stay at home without any Molestation or doing any kind of Duty, and the petition prays that the Premises may be taken under consideration and some adequate remedy applied. Ordered, that the petition be referred to the Legislature. Ordered, that warrants of commitment be issued against John Laurence and Thos. Watson, charged with High Treason. Captain Jacob Oliphan, 2nd Burlington Regiment of Militia desired to resign his commission due to his ill health. The Board accepted his resignation. Thomas Reynolds Esqr. was appointed by the Board, Col., 2nd Battalion of Militia, Burlington County. The Officers of the said Battalion having recommended Joseph Haight as Lt. Col, Thomas Fenimore as 1st Major and Joseph Budd as 2nd Major thereof, their commissions were made and delivered to Col. Haight. The apprehended persons of David McDonald and Thomas Parent, who had been sent to Philadelphia, appeared before the Board and took the Oaths and were discharged. Adjourned till tomorrow 9 o'clock.

10 April 1777 – [Thursday]. The Council met. Present as before. Robert Ellison, John Mildrum, Jacob Cummins and Jacob Goodwin, inhabitants of Sussex County, apprehended by Gen. Heard and sent to this place under guard, on suspicion of aiding and abetting the Enemy and conspiring against the Government. Gen. Heard's letter read. Jacob Goodwin brought before the Board, examined and ordered back to prison. Mr. Muckleroy of Burlington cited to appear as a witness against Saml. Burling. Mr. Helm and John Carty of Burlington cited to appear. William North and John North, two prisoners who had been confined in the Gaol at Philadelphia appeared and examined. The decision of their case was deferred. Adjourned till 3 o'clock.

Met according to adjournment. Examination of Abraham Hendricks against Jesse Woodward taken and written down. Agreed that Justice Symmes take his recognizance to appear as a witness at the next Court of General Gaol Delivery for Monmouth County. Ordered that a warrant for commitment be made for Francis Jones and Moses Mount to the Keeper of the Burlington County Gaol, for being guilty of misdemeanors. The Governor gave the Board a message from Saml. Burling informing that Mr. Helm was confined to his chamber being much indisposed but would appear as soon as his health allowed. John Jones examination taken against Benjamin Helm. Ordered, that Isaac Imlay and Wm. Imlay be cited as witnesses against Jesse Woodward, now in confinement in this place. Adjourned till tomorrow 9 o'clock.

11 April 1777 – [Friday]. The Council met. Present as before. Thomas Fowler brought before Board and examined and notes taken. Capt. Webb, who holds office under the King of Great Britain, appeared by citation, and being heard, agreed that he be given fourteen days to settle his affairs and then remove to the Enemy with a flag. Mr. Muckleroy appeared and was examined on the conduct of Samuel Burling. William North and John North were again called before the Board and they took the required Oaths and were discharged. John Carty of Burlington appeared and refused to take the Oaths but was willing to enter into recognizance, with Surety, for appearance at the next Court of General Quarter Sessions of the Peace, Burlington County; as did Archibald Muckleroy, his surety, in 100 pounds each and were dismissed. Alexander Montgomery appeared and his examination was taken in writing under Oath respecting Jesse Woodward, and he entered into recognizance to appear as a witness against Mr. Woodward at the next Court of Oyer and Terminer and General Gaol Delivery for Monmouth County. Samuel Burling entered into recognizance with William Smith his surety; and Thomas P. Hewlings entered into recognizance with Abraham Hewlings as his surety, Daniel Ellis entered into recognizance with Wm. Smith his surety, and Colin Campbell entered into recognizance with Abraham Hewlings his surety, all for 300 pounds each, for their appearance at the next Court of General Quarter Sessions of the Peace, Burlington County, and were dismissed. Adjourned till 3:00 o'clock

Met according to adjournment. Ordered, that Michael Mount be cited to appear as a witness against Jesse Woodward. John Cleayton, Green Cooke and Samuel Odell, persons apprehended and sent to Philadelphia, were ordered before the Board and examined, took the Oaths and were dismissed. Nathan Allen, who was apprehended and sent to Philadelphia, was examined before the Board, and being a Quaker took the affirmation and was discharged. Robert Ellison of Sussex was brought before the Board was examined on the Plot and Combination in Sussex and reduced to writing. Adjourned till tomorrow 9 o'clock.

12 April 1777 – [Saturday]. The Council met. Present as before. Mr. Camp appeared and took his seat at the Board. William Imlay was examined as a witness against Richard Robbins and Jesse Woodward. Mr. Savage laid before the Board a Resolution of Congress 8 April, 1777, "...recommended to the Governor and Council of Safety of New Jersey not to call into the field such part of their militia not exceeding forty as are necessarily employed in the Salt Works now erecting in their State by Governor of Pennsylvania..." Council replied at the bottom of the document - "The exemption above recommended is inconsistent with the Militia Law of this State, but if the Government of Pennsylvania will carry on the said Works with the inhabitants of their own commonwealth, care shall be taken to have them exempted as above ..." but they may be called if they make their residence here. Isaac Imlay appeared and was examined and he entered recognizance to appear as a witness at the next Court of Oyer and Terminer and General Gaol Delivery for Monmouth County, as a witness against Jesse Woodward. Samuel Lippencut was discharged after taking the Oaths. Agreed that the Governor remit to Mr. Ephraim Philips, Sheriff of Burlington, fourteen pounds five shillings on account. The Board appointed Elisha Boudinot, Esqr., their Secretary and desired the Governor to acquaint him of the appointment. Adjourned till 9 o'clock Monday.

14 April 1777 – [Monday]. The Board met according to adjournment. Present - Governor, Symmes, Paterson, Dick, Camp, Manning, Combes. Letter from Joseph Leonard, of the 10th instant, laid before the Board, excusing his appearance due to "Rash & Fever". Richard R. Crow, an officer of his Britannic Majesty, is desirous of returning to Ireland, his native country. Agreed that he could return to his family near Cheesquakes, Middlesex County, given 14 days to settle his affairs, and apply for to the nearest officer of the United States for a flag to go into the Enemy's Lines. Petition from John Duyckinck stating that he has been in State Prison at Philadelphia since 10th of February last and asking for a hearing. Agreed to write to General Washington being they are at a loss to determine, until some charge is made, whether they have authority to handle it. Adjourned till 3 o'clock.

Met according to adjournment. George Mount, a private in Capt Stillwell's Company, was brought before Board for examination & heard Capt. Stillwell, and he was discharged from confinement after taking the Oaths. Cornelius Williamson, Joseph Thatcher, Morrice Wurts, and Timothy Lake apprehended by Order of Gen. Heard were sent to this place and ordered held in Prison until Board can hear them and witnesses. William Grover, who was apprehended by Order of Gen. Putnam, brought before Board and examined, and being one of the People called Quakers, took the Affirmation and was dismissed. Aaron Robins Brower, apprehended by Col. Randolph, and sent to Philadelphia, ordered before the Board, and George Brown, apprehended as a being dangerous to the present Government, appeared before the Board & both took the Oaths and were dismissed. Adjourned till tomorrow at 9 o'clock.

15 April 1777 – [Tuesday]. Council met. Present – Governor, Scudder, Symmes, Paterson, Dick, Combes, Camp, Manning. Pursuant to Election – the following: Joseph Weaver-Capt., William Dobbins -1st Lt., Henry Howel -2nd Lt, and Abraham Parker-Ensign Lt., in Col. Thos. Reynold's 1st Company, of Militia, 2nd Battalion, of Burlington County. Robert Allison and Jacob Cummins, of Sussex County, apprehended and sent to this place as being dangerous to the present Government, called before the Board, took the Oaths, entered into Recognizance, being mutual Sureties for each other at 500 pounds each before Justice Symmes, for their appearance at the next Court of Year and Terminer in the County of Sussex, and were then dismissed. Joseph Haight was called before the Board and examined in respect to the conduct of John Laurence Senr., his recognizance taken before Justice Symmes, for his appearance as a Witness at the next Court of Oyer and Terminer for the County of Monmouth. The Governor, upon the advice of the Council of Safety, had Capt. Arnold of Morris have two Light Horse of his company attend the Council for carrying dispatches, guarding prisoners, etc. Capt. Arnold sent them but agreed with them that they would be paid 20 shillings a day, without the Board's direction. The Board believing the price was too high agreed to dismiss them but did pay them what they had been promised from the time they left home until they could return – amounting to 10 pounds. Jesse Woodward was called before the Board, told of the charge and being heard respecting the same, was ordered to withdraw. David Condict, Esqr was elected Lt. Colonel and Samuel Hayes Esqr.,

Major, of the 1st Battalion, 2nd Regiment of Foot Militia, Essex County, whereof Philip Van Cortlandt is Colonel. Adjourned till 3 o'clock.

Met according to adjournment. Agreed that a warrant to Col. Bowes Reed to apprehend John Blackwell be issued returnable on or before the 29th of April instant. Ordered that a warrant of Commitment be issued against Jesse Woodward, charged with High treason, and directed to the Gaoler of Sussex. Lewis Bastedo examined as a witness against Thomas Fowler and same written down. Richard Smith of Burlington was cited to appear before the Board as a Person dangerous to the present Government. Adjourn till tomorrow 9 o' clock.

16 April 1777 – [Wednesday]. Met according to adjournment. Ordered, a Mittimus issue to the Gaoler at Freehold to receive custody of Edmund Williams of Monmouth for refusing to take the Affirmations to the effect of the Oaths and giving security for his appearance. John Taylor, Esqr. called in, examined, and ordered that he be committed to the Gaol of Burlington, for maintaining the Authority of the King of Great Britain within the State. Stephen Tallman was called in and examined. John Laurence of Monmouth was called in and examined and ordered that he be committed for High Treason against the State. Adjourned till 3 o'clock.

Met according to adjournment. Ordered that Warrants of Commitment be issued against Thomas Fowler, charged with High Treason, and assaulting Lewis Bastedo, with the intent to murder, with the warrant directed to the Gaoler of Sussex. The assault was committed in Burlington County and the High treason in Monmouth. John Williams, Jr., William Throp and Francis Doyle, were apprehended and sent to Philadelphia, were ordered before the Board and were dismissed. Daniel Laurence was brought before the Board, examined and was ordered to withdraw. Joseph Laurence, Junr. of Monmouth, who was apprehended, sent to Philadelphia, was ordered before the Board, examined, and being one of the People called Quakers, took the Affirmations and was dismissed. Stephen Tallman appeared before the Board and entered into recognizance with Tallman Smith, his surety, in 300 pounds each, for his appearance at the next Court of General Quarter Sessions, of Monmouth County, and in the meantime to be of peace and good behavior, and was dismissed. Col. Dick had leave of absence. Adjourned till tomorrow 9 o' clock.

17 April 1777 – [Thursday]. The Council met. Present – Governor, Scudder, Symmes, Paterson, Coombes, Camp, Manning. Lewis Ellison appeared before the Board, was examined, and being a Quaker, took the Affirmation and was dismissed. The Governor laid a letter before the Board from Gen. Washington of yesterday's date regarding the state of Col. Duycknick's case and the Board determined that he comes properly before them under Military Jurisdiction. Order that Col. Duyckinck be informed of the above. Ordered that a warrant of Commitment be issued against Jacob Goodwin charged with High Treason and directed to the Gaoler in Sussex County. Richard Robins called before the Board, informed of the charge, and under Oath was heard and ordered to withdraw. Daniel Laurence brought before the Board and refusing to take the Oaths was given till tomorrow to find sureties. Benjamin Helme was examined as was Richard Smith of Burlington. Agreed that thirty two blank Commissions be delivered to Col. Freelynhuysen for the Captains and subalterns of his Battalion, to be filled up by him though elections and returned to the Governor. Richard Smith entered into recognizance with Abraham Hewlings in 200 pounds for his appearance at the Quarter Sessions and was then dismissed. Benjamin Helme entered into recognizance and was discharged. Ordered that a warrant of Commitment be issued against Richard Robins charged with High Treason and directed to the Gaoler of Sussex County. Adjourned till 3 o'clock.

Met according to adjournment. Present as before. Lewis Bastedo was examined as a witness against Richard Robins and his deposition taken in writing. Mr. Elmer appeared and took his seat at the Board. Council ordered 1 pound, 10 shillings to be paid to Lewis Bastedo for two days of himself and horse. Adjourned till tomorrow morning 9 o'clock.

18 April 1777 – [Friday]. The Council met. Present – Governor, Scudder, Symmes, Elmer, Paterson, Coombes, Camp, Manning. Ordered that Timothy Lake appear before the Board. Anthony Wooley, John Wooley and Amos Morris took the Oaths and were discharged. The Board appointed the following as Field Officers for the 1st Battalion, of Cumberland Militia – Elijah Hand - Col., Samuel Ogden - Lieut. Col., Dick Paterson -1st Major and their commissions were issued. Captain Wooley was examined against Richard Jeffrey. Nathan Sutton was examined and Jeffrey and Sutton were order to withdraw. Henry Weatherbey was examined. Mr. Speaker appeared before the Council and took his seat at the Board. Col. Symmes had a leave of absence. Timothy Lake of Kingwood, a prisoner, sent to the Council by Gen. Heard was examined. Council adjourned till 3 o'clock.

Met according to adjournment – Present as before – John Severn a prisoner examined, took the Oaths and was discharged. A number of subpoenas and summonses were issued for evidence and disaffected persons. Adjourned till 9 o'clock tomorrow.

19 April – [Saturday]. Met according to adjournment. Present – Governor, Scudder, Patterson, Elmer, Hart, Combs, Manning, Camp. William Lippincot was called into Council Chamber and examined. Henry Weatherby was again called in and upon making further confessions was ordered to withdraw. Daniel Laurence appeared before the Board and entered into recognizance with William Laurence and John Van Matter his sureties in 300 lbs each, for appearance at the next Court of General Quarter Sessions for Monmouth County, and in the meantime to be of peace and good behavior, and dismissed. Adjourned till Monday 10 o'clock.

21 April 1777 – [Monday]. The Council met. Present – Governor, Scudder, Elmer, Paterson, Camp, Manning. Mr. Monice Worts apprehended by order of Gen. Heard and sent to this place, appeared and was examined, took the Oaths and was dismissed. Several resolutions of the Honorable Congress were read and ordered to lie on the table for perusal and consideration of the members. Adjourned till 3 o'clock.

Met according to adjournment – Nathan Stout, Esqr. was examined re: the conduct of Joseph Thatcher, John Mildrum and Cornelius Williamson. Thomas Groom and Joseph Groom were brought before the Board, examined, they took the Oaths and were dismissed. Edward Taylor, Esqr. appeared before the Board and charges against him were read and he being heard in his defense was ordered to withdraw. He was again called and refused to take the Oaths but was willing to be bound with sureties for appearing at the Court of General Quarter Sessions for Monmouth County. He was given time to arrange for his sureties. Adjourned till tomorrow at 9 o'clock.

22 April 1777 – [Tuesday]. The Council met according to adjournment. Present as before. Edward Taylor, Esqr. Entered into recognizance with Joseph Borden and John Imlay, Esqr., his sureties, in 300 pounds each for the Court of General Quarter Sessions for Monmouth County, and in meantime to be of the peace and good behavior and was dismissed. Resolved for the Governor to write to General Maxwell for an exact return of the four Jersey Battalions belonging to his brigade per a Resolution of Congress on the 14th instant and that it be returned to Congress without delay. [Letter recorded.] Edmund Harris apprehended by General Forman in virtue of an order of Gen. Washington, and sent to Philadelphia appeared before the Board, the charges read and he being heard, he was ordered to withdraw. Benjamin Woolley, Jacob Harvey, John Riddle, Richard Jeffrey, Daniel Stukey, William Cooper and Jedediah Lippincot were called before the Board, examined, Oaths given and were discharged. Mr. Hart attended and took his seat at the Board. Adjourned till 3 o'clock.

Met according to adjournment – Mr. Symmes and Mr. Coombes attended and took their seats. Cornelius Williamson appeared and refused to take the Oaths but was willing to be bound with sureties for his appearance at the next Court of General Quarter Sessions of Hunterdon County. He was given till tomorrow to produce his sureties. Joseph Thatcher, John Meldrum, and Daniel Bancroft appeared before the Board, took the Oaths and were dismissed. Ordered that a warrant of Commitment be issued against Edmund Harris of Monmouth County, charged with High Treason. The Board was told that Cornelius Williamson wanted to appear before them, he did, and expressed his desire to take the Oaths, they were given and he was dismissed. Timothy Lake again appeared took the Oaths and was discharged. The examination in writing and under Oath of Lake was taken relative to the conduct of Christopher and John Vaught. Richard Willson was called before the Board, examined, and the Oaths tendered to him but he requested time to think about it or to find sureties in case he could not take them with a "safe Conscience;" whereupon the Board indulged him in his request and ordered him to withdraw. Mr. Manning had leave of absence. Adjourned till tomorrow 7 o'clock.

23rd April 1777- [Wednesday]. The Board met pursuant to adjournment. Present – Mr. Hart, Col. Symmes, Col. Scudder, Mr. Elmer, Mr. Manning, Mr. Camp, Mr. Combs, Mr. Paterson. [They conducted business matters.] Mr. Symmes had leave of absence. Petition of Edmund Harris charged with High Treason asked that he might be able to reside in some private dwelling house in Freehold during his indisposition, upon giving surety, was read and it was ordered to lie on the table. Wm. Sands was called and examined touching the conduct of Henry Wetherby, and others, and after sometime spent therein, further examination was postponed till afternoon. Adjourned till 3 o'clock.

The Board met – Present – Governor, Elmer, Scudder, Paterson, Hart, Combes, Camp. Thomas Forman Esqr. was examined relative to the conduct of Anthony Woodward, John Leonard, Jesse Woodward, William Grover, Ezekiel Forman, Thomas Woodward, (son of Anthony), Robert

Thompson, Wm. Taylor (son of Wm.) and others, and such was written down and sworn to by Thomas Forman. The Board again called Wm. Sands and resumed his examination relative to Samuel Wright, Henry Wetherby, Wm. Smith and Thos. Sherman, Thomas Kerney and others, and such was written down and sworn to by Sands. John Andrews appeared before the Board and was examined about the conduct of Wm. Grover and others, it was written down and sworn to by Andrews. Richard Francis was subpoenaed as a witness, appeared and was examined but his testimony was not material. John Van Mater was called before the Board, examined and he refused to take the Oaths, but was willing to be bound in surety for his appearance in the next Court of Quarter Sessions, with Edmund Bainbridge, his surety in 300 pounds each, for his appearance at the next Court of Quarter Sessions of the Peace in Monmouth County and was dismissed. Daniel Grandine appeared and was examined and the Oaths tendered but he refused them but was willing to be bound in surety for his appearance in the next Court of Quarter Sessions, with Aaron Van Clief his surety in 300 pounds each, and was dismissed. Adjournment till tomorrow at 9 o'clock.

24 April 1777 – [Thursday]. Met pursuant to adjournment. Present – Governor, Elmer, Scudder, Paterson, Hart, Combes, Camp. Samuel Knott appeared and was examined relative to the conduct of Henry Wetherby, Samuel Wright, Stephen Wist, Nathan Allen, and others[not named], which was written down and sworn to by Knott. William Sands and Samuel Knott were examined in reference to the conduct of Obadiah King of Burlington County who was apprehended for making use of expressions which tend to encourage disaffection and to raise tumults and disorders in the State. Ordered he be brought before the Board, he appeared and was examined, took the Oaths and was dismissed. James Bell was called and the Accusation against him was read and being examined relative to same, he was ordered to withdraw. Adjourned till 3 o'clock.

Met pursuant to adjournment. Three blank Commissions were sent to Lt. Col. Vandike to be filled up with the names of officers elected by the Princeton Company of Militia and to make the returns. Thomas Cleayton, Jonathan Burge, Nathan Sutton, David Heslip, and Benjamin Jones were called before the Board, examined, took the Oaths and were dismissed. George Applegate of Burlington County appeared and turned over the Protection given him by the Enemy, which he was prevented from doing so on the Score of Indisposition, he took the Oaths. David Walker and John Carson were ordered before the Board and being they belonged to Pennsylvania, the Board wrote to Mr. President Wharton, with their charges and they were to be sent down to Philadelphia as soon as possible. Wm. Grandine was called before Board, examined, the Oaths tendered to him, and he refused to take them, asking for time in order to provide sureties for his appearance at the next Court of General Quarter Sessions of the Peace of Monmouth County and his request was granted. James Bell, Cornelius Cleayton, William Lippincott and Stephen Harvey were ordered before the Board, examined, took the Oaths and were dismissed. Adj'd till tomorrow 9 o'clock

25 April 1777 – [Friday]. Met pursuant to adjournment. Present as before. Thomas Bennet, Jeremiah Bennet, Joseph Bennet & Theophilus Bennet were ordered before the Board, examined, took the Oaths and were dismissed. William Tice was ordered before the Board, examined, took the Oaths and was dismissed. Simeon Badcock was called before Board, examined, the Oaths tendered to him, and he refused to take them, and was willing to be bound with sureties for his appearance at the next Court of General Quarter Sessions of the Peace of Monmouth County, and he did accordingly enter into Recognizance with Daniel Grandine and John Van Mater in 300 pounds each and was advised to be of good behavior and was dismissed. William Smith was called before the Board, the charge was read, he heard and examined relative to same, and then ordered to withdraw. William Grandine was called before the Board, entered into recognizance with Daniel Grandine and Tallman Smith for 300 pounds each for his appearance at the next Court of General Quarter Sessions of the Peace of Monmouth County, advised to be of good behavior and was dismissed. Robert Hartshorne and Essek Hartshorne appeared before the Board pursuant of a citation, on score of being dangerous and disaffected to the present Government. Oaths were tendered to them, they refused them and the Board called upon them to enter into recognizance with sureties for their appearance at the next Court of General Quarter Sessions of the Peace of Monmouth County, which they also refused, whereupon they were ordered to draw. Adjourned till 3 o'clock PM.

Met pursuant to adjournment. Robert and Essek Hartshorne were again called before the Board and refused to take the Oaths, Affirmations, or to be bound by sureties…whereupon Ordered that Warrants of Commitment be issued against them and directed to the keeper of the Gaol in Monmouth for refusing same. Thomas Kerney was called before the Board, the accusation read to him, and being heard and examined relative to same was ordered to withdraw. Amariah Farnsworth appeared before the Board, took the Oaths and was discharged. Thomas Kerney appeared before the Board and entered into recognizance with Peter Imlay and John Van Mater of the County of Monmouth, his sureties for 300 pounds each, for his appearance before the Court of Oyer & Terminer and General Gaol Delivery to be held in the County of Monmouth, to answer for maliciously and advisedly reviling and speaking contemptuously against the Congress and saying and doing things to encourage disaffection and to raise tumults and disordered, and to now be of good behavior and were then dismissed. Stephen Hedges appeared before the Board by citation as being a dangerous and disaffected to the Government, and being one of the people called Quakers, took affirmations and was dismissed. Henry Wetherby was called before the Board, the charge read, he was examined and then ordered to with draw. Mr. Camp had leave of absence. Adj'd tomorrow morng. 8 o'clock.

26 April 1777 – [Saturday]. Met according to adjournment. Present – Governor, Elmer, Scudder, Paterson, Hart, Combes. Ordered that William Tice and William Smith appear before the Board, both examined again, heard and dismissed on taking of the Oaths. Richard Wilson appeared, entered into recognizance with Edward Taylor Esqr., his surety in 300 pounds, for his appearance before at the next Court of General Quarter Sessions of the Peace of Monmouth County, to be of good behavior and was dismissed. William McMurray, of the County of Monmouth appeared, took the Oaths. Daniel Hendrickson, who was summoned as a person suspected of being disaffected and dangerous attended, was examined, and acknowledged that he had received a Protection from the Enemy which he refused to give up when demanded by the Board. Oaths were tendered and he refused to take them but was ready with his surety Edward Taylor Esqr. at 300 pounds to enter into recognizance to appear at the next Court of General

Quarter Sessions of the Peace of Monmouth County, was told to be of good behavior and was dismissed. John Cotterell appeared before the Board, was examined, took the Oaths and was dismissed. Abraham Smith and Isaac Sharp of Monmouth appeared, were examined, delivered up their Protection, took the Oaths and were dismissed. Joseph Burdge was called, examined took the Oaths and was dismissed. Henry Wetherby appeared and entered into recognizance with Abraham Smith, Wm. Smith and Isaac Sharp as his sureties at 300 pounds each for his appearance at the next Court of Oyer & Terminer and General Gaol delivery of Monmouth County & to be held then and there to answer for advisedly and wittingly by speech writing, open deed and act, maintaining and defending the King of Great Britain over the State of New Jersey, for maliciously doing things encouraging disaffection to raise tumults and disorders, and in the meantime to be good and was dismissed. Adjourned till 3 o'clock PM.

Met pursuant to Adjournment. Daniel Williams was called before the Board, examined and ordered to withdraw. He was again called before the Board and was dismissed upon taking the Oaths. Adjourned till Monday, 3 o'clock.

28 April 1777 – [Monday]. Met pursuant to adjournment. Present - Governor, Elmer, Paterson, Combes. There not being a Quorum to proceed, adjourned till tomorrow morng. 9 o'clock.

29 April 1777- [Tuesday]. Met pursuant to adjournment. Present - Governor, Elmer, Paterson, Combes, Camp. There not being a Quorum, adjourned till 11 o'clock.

Met pursuant to adjournment and there not being a Quorum adjourned till 3 o'clock. Met pursuant to adjournment. Present – Governor, Elmer, Scudder, Paterson, Combes, Camp. Col. Bowes Reed agreeable to his Warrant sent to this place, John Blackwell, under guard. Ordered that subpoenas be issued to cite Joseph Campion, Isaac Merit and William Norton to appear at 10 o'clock tomorrow and give testimony against John Blackwell. A letter was given to the Board from Elisha Boudinot, Esqr., dated the 18th inst., informing the Board that he declined the appointment of secretary that had been conferred upon him. A petition of sundry officers and inhabitants of the Town of New Ark, Essex County, was read, advising them that Militia officers of said town were either dead or by submitting to the enemy were disqualified from acting, and they asked that certain persons named could be commissioned as officers in the militia. The Board sent the petition on to the Legislature. William Halfpenny, sent to this place by Gen. Putnam, ordered before Board, examined, took Oaths and dismissed upon delivering up the Protection he received from the Enemy. William Butler Linch, apprehended by Gen. Putnam and sent here was before Board, examined, took Oaths and was dismissed. Lary Johnston, Thomas Gohem, and Daniel Dancer, apprehended by Major Scudder, sent to Princeton and then to this place under guard by Gen. Putnam, ordered into custody in the Guard Room, until the Board can hear the charge against him and examine witnesses. Governor read a letter from Gen. Putnam, enclosing a letter from Major Scudder in reference to Johnson, Gohem and Dancer. Jacob Dancer called before Board, the charge read, he was examined and then remanded to Prison. Ordered subpoenas be issued for John Anderson and Thomas Smith to appear before Board and give testimony against Stephen Flood. Adjourned till tomorrow 9 o'clock.

1777 April 30 – [Wednesday]. Met pursuant to adjournment. Present – as before. David Burton before the Board, examined on the conduct of Alexander Willson, examination reduced to writing, subscribed and sworn to by Burton. Isaac Meait, cited as a witness, sent his son who appeared & informed Board his father was indisposed and could not attend. Joseph Campion before the Board, was examined in reference to John Blackwell, his examination written down, subscribed and affirmed by Campion. William Norton appeared before Board, examined in reference to John Blackwell but his testimony not material. Ordered that subpoenas be served upon John Wright, James Wells, and a man commonly called "English Thomas" to appear tomorrow at 10 and give testimony against John Blackwell. Ordered that a warrant be issued to bring Alexander Willson, of Upper Freehold, County of Monmouth, before the Board. Adjourned till 3 o'clock PM.

Met pursuant to adjournment. Daniel Dancer was ordered before Board, examined and remanded to Prison. Ordered that a warrant of commitment be issued against Jacob Dancer charged with High Treason and directed to the Keeper of the Gaol at Burlington. Thomas Gohem and Lawrence Johnston were ordered before Board, they being of the state of Pennsylvania, the Board wrote to President Wharton, with the charges and they were to be sent to Philadelphia as soon as possible. Adjourned till 9 o'clock tomorrow.

1777 May 1 – [Thursday]. Met pursuant to adjournment. Present as before. John Jolley, Burlington Co., and one of the prisoners sent here by the Council of Safety of Pennsylvania, ordered before the Board, examined and dismissed after taking Oaths to the State. John Wright before the Board and was examined respecting the charge against John Blackwell, and testimony reduced to writing, subscribed and affirmed by John Wright. James Wills before the Board, examined respecting the charge against John Blackwell, testimony was immaterial. Alexander Willson was before the Board, the charges were read, he was examined and then ordered to withdraw. John Blackwell before the Board, the charges read and he was heard on them, and was then remanded to prison. Ordered that a warrant of commitment be against John Blackwell, charged with High Treason, and directed to the keeper of the Gaol in Burlington. Thomas Maddock, commonly called "English Tom", appeared before the Board, was examined in reference to John Blackwell but his testimony was immaterial. Elias Hollman, Monmouth County, before the Board and took the Oaths. Adjourned till 3 o'clock PM.

Met pursuant to Adjournment. Mr. Boudinot attended as Secretary and took his seat. Governor gave a letter to the Board from Elias Boudinot Esqr, Commissary of Prisoners, requesting an account of the disbursements and expenses of this state in favor of the prisoners taken from the King of Great Britain, and also a return of prisoners as are now confined in this State. Agreed that the Board hadn't the jurisdiction and referred the matter to the Legislature. Ordered a warrant of commitment against Alexander Willson, charged with advisedly and maliciously saying and doing things encouraging disaffection tending to raise tumults and disorders in the State, directed to the Keeper of the Gaol at Burlington. Ordered that 13 pounds, seventeen shillings and six pence be paid to Thomas Powel for his services as Doorkeeper to this Board from 26th March to the 1st of May. The Governor signed the following certificates – to John Combs Esqr. For 16 pounds, ten shillings proclamation money for 27 days attendance at this Board, Nathaniel

Scudder Esqr, 24 pounds for 40 days attendance, Theophilus Elmore, Esqr. 13 pounds, 16 shillings for 23 days attendance, Benjamin Manning Esqr. 18 pounds for 30 days attendance, Caleb Camp Esqr. 15 pounds, 12 shillings for 26 days attendance, John Hart, Esqr. 9 pounds, 12 shillings for 16 days attendance.

1777 May 10 – [Saturday]. Haddonfield – Governor and Members of the Council of Safety met. Present – Governor, Symmes, Elmer, Scudder, Hart, Combs, Camp, Weatherby, Manning. Peter Obart, Francis Letts, and William Lake, prisoners apprehended by Major John Taylor on orders from Gen. Putnam, conducted under guard to this place, were brought before the Board and examined, and there appears to be insufficient evidence against them, they took the Oaths and were discharged. Adjourned till Monday next.

1777 May 12 – [Monday]. Met according to adjournment. Present – Governor, Symmes, Elmer Condict, Paterson, Scudder, Dick. A memorial was presented by Capt. John Dennis, of Shrewsbury Township, Monmouth County, requesting the Council to take cognizance of the case of two Negroes, the property of Peter Parker and John Slocum of the township aforesaid, who were sometime in February last taken prisoners by the Memorialist on suspicion of their having been in Arms & aiding the Enemy, and afterwards went to Philadelphia where they were confined ever since and further setting forth that the Masters of the said Negroes are desirous of having the matter heard here. The Board called Capt. Dennis before them, obtained what information he had, and advised Capt. Dennis to advise the sd. Parker and Slocum to appear on Wednesday, the 21st instant. A Sergeant's Guard detached by Major John Taylor at Cranberry, Middlesex County, arrived with a Prisoner taken by a party of Horsemen near the enemy's lines at Brunswick, who by order delivered them to this place along with a letter stating that the said prisoner has assumed the name John Brown, his real name is John Lee, that he formerly lived in Philadelphia, and had lately introduced a number of recruits into Brunswick for the purpose of joining the British Army, which he has confessed to Major Taylor. Two persons – Thompson and Hall were called in and examined in reference to the prisoner but their evidence amounted to nothing. Adjourned till 6 o'clock PM.

Met according to adjournment. John Brown alias John Lee was ordered to the Board, examined and remanded to prison. Capt. Timothy Shaler delivered to Council two prisoners namely John Martin and William Cowen taken in a Prize, who were ordered into confinement. Council adjourned till tomorrow 11 o' clock.

1777 May 13 – [Tuesday]. The Council met according to adjournment. Present – Governor, Elmer, Condict, Scudder, Camp, Manning. A letter was before the Board from the Secretary of the Board of War, enclosing some resolutions of Congress, respecting Capt. Gamble and Doctor Stapleton at Princeton, who are suspected of being concerned in unwarrantable practices against the United States and requesting an inquiry into their conduct and transmit the results to Congress. Immediate application was made to some persons in or near Princeton to procure every necessary proof and information. Subpoenas were issued for Marshall Isaac Kay, Major William Ellis and Capt. James Tallman citing them to appear before the Board to give testimony against several persons suspected of disaffection and malpractices against this state. Adjourned till tomorrow 10 o'clock.

1777 May 14 – [Wednesday]. The Council met according to adjournment. Present – Governor, Condict, Elmer, Scudder, Camp, Mehelm, Wetherby, Manning. Mr. Isaac Kay appeared before the Board, examined in reference to the behavior of John Henchman Esqr. but he had no personal knowledge. A subpoena ordered for John Sparks Esqr. to appear to give evidence against John Henchman Esqr. John Martin and William Cowen, the two prisoners from Capt. Shaler, were brought before the Board and as they did not choose to enter on board an American armed vessel, they were remanded to the Guard House until application can me made to the Board of War concerning their disposition. The Council adjourned till 11 o'clock AM.

1777 May 15 – [Thursday]. Met according to adjournment. Present – Governor, Elmer, Scudder, Condict, Camp, Manning, Combes. Major William Ellis appeared before Board and was questioned as to the conduct of John Henchman Esqr. but his testimony was founded on information only. Peter Young & Henry Mourisson, two prisoners, sent from General Heard were called before the Board, examined as to their designs and that of their accomplices. It was clear from their testimony that when apprehended, they were on their way to the British Army in company of Richard Stagg (the person who persuaded them to go), Francis Mourisson and Ezekiel Wood, who all three made their escape; and they were remanded into confinement. Peter Young declared that Jacob Hilar and his son Nicholas, Abraham Tiers, John Welcher, Thomas Welcher, Silas Roberts, one Losan and one Tuthill had gone off to the enemy. The Council adjourned to 3 o'clock PM.

Met pursuant to adjournment. Present as before. Jacob Gardner, another prisoner, sent by Gen. Heard was called, examined and remanded to confinement. John Sparks, Esqr. appeared before the Board and although he gave no testimony against John Henchman Esqr. founded on his own knowledge, he furnished the Council with the names of a number of persons whose evidence he believed would be against him. Subpoenas were issued for Joseph Hewlings, William Norton, Zachary Rozel & his wife, William Harrison, Israel Morris, James Sloan, Joseph Hugg, Thomas Denny, Samuel Harrison Esqr. and Joseph Ellis Esqr. for their appearance to give testimony against John Henchman Esqr. Adjourned till tomorrow morning 10 o'clock.

1777 May 16 – [Friday]. Council Met pursuant to adjournment. Present – Governor, Elmer, Condict, Scudder, Combes, Manning, Camp. The Council informed that Capt. Webb, who, on the 11th of April last, obtained permission of this Board to settle his affairs within 14 days, and then remove to the Enemy with a Flag, had, instead spent a considerable time beyond those limits in passing though this State and Pennsylvania and to Baltimore in Maryland; and in his return he was apprehended by Gen. Schuyler and was put on parole until the Council of Safety wanted him. Capt. Webb was called before the Board and being heard as to the reasons, he desired to withdraw. However, the Council was of the opinion that Capt Webb had forfeited all, and it was therefore resolved that he be ordered forthwith to return to Gen. Schuyler at Philadelphia and that it be left to Gen Schuyler to determine whether he ought to be permitted to pass over to the

Enemy with a flag, or be detained as a Prisoner of War. A detailed account of the whole process involving Capt. Webb was to be transmitted to Gen. Schuyler. Adjourned to 4 o'clock PM.

Met pursuant to adjournment. Present as before. Mr. Zachary Rossell, happening in town, was called upon and attended before Council but it appeared by his testimony that he didn't know anything relating to John Henchmen Esqr. He also declared that he really believed it was not in the power of his wife to communicate anything material, the Council concluded to dispense with her appearance at Haddonfield. He also informed Council that Joseph Hewlings is missing from the neighborhood of Mount Holly and that he supposes he went off with the Enemy; his subpoena was suppressed. Thomas Denny Esqr. appeared before the Board to give evidence against John Henchman, Esqr., and after examination, his testimony was committed to writing and sworn to. Subpoenas were issued for Jacob Roberts and Captain Samuel Hugg to appear before Council tomorrow at 10 o'clock for giving evidence, etc. Israel Morris appeared by subpoena, examined but he had nothing that was material. Council adjourned till tomorrow 11 o'clock.

1777 May 17 – [Saturday]. Met pursuant to adjournment. Present – Governor, Condict, Elmer, Scudder, Camp, Manning. Joseph Hugg, Esqr. appeared before Council and gave testimony against John Henchman Esqr, which was written down and affirmed by Mr. Hugg. A memorial was presented to Council in behalf of Francis Hingston, praying permission for him to return to his friends in England, which was granted. Council adjourned to 3 o'clock PM.

Met according to adjournment. Present – Governor, Condict, Elmer, Paterson, Scudder, Camp, Manning. James Sloan appeared by subpoena, was examined, but testimony was deemed immaterial. Capt. Samuel Hugg appeared and examined about the suspicious conduct of John Henchman Esqr., his testimony written down, which he affirmed. Capt. Hugg gave some account of Henchman producing his former Commission under the Crown to some British officers at the Black Horse as a pass and of his inviting some British officers to his sister's at Mount Holly. Samuel Harrison Esqr. appeared and was examined but his testimony was already heard from others already in evidence. Col. Joseph Ellis being called declared that he heard John Henchman acknowledge that he wished the regular troops would come among us. Jacob Roberts being called, testified, his testimony written down which he affirmed. The Council adjourned till Monday 4 o'clock PM.

1777 May 19 – [Monday]. The Council met pursuant to adjournment. William Norton appeared, was examined re: the conduct of John Henchman Esqr. among the Hessians at Black Horse & Mount Holly, but his testimony was not written down. Capt. William Harrison was called, examined but his testimony was the same as others and was not written down. A subpoena was issued for John Estaugh Hopkins to appear tomorrow to give evidence against John Henchman Esqr. Adjourned till tomorrow 4 o'clock PM.

1777 May 20 – [Tuesday]. The Council met pursuant to adjournment. Present – Governor, Paterson, Symmes, Elmer, Scudder, Combs. Garret Rapalje and his son, George Rapalje appeared before the Board, the Oaths were tendered but both refused and desired time till tomorrow to consider them, which was granted. James Nevill, a prisoner sent by Gen. Heard to the Council was called, examined, and it appeared to the Board that the prisoner had been detained a long time as prisoner in New York, where he had suffered great hardship and abuse. He also explained to the Board to their satisfaction how he had a large sum of money on his person causing him to be detained by Gen. Heard. The Oaths were given to him, he money was returned to him and he was discharged. The Council adjourned till tomorrow 8 o'clock AM.

1777 May 21 – [Wednesday.] Met pursuant to adjournment. Present as before, except Mr. Combs, with the addition of Mr. Camp and Mr. Dick. Garret Rapalje appeared and entered into recognizance with Jacob Drake, his Surety, for 300 pounds each, for his appearance at the next Court of General Quarter Sessions of the Peace for the County of Sussex, warned to be of good behavior and was dismissed. George Rapalje appeared and he was offered to either take the Oaths or be a Prisoner of War, he begged for further time to consider the matter and was ordered to withdraw. A memorial from Lieut. Gilbert Imlay, praying that a number of former inhabitants of this state, who have been a long time confined to the city of Philadelphia, who had enlisted in the company to which he belongs, that they may be released from confinement and allowed to join his company. The Council decided to send for them together with all prisoners taken in Monmouth County by Major Mifflin, and the Council issued the papers for that purpose. Thomas Williams was brought before the Board, examined and remanded to confinement and determination of the case referred for further consideration. Thomas Woodward gave testimony against Thomas Williams, written down and he affirmed same. Thomas Woodward, son of Anthony, was called who appeared before the Board and questioned as to his disaffection and suspicious conduct and as about his "late Elopement" from the Guard in Haddonfield, and he was then ordered to withdraw and further consideration of his case to be deferred. Council adjourned till 4 o'clock PM.

Met pursuant to adjournment. Present – Governor, Symmes, Elmer, Condict, Scudder and Manning. A subpoena ordered for John Estaugh Hopkins to appear tomorrow morning to give evidence against John Hincksman, Esqr. Council took up the case of George Rapalje and finding that sometime in January he admitted having voluntarily gone over to the Enemy at New Brunswick, where he had taken the Oath of Allegiance to the King of Great Britain, then he went to Staten Island, New York and Long Island, and has continued with the Enemy since till within a few days, and is now back into this State, without Flag or Passport. The Board after deliberation ordered that a warrant of commitment directed to the Sheriff of Gloucester be issued against George Rapalje for by speech, writing, open deed and act, maintaining and defending the King of Great Britain, with this State. The Council adjourned till tomorrow morning 8 o'clock.

1777 May 22 – [Thursday]. Met pursuant to adjournment. Present – Governor, Elmer, Condict, Col. Scudder, Manning, Camp. A Memorial by Col. John Cox in behalf of his sister, Mrs. Mary Allen, setting forth that her son now in New York is dangerously ill from consumption and she is anxious to see him before his death, as well as desirous of taking care of her property there, etc. The Board agreed that Col. Cox be permitted to apply to General Putnam for a Flag of Truce in behalf of his sister, Mary Allen, and in case the General shall think proper to grant such Flag, that Mrs. Allen have leave to depart the State. Peter Parker of Shrewsbury Township appeared before the Board and took the Oaths, and offered to pay the costs regarding the apprehension and imprisonment of his Negro Man Sip, now confined in Philadelphia, and willing to give Bond to full value of said Negro, for his future good behavior. It was agreed that his Negro be released upon Parker complying with his forgoing conditions. John Estaugh Hopkins appeared by subpoena, but Council couldn't hear his testimony, and being he lives near, he agreed to appear at 8 o'clock tomorrow. Council adjourned till 6 o'clock PM.

Met pursuant to adjournment. Present – Governor, Elmer, Condict, Scudder, Manning, Combs. John Slocom, of Shrewsbury Township, appeared before the Board and offered to pay the costs regarding the apprehension and imprisonment of his Negro Man Sip, now confined in Philadelphia, and willing to give Bond to full value of said Negro, for his future good behavior. It was agreed that his Negro be released upon Parker complying with his forgoing conditions. It was also agreed that Peter Parker's Negro be valued at 100 pounds and Slocum's Negro be valued at 70 pounds. Adjourned till tomorrow 8 o'clock.

1777 May 23 – [Friday]. Met pursuant to adjournment. Present – Governor, Symmes, Condict, Elmer, Scudder, Camp, Combs, Manning, Dick. John Estaugh Hopkins appeared, gave testimony against John Henchman, Esqr., which was written down and affirmed by him. A summons issued for John Henchman Esqr. to appear before the Governor and the Council of Safety in Haddonfield on the 5th of May next at 8 o'clock AM. John Kite, William Parker, John Allen, John Sears, William Thompson, Jonathan Burge, James Cumpton & Stout Havens, prisoners taken by a detachment commanded by Major Mifflin in Monmouth County about the beginning of January last, and since confined in Philadelphia were brought under guard yesterday, were examined and all being willing to enter into the Continental Service during the War, to serve in Capt. John Burrowe's Company of Col. David Forman's Regiment, agreeable to a former Engagement with Lieut. _____ Patterson, and upon the condition that they may obtain a full & free pardon for all past treasonable offenses against the State of New Jersey; as did Richard Margison, another prisoner, who had not entered into any previous engagement with regard to said Company. William Newman another prisoner in the same predicament refused to enter the service and was remanded to the guard house to be held for future trial. Council adjourned till half past two o'clock PM.

Met pursuant to adjournment. Present – Governor, Paterson, Condict, Scudder, Manning, Camp. Aaron Cumpton another of the prisoners taken by Major Mifflin, was called to appear and upon his own confession that he had previous to his engagement with Col. Morris' party, deserted Capt. Thomas Patterson's Company in Col. Dayton's Battalion. He was remanded to confinement. James Peirce and John Barber, two more of the same prisoners, were examined and agreed to enter into American Service in the same Company as had the others. Adjourned till tomorrow morning 8 o'clock.

1777 May 24 – [Saturday]. Met pursuant to adjournment. Present – Governor, Condict, Scudder, Camp, Manning, Combes. Joseph Pierce, one of the prisoners taken by Major Mifflin was called in, and examined, but didn't want to enter service, and was remanded. Joseph Throckmorton, Esqr., who previously presented a Memorial to the Governor and Council on behalf of his son, John Throckmorton, then and still in confinement in Philadelphia, appeared before the Board and prayed that his son could be removed to the State and confined in his own house in Colts Neck, Monmouth County, offering to enter into Bond for "2.000 to 3.000" pounds, for his future good behavior and his appearance whenever required. The Board believed that they could not form an opinion without having the prisoner before them and since they didn't have the time to deal with it, they deferred it to another time. Jacob Cooper, a prisoner taken by Major Mifflin, appeared, was examined and as it appeared he had joined the Enemy and was enlisted with them, before the Publication of the Act for Punishing Traitors, etc., he was considered a Prisoner of War. John Sears, Stout Havens, Richard Margison and John Barber, four of the eleven prisoners, who had consented to enlist into the Continental Service, being called to enroll, declared that they had changed their minds, and refused to comply, whereupon the were remanded to the Guard House. The other seven took the Oaths, enrolled themselves and were delivered to Lieut. Gilbert Imlay. Adjourned till Monday next.

1777 May 26 – [Monday]. Met pursuant to adjournment. Gershom Ayres was discharged on taking the Oaths. Adjourned till Wednesday next.

1777 May 28 – [Wednesday]. The Council met. James Cornelius sworn, etc., Walter Curtis and Peter Brewer examined and remanded to confinement. Adjourned till tomorrow.

1777 May 29 – [Thursday]. The Council met. Present – Governor, Elmer, Condict, Combs, Camp, Manning. Jacob Cooper being considered a Prison of War, was put on parole and Thomas Curtis of Shrewsbury became his surety at 100 pounds. Ordered that Walter Curtis be discharged upon taking the Oaths, and entering into recognizance with Thomas Curtis, for 100 pounds, for his appearance at the next Court of General Quarter Sessions of the Peace to be held for Monmouth County, and giving his note for 16.16.10 payable the 1st July next (with Thomas Curtis for security) and being his proportion of the expense by bringing him and Williams to Haddonfield. Ordered that Peter Brewer be discharged on his taking of the Oaths. Council adjourned till tomorrow morning 9 o'clock.

1777 May 30 – [Friday]. Met pursuant to adjournment. Present – Governor, Condict, Elmer, Manning, Combe, Camp. Walter Curtis having complied with yesterday's order, and this morning discharged his note for such expense, is at liberty to go home. Richard Stanton, late of Essex County, took the Oaths and entering his recognizance with Thomas Dey, Esq., of Bergen County, for 100 pounds for his appearance at the next Court of General Quarter Sessions of the Peace to be held for Essex County and to be on good behavior was discharged. Adjourned till three o'clock PM.

Met pursuant to adjournment. Present – Governor, Condict, Elmer, Combs, Camp, Manning. John Ederson called in and examined and on taking the Oaths, entering his recognizance with Richard Stanton, for 100 pounds for his appearance at the next Court of General Quarter Sessions of the Peace to be held for Essex County and to be on good behavior was discharged. Adjourned till tomorrow 12 o'clock.

1777 May 31 – [Saturday]. Met pursuant to adjournment. Present – Governor, Condict, Elmer, Scudder, Manning, Combs. Richard Snowden attended the Board under citation but refused the Oaths or to be bound by sureties for his appearance at the next Court of General Quarter Sessions of the Peace to be held for Gloucester County. Therefore, a warrant of Commitment was issued against him and was directed to the Sheriff of the county. Adjourned till Wednesday next.

1777 June 4 – [Wednesday]. Met pursuant to adjournment. Present – Governor, Elmer, Condict, Scudder, Manning, Combs, Cramp, Mehelm. Stout Havens, one of the prisoners taken by Major Mifflin petitioned for another hearing before the Board, was called in, and after hearing proposals by friends in his favor, and a further examination, he was ordered to return to the Guard House. John Barber, Joseph Pearce, John Sears, Richard Margison, and William Newman, five of the prisoners taken by Major Mifflin also petitioned for another hearing, were called before the Board and after examination were remanded to the Guard House. The Council having listened to the above prisoners and finding by their confession that they were taken in arms in the service of the King of great Britain on the 2nd of January last, in which none of them had been engaged more than a fortnight, they were of the opinion that the prisoners were neither Prisoners of War, nor admitted to bail and therefore ought to be continued in confinement. Adjourned till tomorrow morning 7 o'clock.

1777 June 5 – [Thursday]. Met pursuant to adjournment. Present – Governor, Condict, Symmes, Scudder, Elmer, Combs, Hart, Camp, Mehelm, Manning. John Henchman, Esqr. appeared before the Board, charges were read and he was permitted to offer anything in his power by way of palliation and after being heard was ordered to withdraw. Council felt Henchman's case did not fully indicate a malicious intention but put him under strong suspicion of disaffection to the United States. Agreed, that Henchman be called back and that the Oaths be tendered to him, which he refused, but said he was willing to be bound with surety, and did so with Jacob Clement as surety at a sum of 300 pounds each, for his appearance at the Council of Safety and the next Court of General Quarter Sessions of the Peace to be held for Gloucester County, and to maintain his good behavior, and was dismissed. Adjourned to meet again at 11 o'clock.

Met pursuant to adjournment. Jacob Bogart, of Bergen County, one of the prisoners sent down by Gen. Heard, was called and examined, and it appearing that he had enlisted and had joined the enemy and had been actually in arms with them, since the publication of the act, for punishing traitors and disaffected persons, Council was of Opinion --- [The determination of Council is not given.] Giles Williams a prisoner brought down by Col. Briarley was called and examined; but as it appeared that he had been persuaded away by Elihsa Laurence and others, and that he had not either enlisted or taken up arms with the enemy, but had returned, the first opportunity to his neighborhood, but had neglected to turn himself in, he was tendered the Oaths, which he took, and was discharged. Thomas Woodward petitioned for another hearing and went before the Board, and after a further examination was ordered to withdraw. Adjourned till 3 o'clock PM.

Met pursuant to adjournment. Peter Young and Henry Mourison petitioned for another hearing, called in, examined and they appeared very penitent, and were given the Oaths, which they cheerfully took and subscribed and were dismissed. Jacob Gardner also requested another hearing, was examined, heard in his own behalf, but due to General Heard's letter, his confession, and other circumstances, he was a person too dangerous to the liberties of the State to be discharged, and ought to be confined, and he was remanded accordingly. Ordered that 15 shillings be paid to John Hendry for service of himself and horse in bringing a letter express from Burlington to Haddonfield. Adjourned till tomorrow afternoon.

1777 June 6 – [Friday]. Met pursuant to adjournment. Present – Governor, Symmes, Condict, Scudder, Manning, Combs, Camp. Ordered that a warrant of Commitment to the Sheriff of Gloucester issued against Thomas Woodward, son of Anthony, charged before the Council of Safety for the State of New Jersey, with maliciously saying and doing things…such as false rumors concerning the American Forces and the Force of the Enemy as to tend to alienate the affections of the people from the Government…and to dispose them to favor the pretensions of the Enemies of the State. Adjourned till Monday next.

1777 June 9 – [Monday]. The Council met. Present – Governor, Symmes, Combs, Camp, Wetherbee, Elmer, Scudder. Ordered that one pound, ten shillings be paid to Isaac Kay for use of his wagon and horses hauling provisions from Philadelphia for the Guards. Also ten shillings for a load of wood for the guard house. Also seven shillings and six pence to Mrs. Phebe Wallington for House Room and Trouble with a wounded prisoner. The Governor gave a draft of an Appointment of Officers to grant passports and permissions to pass to the Board; which was approved of & is in the words following, to wit:

"State of New Jersey,

In Council of Safety, Whereas in and by a certain Act, of the Legislature of this State, passed at Haddonfield the fourth day of this present month of June, entitled "An act for rendering Effectual two certain Acts therein mentioned," it is among other things enacted, that the Governors or Commanders-in-Chief for the time being, and Council of Safety, be Authorised and Impowered, to grant passports and Permissions to pass through any parts of the State; and also to Authorise such and so many Persons and permissions, and under such Regulations as they shall think necessary, and to detain under guard all Persons Suspected of dangerous Designs, against this State, travilling without such Passports or permissions, until they shall satisfy the Governor and Council aforesaid or the Persons so by them Authorized, of their being well Effected to the State, or of their traveling without any designs Injurious to it; and that every Person who shall be convicted of counterfeiting such passports, or Permissions shall suffer Six Months Imprisonment, as by the said Act, reference being thereunto had, may appear,

We do therefore, by these Presents, Authorize and appoint to Grant such passports and permissions as aforesaid, the Officers following, to wit: All the Members of the Council and of the General Assembly of the State, the Justices of the Supreme Court, the Judges of the Inferior Courts of Common Pleas, the Justices of the Peace and field Officers of the Militia of this State, that-is-to-say Such of the Justices of the Piece and field Officers as have been duly qualified, and taken the Oaths of Abjuration and Allegiance, prescribed by Law; which passports or permissions are hereby directed to be to the following Effect, to wit: County of _____. The Bearer

hereof, _____ aged about _____ years, complexion rather _____ of stature _____ with _____ eyes, a Traveller from _____ to _____, has permission to pass to sd. _____ behaving himself civilly.
Dated: _____.

Which passport or permission the said Officer is to subscribe with is Name and Title of Office; - And all ferrymen and Inn-keepers within this State are hereby prohibited to convey over any creek or River, or to entertain any Traveller, (excepting the said Officers hereby Authorised to grant such Passports or Permissions and all Persons belonging to the Army of the United States) who shall refuse to produce such passport or permission upon being thereunto requested, which every Ferryman and Innkeeper is hereby Enjoined to do. Dated at Haddonfield the ninth day of June in the year of Our Lord One Thousand Seven Hundred and Seventy Seven. Wil Livingston, President."

1777 June 17 – [Tuesday]. Met at Morristown - The Governor and members of the Council of Safety met pursuant to adjournment. [No entry of an adjournment appears.] Present – Governor, Symmes, Condict, Camp, Manning. There being no quorum to proceed, adjourned till tomorrow morning.

1777 June 18 – [Wednesday]. Met pursuant to adjournment. Present as yesterday. There being no quorum to proceed, the Council sent for Benjamin Halsey, Esqr., one of the Judges of the Inferior Court of Common Pleas, Morris County, who attended and took his seat. Ordered, that Isaac Arnot be appointed a Commissioner in the County of Essex, to inventory and dispose of all the Estate & personal effects of certain offenders described in the act of free and general pardon, in the room of Robert Clark who refuses to act. Agreed that a Court of Oyer & Terminer he held, in Essex County, on the first Tuesday of August next. Adjourned till 3 o'clock.

Met pursuant to adjournment. Present – Governor, Condict, Symmes, Camp, Manning, Halsey. John Drummond a prisoner committed by Capt. O'Harra was discharged upon taking the Oaths being there was no evidence against him. Benjamin Foster of Wendham took the Oaths. Adjourned till 9 o'clock tomorrow morning.

1777 June 19 [Thursday]. Met pursuant to adjournment. Present Governor and members as before. Major Gordon appeared before Council from General Heard with a complaint against several persons for plundering tea. Referred him to the possessors of the plundered tea to bring due process. Mr. Hampton, one of the Continental Quarter Masters complained to Council that the Essex Militia was plundering Middlesex and the Council told him to have the owners bring action against those responsible. Adjourned till 3 o'clock in the afternoon.

Met pursuant to adjournment. Levi Lewis, Adam Hebler & Conrad Silpan appeared before Council, examined, and were referred to a further hearing when witnesses can be examined. William Newman, Joseph Pierce, John Sears, Richard Margison, John Barber, Stout Havens, and Jacob Bogart were committed to the Morris County prison for high treason. Adjourned till 9 o'clock tomorrow morning.

1777 June 20 – [Friday]. Met according to adjournment. Present as before – Governor, Condict, Symmes, Camp, Manning, Halsey. Nicholas Smith, Jacob Smith, Levi Lewis, Adam Hebler and Coonrad Silback, prisoners from Sussex County were called before Council, and no witnesses appearing against them, nor any charges brought against them, the Council decided to take recognizance for their appearance at the next Court of General Quarter Sessions of the Peace to be held in Sussex County, and to discharge them from confinement, with them taking the Oaths. Henry Smith of Sussex being very sick in the prison and the Council thought it best to release him from confinement, with him taking the Oaths, with no charge being made against him. Adjourned till 3 o'clock afternoon.

Council Met. Present as before. Captain Marsh appeared before Council in reference to the pay due his company of Light Horse, praying directions in the premises; and desiring to have his company put on a respectable footing for the future. Col. Cortlandt waited upon the Council complaining of Aquacknunk Township neglecting to chose assessors whereby those of the militia who neglect their duty there go unpunished…. Adjourned to 8 o'clock tomorrow morning.

1777 June 21 – [Saturday]. Council met according to adjournment. Present – Governor, Condict, Symmes, Camp, Manning, Halsey. Isaac Ogden, one of the prisoners in Morris Gaol, appeared and professed himself to be a subject of the King of Great Britain, whereupon he was committed to the Morris County Gaol. Thomas Philips and Hendrick Bross, two prisoners in Morris Gaol, appeared and with nothing against them, ordered that they enter into recognizance at 300 pounds each for them to appear at the next Court at Essex, and that they be discharged from confinement, they taking the Oaths. Order that Mr. Camp do advance twenty dollars to Hiram Howard, a wounded soldier of Morris County. Benjamin Morgan Esqr, a prisoner in Morris County (committed by order of his Excellency George Washington) petitioned to be removed from prison to some private house. Ordered that Benjamin Morgan be removed to the house of Widdow Jemima Lum of Morristown, and to remain there or within 100 yards thereof, until further order of the Council of Safety or discharged, on his giving a bond 2,000 pounds, which bond was executed. Peter Fell, one of the Commissioners appointed in an "Act of Free and General Pardon…" for Bergen County, appeared and declined accepting the appointment. Adjourned to Monday 23 June, 3 o'clock afternoon.

1777 June 23 – [Monday]. Met according to adjournment. Present - Governor, Condict, Symmes, Camp, Halsey. There being no quorum to proceed.

1777 June 24 – [Tuesday]. Met according to adjournment. Present - Governor, Condict, Symmes, Camp, Halsey, Manning. Agreed that Major Hayes or the Commanding officer of the Militia at Newark, be ordered to remove from Essex County to the South side of Hackensack River in Bergen County, the following to go into the Enemy's lines: the following women (with their children) being the wives and children of persons, lately residing within this State, who have gone over to the enemy, to wit: Mary Longworth, Catharine Longworth, Elizabeth Wheeler, Phoebe Banks, Mary Wood, Hannah Ward, Elizabeth Betty and Anne Clarke, and make a return thereof to the Council of Safety. Agreed, that Joseph Hodden, Jr, Esqr. be appointed a Commissioner of Essex County for signing and inventorying the estates and effects of persons gone over to the Enemy, in place of Isaac Dodd, who refuses to act. Issac and Cornelius Van Saen, two prisoners in Morris Jail appeared and nothing against them, they were discharged upon taking of the Oaths and entering into recognizance to appear at the next Court of General Sessions of the Peace for Bergen County. Cornelius Van Saen declared that he sold to Capt. Campbell, four bags or flour and five bushels of rye, which he threatened him into the sale and was never paid. Isaac Van Saen says that Campbell compelled him to sell to him ten bushels of wheat for which he paid him nothing, and also took two horses that have nor been returned. Mr. Chief Justice Morris happening to come into the Council gave them such information concerning both Isaac and Cornelius Van Saen, as induced the Council to remand them to prison. Adjourned to 3 o'clock in the afternoon.

Met pursuant to adjournment. Present – as before. Mr. Peter Mackie summoned before Council, suspected of being disaffected, was offered the Oaths, which he refused, and appearing too dangerous to be let go, was ordered committed to the Gaol. Ordered that Isaac Ogden, now in the Morris County Gaol, be removed for trial to Essex County in which he resides. Peter Mackie offering to take the Oaths after a warrant of commitment was made, was sworn, and then discharged. Agrees that William Manning be appointed Commissioner for Middlesex County for seizing and disposing of the goods and effects of persons gone over to the Enemy in place of Thompson Stelle, disabled by being taken a prisoner by the Enemy. Ordered that the Governor draw on the treasurer for the use of the Council of Safety, the sum of five hundred pounds by Frederick King. Adjourned till Friday morning at 9 o'clock.

1777 June 27 – [Friday] – Met according to adjournment. Present – Governor, Col. Symmes, Col. Scudder, Paterson, Camp, Mehelm, Manning, Condict. Mr. King brought 500 ponds drawn on the Treasurer by the Governor which was given to Mr. Camp for disposition of the Council of Safety. A petition from sundry inhabitants of Bergen, was read and setting forth, that Isaac Van Saen and Cornelius Van Saan, inhabitants of Bergen County, and now in jail in Morris Town, have not acted in opposition to the United States, or been aiding the Enemy, otherwise than by compulsion, and pray that they may be released on certain terms. Order that the petition be laid on the table. Agreed that Oake Hoagland Esqr. be appointed Commissioner for Burlington County for the purposes mentioned in the Act of free and general pardon, in place of Nathaniel Lewis, Esqr., who refused to act. Whereupon, Oake Hoagland was so commissioned. James Ackerman and William Drummond, Bergen Inhabitants, appeared before the Board and took the Oaths. Adjourned till 3 o'clock PM.

Met pursuant to adjournment. Lt. Col. Vandike made return of the names of the officers elected by the Princeton Company of Militia pursuant to a resolution dated 24th April last. The Governor submitted a bill from the Court of Oyer & Terminer, Sussex County on 28 May 1777. The Court having to detain a number of persons as witnesses for a longer time than usual and expenses being very high, recommended the Council of Safety, pay the following persons their expenses: Josiah Quimby and George Harrison 6 days, each from Essex; William Bouton's horse 6 days and himself 2 days; Capt. Thomas Kinney for summoning witnesses, himself & horse 5 days; Capt. Campbell's account, Francis Miller's account, and Phillip Hoffman's Bill for boarding of Miller –

Total 24 pounds, 9 shillings, 6 pence. Mr. Symmes had leave of absence. Adjourned till tomorrow morning 9 o'clock.

1777 June 28 – [Saturday]. Met pursuant to adjournment. Present – Governor, Scudder, Condict, Paterson, Mehelm, Camp, Manning. Robert Norris and James Smith appeared before the Board and took the Oaths. Abraham Ogden, Esqr. appeared and produced a certificate saying he had taken the Oaths before Justice Tuthill, whereupon he was dismissed. A memorial from Lardner Clark was presented praying the Board would recommend him to Major Gen. Mifflin, for some higher appointment in the Quarter Master Department than what he presently has. The Board took it under consideration and asked the Governor to recommend the said Lardner Clark to Maj. Gen. Mifflin agreeably to the prayer of the memorial. Agreed that Capt. Gifford Dakey have leave to remove Gertrude Tillford, _____wife of _____ Tillford and her children to Staten Island in the State of New York; which said _____ Tillford formerly resided in this State and hath lately gone over to the Enemy. Adjourned till Monday morning 9 o'clock.

1777 June 30 – [Monday]. Met pursuant to adjournment. Present – Governor, Scudder, Condict, Paterson, Mehelm. There not being a number to make a Quorum, adjourned till 3 o'clock PM.

Met pursuant to adjournment. Present – Governor, Scudder, Mehelm, Condict, Camp, Paterson. Agreed that Isaac Van Saan & Cornelius Van Saan, now in confinement in Morristown, be exchanged for John & David Demarest, now in confinement in New York and that Col. Boudinot, Commissary General of Prisoners, negotiate the Exchange. Richard Kemble, Elisha Beach, Samuel Wells, Hartshorne FitzRandolph appeared before the Board by citation and took the Oaths. Pursuant to Order, Major Hayes made a return of the removal of the following persons into the Enemy's lines, to wit: Catharine Longworth, Mary Longworth, Elizabeth Batey, Hannah Ward & Mary Wood; that Phoebe Banks had gone to New York by the way of Hackensack, before the Order of Removal reached his hands; and that Elizabeth Wheeler was in such circumstances that it was judged that her removal would endanger her life. Adjourned till 9 o'clock tomorrow morning.

[The end of the Volume 1]

Council of Safety, State of New Jersey

Volume 2

[Minutes Are Out of Order]

1777 September 12 – [Friday]. Haddonfield - The Council Met. Present – Governor, Paterson, Symmes, Camp, Combs, Condit. Whereas John Ogden, Smith Hetfield & John Willis, of Essex County, have gone over to the Enemy and left their families behind, then agreed that Col. Frelinghuysen cause the wives of the above named and such of their children as are under age to be removed within the Enemies lines, or some place within their possession.

1777 July 1 – [Tuesday]. Morristown – Met pursuant to adjournment. Present- Scudder, Condict, Mehelm, Camp, Paterson. Samuel Ogden appeared before the Board by citation and took the Oaths. Letter from Joseph Hedden Esqr. representing the removal of the prisoners confined in the Newark Gaol, read and answered. Letter from Mr. Symmes setting forth the necessity of the Board sitting for a short time in Sussex, was read and answered. Adjourned to 3 o'clock PM.

Met pursuant to adjournment. Present – Governor, Scudder, and Mehelm, Camp. Not being a Quorum, adjourned till tomorrow morning 8 o'clock.

1777 July 2 – [Wednesday]. Met pursuant to adjournment. Present – Governor, Condict, Scudder, Camp, Mehelm, Paterson. Peter Dubois, John Robinson, Eliphelet Johnson, Thomas Codmus Jr & James Nuttman, committed in the New Ark Gaol, Essex County, for six months, by order of the Court of General Quarter Sessions of the Peace, for refusing to take the Oaths, and whereas John McGinness and John Haveris were by order of the same Court imprisoned for nine months on being convicted of a misdemeanor for attempting to go over to the Enemy; and whereas Isaac Ogden, George Watts and John Edison, are committed to the Gaol charged with High Treason; and also Aaron Kingsland, Morris Hetfield & Baker Hendricks are confined the first in the Gaol and the two latter in the Gaol at Elizabeth Town, for uttering & passing counterfeit bills of credit, that the vicinity of Newark & Elizabeth Town to Staten Island, and other places in possession of the Enemy, and the exposure to incursions, render it necessary for the persons above named, should be removed to some more distant and secure place in the State – The Board agrees that the persons aforesaid be confined in the Common Gaol at Morristown and that the orders of removal be immediately made out and executed. Adjourned till 3 o'clock PM.

Met pursuant to adjournment. Present – Governor, Scudder, Paterson, Mehelm, Camp. Mr. Condict had to attend the Court of Common Pleas, the Board adjourned till 8 o'clock tomorrow morning.

1777 July 3 – [Thursday]. The Council met. Present – Governor, Scudder, Condict, Mehelm, Camp, Paterson. The Memorial of John Clawson was read indicating that the Memorialist was a Sergeant & then an Ensign in a Company of Militia, in Sussex County and that on the 9th of

January last, he was on his way under Col. Winds at Quibbletown, and that by firing off his musket, it burst, and his left hand was so injured that it was immediately cut-off a little above the wrist and that he is now in low circumstances and unable to procure his livelihood and & prays that the Board would grant him some relief; a testimonial of Abia Brown Esqr in favor of the above was likewise read. The Board referred it to the Legislature as they could not decide upon it. The petition of Benjamin Morgan, now confined at Morristown, was read indicating that he wants to take the Oaths, willing to have boundaries set-up and accept whatever penalties the Board may think necessary; and prays he may be permitted to return home. Agreed that Morgan had been apprehended by order of General Washington and is to be considered a military prisoner and the petition to be referred to the General. Agreed, that the Governor direct Genl. Winds to detach 200 men of the militia; to wit: 100 from Morris and the remaining 100 from Sussex and Essex, to be employed in apprehending certain disaffected persons in this State. Board adjourned to meet at Newtown in Sussex, Saturday, the 5th instant July, at 9 o'clock in the forenoon.

1777 July 5 – [Saturday]. Met pursuant to adjournment. Present – Governor, Elmer, Camp, Condict, Paterson, Scudder. A memorial from Elijah Clark, Richard Wescott, and John Cox was read, stating that the Enemy's ships of War entered Little Egg Harbor inlet and seized two brigs lying at the Fox-barrows, just within the inlet & carried them off, a quantity of stock, etc, a praying that Little Egg Harbor may be fortified and that the Board would issue the necessary orders. Agreed that the matter must be referred to the Legislature. Adjourned to 9 o'clock Monday morning.

1777 July 7 – [Monday]. Met pursuant to adjournment. Present – Governor, Scudder, Elmer, Condict, Paterson, Camp, Symmes. Agreed that letters be written to Major Samuel Meeker and Samuel Kirkendall, Isaac Martin, Jacob McCollom and George Allen Esqrs. to appear before the Board, and give a list of persons in this County, who are disaffected or dangerous to the present Government. Adjourned till 3 o'clock PM.

Met pursuant to adjournment. Present – Governor, Scudder, Elmer, Camp, Symmes, Condict. Ordered – Lieut. Aaron Ross Westbrooke take by warrant William Briton, Ephraim Drake, Richard Schackelton, William Honeywell, John Honeywell, Joseph Reed, and Nathan Manning, all of Knowlton, and have them before the Council of Safety without delay, as suspect persons. Adjourned till 9 0'clock Tuesday morning.

1777 July 8 – [Tuesday]. Met pursuant to adjournment. Present – Governor, Elmer, Condict, Symes, Scudder, Paterson, Camp. Governor had a letter before the Board from Brig. General Winds informing that he had collected 200 militia as ordered at Morristown, excepting the detachment from Sussex, which he expected to join them soon at Morristown. He informed that they only had provisions for three days, which they had brought with them and was requesting directions for further supply. Mr. Camp was ordered to furnish Gen. Winds with 100 pounds to procure provisions for the Militia at the direction of the Gen. or Commander, who is to account to this Board for the expenditure of same. He further asked if the Governor would apply to General Washington to have them supplied with ammunition out of the Continental Magazine, and if the can be supplied from the Continental Store, the above money will be returned. Agreed that Teunis Dey Esqr. be appointed Commissioner of Bergen County in reference to the Act of free and general Pardon, in place of Peter Fell Esqr. who refused to act; whereupon Teunis Dey was commissioned accordingly. Agreed that a letter be written to Major Hayes, commanding a detachment of Militia ordered into Bergen County, directing him to aid the Commissioners of said County in the discharge of their duties, and to advise the Commissioners by letters the orders given to Major Hayes. Adjourned to 3 o'clock PM.

Met According to adjournment. Present – Governor, Scudder, Elmer, Condict, Paterson, Camp, Symmes. Ephraim Drake appeared before the Board by citation and took the Oaths. Wm. Britton, Wm. Honeywell and Joseph Reed appeared before the Board by citation and were tended the Oaths and all requested time to consider them upon entering into recognizance with surety for their appearance before the Board tomorrow. They all used each other and Ephraim Drake as their surety at 100 pounds each. Adjourned till tomorrow morning 10 AM.

1777 July 9 – [Wednesday]. Present – Governor, Elmer, Scudder, Condict, Paterson, Symmes. Wm. Honeywell, Nathan Manning and Joseph Reed appeared before the Board, took the Oaths and were dismissed. Wm. Britton appeared before the Board, refused to take the Oaths, and being deemed a dangerous person to be at large by the Council, it was agreed that he should be committed to close custody in the common Gaol at New Town, Sussex County, whereupon a warrant of commitment was made out and directed to the Sheriff of Sussex County. Isaac Carey, Esqr. appeared before the Board and was examined in reference to certain seditious words and expressions made by Wm. Britton, which was reduced to writing and sworn to by Carey. Mr. Meeker, Mr. Kirkendall, Mr. Martin, Mr. McCollom, Mr. Allen and others appeared before the Board and gave the name of the following persons as disaffected and dangerous to the present Government: Gabriel Wilson Senr., Simeon Boiles, Samuel Lundy, Nathaniel Hart, Thomas Lundy, John Green, Jacob Lundy, Charles Pettit, John Collins, Adam Green, Edmund Thatcher, Simpson Howell, James Hannah, Ralph Hunt & Capt. John Shaw in the township of Hardwick; Frederick Limbock, Frederick Bloom, John Mushpan, Charles Crissman, Henry Weighman, James Clandening, Mw. Dilts and Alexander Adams of the township of Knowlton; Solomon Cartwright in Wantage; Henry Slack, Job Slack and Abijah Chambers in New Town; John De Cond. in Oxford. Ordered that a subpoena be issued for Margaret Martin, widow, to appear and give testimony against James Hughstus in Hardeston. A Memorial from Peter DuBois, Eliphelet Johnson, Thos. Cadmus Jr., James Nuttman and John Robinson, certain criminals removed from the Gaol of Essex to the Gaol in Morris, indicating that the distance from their families made it difficult to procure the comforts of life, that the Gaol of Morris has been occupied by prisoners of War, that the filth and stench of the rooms was great and offensive, and that they fear fatal consequences may come from their confinement and asked that they be moved back to their former place of imprisonment in the Gaol in Essex. The Board agreed that the Sheriff of Morris receive orders to clean the Gaol without delay but they cannot at present be moved. They further ordered that the Sheriff of Morris be directed to make a report to the Board of the expense, which may arise for the cleaning of his Gaol and the account of it being inspected and approved, which will be paid. It was further noted to the Board that one of those, James Nuttman, is far advanced in life and has never had smallpox, and that the Disorder now prevails in the Gaol of Morris, in which Nuttman in confined. Therefore, it was agreed that James Nuttman be permitted to move to and be confined in the Gaol of Sussex but he paying for the cost of his move. Adjourned to 3 o'clock PM.

Met pursuant to adjournment. Present – Governor, Scudder, Symmes, Condict, Elmer, Paterson, Camp. John Honeywell, Richard Schackleton, John Shaw, Ralph Hunt, Charles Pettit, Adam Green, John Green, Sampson Howell appeared before the Board by citation and took the Oaths. The Petition of Nathl. Pettit, Thos. Woolverton, Francis McGee, Timothy Skinner, Robert Rosbrook, William Green, Jonas Johnson, Sebastian Chesnutwood, and Felix Hassen, persons duly convicted, fined and imprisoned by the Court of Oyer & Terminer, at late session at Newtown, Sussex County, was read where they asked that some part of their fines and time of imprisonment may be remitted. The Board agreed that they could not handle this request and sent it to the Governor and his Privy Council. Petition of Wendle Lance, Jacob Lance, George Lance Christopher Lance, Peter Lance, Casper Snooke, and Frederick Tatticker was read asking that Henry Shizzler, who was committed by the Court of Oyer & Terminer, at late session at New Town, Sussex County, for the negligent escape of John Eddy, who was charged & indicted for High Treason, might have some part of his punishment remitted. The Board agreed that they could not handle this request and sent it to the Governor and his Privy Council. Petition of Richard Robins, Jesse Woodward & Thos. Fowler, persons confined in the Gaol of Sussex for crimes committed in other Counties, praying that they make take the Oaths of Government & be thereupon released from confinement was read & ordered to lie on the Table. Adjourned till tomorrow morning 9 o'clock.

1777 July 10 – [Thursday]. Met pursuant to adjournment. Present as before. George Augustus Seagrave, a person apprehended by some Military officers & confined in the Gaol of Sussex, was called before the Board, examined and took the Oaths. It was agreed that before Seagrave be permitted to return to his abode he needed to procure by Tuesday surety for his appearance before the next Court of General Quarter Sessions of the Peace for the County of Sussex, to answer such charges by the State, and to be on good behavior and not to depart the Court without Leave. Also, agreed that Mr. Justice Barber be desired to take the recognizance. Adjourned to 3 o'clock PM.

Met pursuant to adjournment. Edmund Thatcher appeared before the Board pursuant to citation and took the Oaths. Joseph Alward of Middlesex appeared before the Council charged with High Treason, upon his own confession, and was committed to Sussex Gaol. Silas Alward was brought before Council and it appeared that he was a prisoner of War. James Morris was called before the Council, and by his own confession charged with High Treason, whereupon a Mittimus was ordered to issue against him, directed to the Sheriff of Sussex County. Adjournment till tomorrow morning 9 o'clock.

1777 July 11 – [Friday]. Present as before. Agreed that Major Hayes be directed to apprehend with the party under his command, and send them to the Gaol in Morristown, the following disaffected persons: Dr. William B. Peterson of Elizabeth Town; Nicholas Governeur of Newark; Peter Duboise of Second River; Aaron P. Schuyler and Henry Kingsland of New Barbadozneck; John Demerest Esqr., Laurance E. Ackerman, John Earle, Andrew Van Buskirk and Dr. James

Van Buren of New Barbados; John Zabriskie Esqr of Newbridge; Gabriel Van Orden of Steen Rapie; Cornelius Banta of Stuckup; John Van Buskirk Esqr and Daniel Van Buskirk of Kinderkamack; Captain John Banta, Caspavus Westervelt, Captain Garret Demerist of Pashack; Captain Cornelius Harring, Cornelius Harring Esqr, John Debauc, Peter J. Harring Esqr of up Hackensack River; John Durzee (Miller) of Old Tappan; Samuel Peck, Jacobus Peck (Prisoner at Morris) and Daniel J. Durzee of Schralenberg; Derick Banta, Peter Bogert, Cornelius Banta of Winkleman; Simon Simonson of Old Hackensack; Seba Brinkerhoff, John Paulison, and Cornelius Bogert of Old Hackensack Point; James Campbell of Teaneck; Samuel Lugdecker, Jacob Degrote, Jacob Dermott, Laurance Vanhorne, Derrick Vreelandt, Abraham Dey, Jacob Dey (his son), Michael Smith, Capt. John Brinkerhoof, Peter Degrote, and John Degrote of English Neighborhood; Garret Van Gieson, Daniel Smith Esqr and Job Smith of Secaucus.

The Board received information that the Women hereafter mentioned, being the wives of Disaffected persons who have gone over to the Enemy, obstruct the Commissioners for seizing and disposing of the personal estates and effects of their husbands, by secreting & concealing the same and that it will be an advantage to the State to send them after their husbands. Agreed that Col. Van Courtlandt be directed by a detachment of the Militia under his command to remove to the South side of the Hackensack River, in order that they may go into the enemies lines, the said women together with their children, to wit: Mary Kingsland, Mary Shagor, Elizabeth Howell, Martha Hicks, Mahitabel Handinot, Labbitee Vanriper, Joanna Wieks, Altia Van Riper, Mary Ganalvant, Jane Drummond, Lydia Sayer, Margaret Nichols, Elisabeth Brown, Sarah Crawford, and Abigail Wood, and that the said Col. make a return of his proceedings to this Board with all convenient speed.

Ordered that the following persons be sent for from Knowlton: William Little, John Mills, Asher Reed, John Bugner, William Wilgurst, John Wilgurst, John Misner, Peter Misner, George Fitcher, John Wars, Andrew McClan, Jonathan Collins, Malon Collins, Liga Collins, John Laun, Reuben Lundy, John Stephenson, Peter Smock, Robert Wilson Senr., Abuson Wilson, Jonathan Wilson, Thomas Parker, John Wooley, John Willis, John Hoole, and Titus Doane who are all suspected of Disaffection to the State and that the Oaths are to be tendered to them. Frederick Leinback appeared by citation and refused to take the Oaths, and entered in recognizance with Frederick Bloom, his surety at 300 pounds each, for his appearance before the next Court of General Quarter Sessions of the Peace for the County of Sussex, and to be on good behavior in the meantime. Frederick Bloom and John Mushback appeared and refused to take the Oaths and entered in recognizance each with Frederick Leinbach their surety in sums and manner as abovesaid. A Memorial was presented by William Hebler of Sussex County in behalf of his son, John Hebler, who is now a prisoner in the State of Pennsylvania, which was read and referred for further consideration. Adjourned till 3 o'clock PM.

Met pursuant to adjournment. Present as before except Mr. Camp who being indisposed had leave of absence. Thomas Lundy appeared by citation, the Oaths were tendered and he asked for time till tomorrow morning to consider them, which was given. Alexander Adams, Simeon Boyles, and Nathaniel Hart appeared and took the Oaths of Abjuration and Allegiance as prescribed by Law. Agreed that Capt. Cyrus Beckwith be instructed to convey Mary the wife of

Silas Hopkins, Rachel the wife of Richard Crowel, and the wife of Allen Wager, with their children to the South East side of Hackinsack River, that they may go to their husbands, who are gone within the Enemy's lines. Adjourned till tomorrow morning 9 o'clock.

1777 July 12 – [Saturday]. Met pursuant to adjournment. Present – Governor, Elmer, Condict, Scudder, Paterson, Symmes. Thomas Lundy appeared before the Board, the Oaths were tendered and he refused to take them, but was willing to be bound, with surety for his appearance before the next Court of General Quarter Sessions of the Peace for the County of Sussex, with Samuel Lundy, his surety, entered into recognizance at 300 pounds each, and to be on good behavior in the meantime. Jacob Lundy appeared before the Board, the Oaths were tendered and he refused to take them, but was willing to be bound, with surety for his appearance before the next Court of General Quarter Sessions of the Peace for the County of Sussex, with Thomas Lundy, his surety, entered into recognizance at 300 pounds each, and to be on good behavior in the meantime. Samuel Lundy appeared before the Board, the Oaths were tendered and he refused to take them, but was willing to be bound, with surety for his appearance before the next Court of General Quarter Sessions of the Peace for the County of Sussex, with Jonn. Collins, his surety, entered into recognizance at 300 pounds each, and to be on good behavior in the meantime. Jonathan Collins appeared before the Board, the Oaths were tendered and he refused to take them, but was willing to be bound, with surety for his appearance before the next Court of General Quarter Sessions of the Peace for the County of Sussex, with Jacob Lundy, his surety, entered into recognizance at 300 pounds each, and to be on good behavior in the meantime. John Stevenson appeared before the Board, the Oaths were tendered and he refused to take them, but was willing to be bound, with surety for his appearance before the next Court of General Quarter Sessions of the Peace for the County of Sussex, with Thomas Lundy, his surety, entered into recognizance at 300 pounds each, and to be on good behavior in the meantime. A Petition from Richard Robins, Jesse Woodward & Thomas Fowler, offenders confined in the Gaol of Sussex, pray that they may at their own expense be removed to the Gaol at Burlington was read and it was agreed that the petition be granted, and an order of removal was issued. John Buganer, Aza Reed, William Little, John Mills, William Willgus and John Willgus, and John Misener appeared by Citation and took the Oaths. Mr. Condict had leave of absence. Adjourned to 3 o'clock PM.

Present – Governor, Elmer, Scudder, Symmes, Paterson. There not being a Quorum, Thomas Anderson Esqr., a Magistrate in Sussex County was called in & took his seat accordingly. Abraham Howey appeared before the Board by citation and took the Oaths. The Memorial of Isaac Coult Junr. was read, setting forth that Samuel Shewed, an apprentice of the Memorialist in May last, was in the service of the State, as a Militia Soldier at Succasunny Plains, and was enlisted in the Continental Army in a regiment under Col. Oliver Spencer, for three years, but had not joined the Regiment, but still continued and was in the Militia. Samuel Shewed was very dangerously wounded, etc. and praying that the Board would take his case under consideration and grant relief. The Board agreed that they couldn't handle the matter and would refer it to the Legislature. Titus Doan appeared before the Board by Citation, the Oaths were tendered and he refused to take them, but was willing to be bound, with surety for his appearance before the next Court of General Quarter Sessions of the Peace for the County of Sussex, with Reuben Lundy, his surety, entered into recognizance at 300 pounds each, not to depart the Court without Leave and to be on good behavior in the meantime. The following individuals entered into recognizance: Reuben Lundy with Mahlon Collins his surety; Mahlon Collins with Jonn. Willson his surety, Jonn. Willson with John Wear his surety, John Wear with Ebenezer Wilson his surety, Jonn. Willson with John Wear his surety, Ebenezer Wilson with John Willets his surety, John Willets with Elijah Collins his surety, Elijah Collins with Thos. Parker his surety, Thomas Parker with John Hole his surety, John Hole with Thos. Parker his surety. Peter Misner appeared before Board with Citation and took the Oaths. The Memorial of Thomas Gustin was read setting forth that he attended at Morristown to hear Testimony on behalf of the State against sundry disaffected persons for 16 days, at his expense for himself and his horse, and that he has not received any compensation for same and is Praying that the Board would take the same into consideration. The Board agreed that they couldn't handle the matter and referred it to the Legislature. Andrew McClean and Joseph Leamon took the Oaths. The Board adjourned to meet at New Germantown, in Hunterdon County, Tuesday, the 15th of July, at 3 o'clock PM.

1777 July 15 – [Tuesday]. Present – Governor, Scudder, Symmes, Paterson, Mehelm, Elmer. Ordered that Warrants be issued for the appearance of the following persons to appear before the Board and take the Oaths: Jacob Hager, Wm. Meerakey, Henry Smith, David Welsh, Mw. Pew, Wm. Buth, Jacob Rose, Jacob Stine, John Hen, Andrew Anbel, Anthony Sharp, Adam Perry, Adam Rhinehart, Adam Crips, Adam Shanket, Christian Oest, Coonrad Bume, Christian Kimpel, Christopher Kain Junr, Daniel Pane, David Crestley, David Trimer, David Safrene, Frederick Safrene, Fredk. Young, George Sliker, George Konk, George Sharp, Henry Sager, Jacob Tovert, Jeremiah Hendershed, John Bunn, John Colver, Jacob Frayee, Jacob Bodine, Jacob Sharp, Jacob Trimer, John Sharp, John Lick, John Morehouse, and James Colver, inhabitants of Morris County. Adjourned till tomorrow morning 9 o'clock.

1777 July 16 – [Wednesday]. Met pursuant to adjournment. Present as before. Ordered that Warrants be issued for the appearance of the following persons to appear before the Board and take the Oaths: Jeremiah Cramer, John Fonger, Jacob Hile, John Hager, Isaac Cowel, John Mann, Laurence Bunn, Laurence Sliker, Laurence Rocloffson, Leonard Shankel, Leonard Trimer, Morris Sharp, Mathias Thomas, Matthias Auled Jr., Martin Stine, Michael Beron, Nicholas Trimer, Powel Cretsley, Philip Hen, Peter Hen, Peter Smith, Peter Luce, Richard Sutton, Robert Colver, Samuel Pew, Stephen Tovert, Thomas Pew, Thomas Man Jr., Thomas White, William Albough, William Nitzer, William Hen Junr, William Trimer, William Patre, William Porter, William Young, William Pew, William Puce, Wm. Duggen, Moses Goodwin, Michael Puce Jr., Samuel Smith, Wm. Mann, Fenwicke Taylor, Philip Wiser Junr., Rocloff Roloffson, Thomas Neal, Daniel Puce, John Stine, Henry Fraze, Jacob Stile Senr., Peter Young, Mathias Trimer, William Welsh Senr., Gabriel Philips, Laurence Hager, Philip Wiser, Leonard Neighbour, Christopher Kam, John Walder, Morrice Sharp, Tretrick Stubel, Coonrad Rerick, Frederick Safrene Senr., John Sagar, William Hen, Gasper Eick, John Pizer, Jacob Hen, Robert Colver Senr, John Inman, Michael Lefan, Doctr. Adam Laurence, Andrew Flock, Thos. Colven, Michael Aubal Senr., Morrice Creter, Philip Creter, William Welsh Junr, Philip Shiler, Samuel Swackhamer, Joseph Corp, Arnold Cleehaws, Henry Lever, Thos. Hills, and Andrew Flock Junr., inhabitants of Morris County. The Petition of David Campbell was read putting forth that he was a native of Britain, that he has resided in America 11 years, for many years has labored under a disorder of the Scorbutick kind that has baffled experienced physicians, that his estate is considerably reduced, that he desires to return to Britain, and praying that the Board would grant him a passport for that purpose. Agreed that he be given three weeks to settle his affairs and then taking an Oath not to say or divulge any matter or thing prejudicial to the United States, and to remove from the City of New York with his effects. Adjourned to 3 o'clock PM.

Met pursuant to adjournment. Present as before. None of the persons who had been sent for appeared, the Council spent the rest of the afternoon in drawing recognizances and etc. in the blank, and then adjourned to 9 o'clock tomorrow morning.

1777 July 17 – [Thursday]. Met pursuant to adjournment. Present as before. John Stine, Wm. Welsh Junr., Fenwick Taylor, Christian Oart, Jacob Stine, Jacob Hyd, Thomas Neal, Hendrick Fraze, Leonard Neighbur, Wm. Wilsh Senr., Jacob Coleman, Joseph Layboyteaux, Wm. Porter, Peter Laboyteaux, Joseph Coble, Christopher Hendershut, Michael Pace, John Horton, Tedrick Strubel all appeared before the Board and took the Oaths. Mr. Condict appeared and took his seat on the Board. Adjourned till 3 o'clock PM.

Met pursuant to adjournment. Present as before. Col. Van Cortlandt and Potter and the Rev. Mc Whorter and Caldwell, requested to appear before the Board, which was granted. They gave a particular account of the situation of Essex, Middlesex & etc. that the two Continental Regiments stationed along the Essex Coast, would be ordered to join the Grand Army, as soon as the Enemy's movements are indicated; that in such case, the Coast would be exposed to the depredation and incursions of the Enemy on Staten Island, in which place it is probable a body of troops would be placed during the summer in order to plunder the Jersey Shore; and requested a detachment of the Militia be stationed as Guards in that part of the State, that Beacons and alarm posts be fixed upon and appointed, etc. Memo – The above entry must be inserted in the Minutes of the Privy Council. Adjourned till tomorrow morning 9 o'clock.

1777 July 18 – [Friday]. Met pursuant to adjournment. Present – Governor, Scudder, Elmer, Condict, Symmes, Paterson, Mehelm. Daniel Johnson, Essex County, voluntarily appeared before the Board and took the Oaths. On motion, agreed that Peter Dubois, Eliphelet Johnson, James Nuttman, Thomas Cadmus Junr., John Robinson, John McGinnis & John Havens, be remanded to their former place of imprisonment in the Gaol of Essex; they bearing the expense. Mr. Camp appeared and took his seat at the Board. Morrice Sharpenstein and William Allpaugh, of Morris County, appeared before the Board by Citation and took the Oaths. Adjourned to 3 o'clock PM.

Met pursuant to adjournment. Present - Governor, Elmer, Condict, Symmes, Paterson, Mehelm, Camp, Scudder. Gabriel Phillips appeared before the Board by Citation and took the Oaths. The Memorial of Brian Leferty was read, praying that he be permitted to go to Philadelphia and memorialize in the Congress or Board of War respecting the Situation and Case. Agreed that Mr. Leferty be discharged from his Parole, as to have leave to go to Philadelphia respecting his situation & case, and return to his present place of abode in 3 weeks from this date; unless otherwise Ordered by the Congress or Board of War. Agreed that Mr. Condict have leave of absence until Monday next in the afternoon. Isaac Smith, Jacob Hagar, Anthony Sharp, Edward Hall appeared before the Board and took the Oaths. Adjourned till 9 o'clock tomorrow morning.

1777 July 19 – [Saturday]. Met pursuant to adjournment. Present – Governor, Scudder, Elmer, Symmes, Paterson, Mehelm, Camp. Mr. Camp laid before the Board an Acc't from Ichabod Gronman Junr. – To Council of Safety – 1777 – June 10, re: 6 days riding Express – 3 pounds; July 2, re: Jacob Foster, 3 days riding Express – 1 pound, 10 shillings – Total Due – 4 pounds, 10 shillings. It was ordered that the bill be paid. Michael Brean appeared before the Board by Citation and took the Oaths. Mr Scudder and Mr Symmes had leave of absence. Ordered that Warrants be made out to apprehend William Grover, Harry Waddell, Joseph Leonard, Richard Waln & Robert Cooke of Monmouth County, and bring them before the Board without delay. Adjourned to Monday morning 9 o'clock.

1777 July 21 – [Monday]. Present – Governor, Elmer, Condict, Paterson, Mehelm. There not being a Quorum, Oliver Barnet Esqr., one of the Magistrates of Hunterdon County was called in & took a seat accordingly. John Pizor, Casper Eick, Robert Colver, Jacob Bodine, Laurence Rocloffson, William Booth & Samuel Smith, persons cited to appear before the Board, on the score of being dangerous to the present Government, appeared before Mr. Mehelm, one of the members, on Saturday last after the Board adjourned, and they all took the Oaths. Peter Young, Michael Pace, David Crosly, Laurence Hager, Wm. Trimmer, Adam Parry, Paul Crosly, Moses Goodin, Wm. Pace, Jacob Frieze and George Sliger appeared before the Board and took the Oaths. Agreed that Thomas White, of Morris County, taylor, to have leave to go into the Enemy's lines on Staten Island with his wife & 3 children, between this and next Thursday morning; and if seen in this State after that day, all officers, civil & military, are directed to apprehend him & bring him before the Governor and the Council. Adjourned to 3 o'clock PM.

Met Pursuant to adjournment. Present as before. Ordered, that Warrants be issued to cite the following persons to be and appear before the Governor & Council on Friday the 25th instant, to take the Oaths: Joseph St. Clair, John Allen, Nathaniel McPherson, John Davis, Aaron Large, John Large, John Emley, John Rockhill, Barthlw. Thatcher, Thomas Cahill, Aaron Furman, Dr. Robert Taylor, at the Union, Robert Large, John Grandine & Jerh. King, all inhabitants of Hunterdon County. Ordered that James Parker of Hunterdon be by letter warned to appear before the Board and take the Oaths. Daniel Pace, Thomas Hill & Timothy Colver appeared before the Board and took the Oaths. Joseph Collver, one of the people called Quakers, appeared before the Board and took the Affirmations, to the effect of the Oaths to the State. The petition of sundry persons, inhabitants of Bergen, apprehended by order of the Governor and Council of Safety, and now confined in the Gaol at Morris, was read: Setting forth that the Gaol is exceedingly unhealthy, dangerous and disagreeable, and praying that they may be brought to a speedy hearing, and in the meantime, that they may be permitted to take private lodgings within the limits of the Morristown Township, giving parole or security that they will not depart from the limits prescribed them until they are discharged by the Board. Agreed that the petitioners may take private lodgings within one mile from the Gaol of Morris, on giving Bond, with Surety, to the Sheriff of Morris, in the sum of 1,000 pounds each, and not to depart from the limits prescribed them until they are permitted by the Governor and the Council of Safety of this State.

The petition of Isaac Ogden, George Walts and Aaron Kingsland was read, setting forth that they were removed from the Gaol of Essex to that of Morris by the Board, and from the difficulty of getting their provisions, from the stench and filth of the Gaol, the unhealthy state of the air of the town of Morris, and the prevalence of the Bloody Flux and Camp Fever in said town, their lives are in great danger, and praying they may be speedily tried for the crimes of which they stand charges, and in the meantime they may be remanded to the Gaol of Essex. Agreed that Isaac Ogden, George Watts and Aaron Kingsland be remanded to their former place of imprisonment in the Gaol of Essex; they bearing the expense of such removal. Mr. Camp appeared and took his seat at the Board. Adjourned till tomorrow morning 9 o'clock.

1777 July 22 – [Tuesday]. Met pursuant to adjournment. Present – Governor, Elmer, Condict, Camp, Paterson, Mehelm. Jacob Engellman and Samuel Arlas voluntarily appeared before the Board and took the Oaths. Ordered that Warrants be issued to apprehend and bring the following persons forthwith to take the Oaths: Christopher Vandevender, Jacob Vandevender, John Teeplenn T. keeper; Jacob Eoff Senr., Jacob Eoff Junr., John Thompson, Samuel Siloy, Joseph Kelly, Thomas Willot, John Fossey, Aaron Craig, Dr. John Brown, John Castner Senr., John Castner Junr. Abraham Castner, David King Senr. & David King Junr., of Pluckemin. Ordered that Warrants be issued to apprehend & bring the following persons forthwith forthwith to take the Oaths: James Castner, Peter Seeple, Samuel Perry, John Steel, Jacob Fussler, John Aupelman, Tice Aupelman, Philip Meelick, Jacob Castner, Peter Meelick, John Shaw & Elisha Laurannce, of Somerset County. Mathias McKinstey, of Hunterdon, voluntarily appeared before the Board and took the Oaths. Mr. Mehelm had leave of absence. Adjourned to 3 o'clock PM.

Met pursuant to adjournment. Present – Governor, Elmer, Condict, Paterson, Camp. There not being a Quorum, Oliver Barnet Esqr, one of the Justices of the Peace in Hunterdon County was called in and took his seat accordingly. John Waldorf, Conrad Rerick, George Sharp & Rocloff Rocloffson appeared and took the Oaths. Joseph Shea voluntarily appeared, as did John Sharp of Morris County, and took the Oaths. Ordered that a Warrant be issued to the Constable of Lebanon to apprehend George Horthrun, Nicholas Linnerberry, Fredk. Fritz, George Bangheart, Henry Connolly, and John Croley to bring them to take the Oaths on Thursday next. John Inman, Jacob Hann, John Fouger, David Sovereign, Wm. McCrakan & Matthias Thomas appeared by Citation and took the Oaths. William Hann of Morris County appeared & took the Oaths. Ordered that a Warrant be issued to apprehend and bring before the Board, John White said to be a deserter from Capt. Stout's Company, and now at work for & in the employ of Mr. Justice Cole of Hunterdon. Adjourned to tomorrow morning at 9 o'clock.

1777 July 23 – [Wednesday]. Met pursuant to adjournment. Present – Governor, Camp, Elmer, Mehelm, Condict. There not being a Quorum, Oliver Barnet Esqr, one of the Justices of the Peace in Hunterdon County was called in and took his seat accordingly. Henry Smith, George Conck, Jacob Wise, Jacob Dufford, Adam Segor, David Trimmer, Morris Cretor, Stephen Dufford, Christopher Babel, Michael Levet, Philip Dercberah, Peter Hen, Christohper Kann, Philip Weis, William Nitzer, and Saml. Sego, of the County of Morris, appeared before the Board and took the Oaths. Robert Culver of Morris County being excited to take the Oaths, refused and entered into recognizance to appear at the next General Quarter Sessions of the Peace to be held for said County. Adjourned to 3 o'clock PM.

Met pursuant to adjournment. Christopher Kimball of Morris County appeared before the Board by Citation and took the Oaths. Walter Rutherford & Jas. Parker of Hunterdon County appeared being cited to take the Oaths, refused and entered into recognizance to appear at the next General Quarter Sessions of the Peace to be held for said County. Adjourned to tomorrow morning 9 o'clock.

1777 July 24 – [Thursday]. Met pursuant to adjournment. Present – Governor, Condict, Camp, Elmer, Mehelm, Paterson. After adjournment last evening, Saml. Ketcham of Morris County appeared before his Excellency the Governor & took the Oaths. Abijah Merrit, Robt. Nisbett, Fredk. Ferriberry, Frederick Fraze, Peter Hind, Thos. Colver, Lambert Van Sicklen, Simon Colver, John Winckler, Ephraim Tuthill Junr., David Hagar, John Fisher, Wm. Giston, Isaac Lockman, George Hover, John Dusenberry, Martin Gates, Thos. Betson & Peter Lewis appeared by Citation and took the Oaths. Richard Mann appeared before the Board pursuant to Citation and being one of the people called Quakers, took the affirmations to the effect of the Oaths. William Hedden, Levi Mann, John Kelly, Frederick Fritz, Wm. Anderson of Morris County pursuant to Citation, and Giles Lee, 1st Lieut. in the Company of Militia, of the County of Morris, voluntarily appeared & took the Oaths. Adjourned to 3 o'clock PM.

Met pursuant to adjournment. Present as before. Daniel McDonald Esqr., 2nd Major of the 2nd Regiment of Foot Militia, in Hunterdon County, under the command of Col. Beavers, having removed into the County of Sussex, the Board elected Garrat Albertson Esqr. to be 2nd Major of the said Regiment. George Banghart of Hunterdon appeared before the Board by Citation and took the Oaths. John White, a deserter from Capt. Stout's Company was apprehended & brought before the Board, and on his examination having confessed that he belongs to the said company, the Board delivered him to the care and committed him to the charge of Mr. Justice Cole, who promised and engaged to convey him to his Company without delay. Wm. Dals was brought before the Board and took the Oaths. Adjourned till tomorrow morning 9 o'clock.

1777 July 25 – [Friday]. Met pursuant to adjournment. Dr. Aaron Craig & John Teeple, Tavern Keeper, John Thompson, Saml. Selby, David King Senr., Jacob Eoff Esqr. Junr., Jacob Eoff, Senr., John Castner Junr., Coonrad Castner, Joseph Kelly appeared before the Board by Citation and took the Oaths. John Castner Senr. of Morris County appeared before the Board and took the Oaths. Jacob Castner, John Castner Junr., John Castner Senr. & David King Junr., of Somerset, appeared before the Board and took the Oaths. John Aupelman & Mathias Aupelman being too much indisposed to attend sent certificates of their having taken the Oaths before Mr. Justice Sebring and the Board agreed that the certificate was sufficient & they did not have to attend. Philip Meelick appeared before the Board by Citation and produced a certificate of having taken the Oaths on the 12th of this instant, July, whereupon he was dismissed. Adjourned till 3 o'clock PM.

Met pursuant to adjournment. Present as before. The Memorial & Petition of Maria Elizabeth Lesten was read, setting forth that she was a native of Holland, from whence she removed with her husband, Michael Henry Lesten, to Rio Demarari, a Dutch settlement in the West Indies, where they had lived for 10 years; that upwards of 3 years ago, she lost her health in Demarari and she undertook a voyage to North America, and landed in New Hampshire with 3 young children; that her husband intended, after he had settled and adjusted his business, to follow her to America, in order to reside the remainder of their days; that the difficulty of settling his business in the West Indies prevented his intended voyage until the present unhappy disputes in America obliged him to lay aside all thoughts of carrying those his intentions into execution at present; that she has lived a great part of the time she has been in America at Amboy, which place she was obliged to quit in Fall, and now resides at Mr. Crooks at Rariton with her 3 children; that she has been at a very great expense in the maintenance & several removals of herself & family, and from the disappointment in remittances intended for her by her husband is reduced very low in her finances and seeing no end to the present disputes, thinks it prudent for her to endeavor to recover such of her effects as may have been taken by the British Ships of War, or to procure leave of the Commander of British Troops to return to Demerari, and upon obtaining such leave to procure passage thither for herself & family; and praying that the Board would be pleased to grant her a passport to New York where she expects she may be advised of and assisted in such steps as may be proper & necessary for her to take for the attainment of the ends proposed; And, if she cannot attain them, that she may return and provide for herself in the best manner she can.

The Board agreed that Mrs. Maria Elizabeth Lesten have leave to go to the City of New York with her children, agreeably to the Prayer of her Memorial, and if she thinks proper to return to this State, on taking an Oath that she will not carry nor bring with her any dispatches respecting the present War between Great Britain and the United States of America, nor on any political subject relative to the said War, nor say nor do anything prejudicial to the State, or the United States. Adam Leake, Thos. Kellyham, Nathaniel Bedson, Thos. Kendry, John Taylor, Wm Thornhill, Thos. Willet, Jacob Vandevender, John Hagar, appeared before the Board by Citation and took the Oaths. Jacob Schuyler, John Schuyler, Wm. Weir and Philip Cramer, of Morris appeared before the Board by Citation and took the Oaths. The Governor laid a letter before the Board from John Emley of Hunterdon, who was cited to appear, who asked to be excused for his non-attendance, as he had been for some days sick and confined to his room. Dr. Aaron Furman of Hunterdon, being brought before the Board, by Warrant, refused to take the Oaths and he being deemed too dangerous to be suffered to go at large, upon giving security for his appearance at the next Court of Quarter Session of the Peace in Hunterdon County, agreed that he should be committed to close custody in the Common Gaol at Trenton in the county aforesaid, whereupon a warrant of commitment was made out accordingly. Joseph St. Clair, John Allen and Nathaniel McPherson of Hunterdon, were brought before the Board and they, too, refused to take the Oaths and being deemed too dangerous to be suffered to go at large upon giving security for their appearance at the next Court of Quarter Session of the Peace in Hunterdon County, agreed that they should be committed to close custody in the Common Gaol at Trenton in the county aforesaid, whereupon a warrant of commitment was made out accordingly. Aaron Large was brought before the Board by Warrant, and being one of the people called Quakers, refused to take the affirmations to the effect of the Oaths, and being deemed too dangerous to be suffered to go at large, upon giving security for his appearance at the next Court of Quarter Session of the Peace in Hunterdon County, agreed that he should be committed to close custody in the Common Gaol at Trenton in the county aforesaid, whereupon a warrant of commitment was made out accordingly. Daniel Cahill, being brought before the Board, by Warrant, refused to take the Oaths but was willing to be bound with surety, whereupon he entered into recognizance with Mr. Campbell, his surety, at 300 pounds each, for his appearance at the next Court of Quarter Session of the Peace in Hunterdon County, and in the meantime to be of good behavior, and not depart the Court without leave and as dismissed. The Petition of Mathias Sharp, Peter Dumont, John Berry, and John Brockman, was read: Setting forth that some time ago in Decr & Jany last, when the Continental Army was marching through the State, several horses were taken from them by order of the commanding officers for the use of the Army, for which they have received certificates; that they have applied to the Q. M. Genl. For payment, but it was refused, and praying that the Board would pay them. Ordered that the petition lie on the table for consideration. Adjournment to 8 o'clock tomorrow morning.

1777 July 26 – [Saturday]. Met pursuant to adjournment. Present as before. John Todd of Somerset voluntarily appeared before the Board and took the Oaths. Whereas, _____ Howard and _____ Rodney, who were lately residents of this State, have gone over to the enemy & have left their families behind them; it is ordered that Capt. Cornelius Tunison, of Somerset, be directed to remove Bloomy Howard, wife of said _____ Howard, and Elizabeth Rodney, wife of _____ Rodney, and her two children from the County of Somerset, to Staten Island, or the South east side of Hackensack River, in order to go into the Enemy's lines, and the Captain is to make a report of the proceedings and the expense of such removal. William Hughes, Henry Weaver, Hezekiah Drake, Joseph Drake, Daniel Laurance & Christian Hoffman, all of Morris County appeared by Citation before the Board and took the Oaths. Andrew Sergeant, Mathias Harris & David Sergeant, Captain Wm. Laurance of Morris appeared voluntarily before the Board and took the Oaths. Peter Hartsaugh, Abraham Sickle, Jacob Van Sickle, and Peter Weaver appeared by Citation before the Board and took the Oaths. John Grandin of Hunterdon County appeared and took the Oaths. Robert Taylor, Esqr., of Hunterdon, appeared by Citation before the Board and produced a certificate of having taken the Oaths before Mr. Justice Johnson on the 28th of May last. Mr. Paterson had leave of Absence. The Council adjourned to meet at Morristown, on Monday, the 28th instant, July at 3 o'clock PM. After Council adjourned, Jacob Evert of Morris, and Peter Massig appeared by Citation and took the Oaths.

1777 July 28 – [Monday]. Met pursuant to adjournment. Present – Mr. Camp, Mr. Condict, Mr. Elmer. There not being a Quorum, adjourned to tomorrow at 2 o'clock PM.

1777 July 29 – [Tuesday]. Met pursuant to adjournment. Present – Governor, Hart, Manning, Elmer, Condict, Camp. John Van Orden, Abraham Allen, and David Anderson were called to give evidence against prisoners from Bergen, in Hackensack, were sworn but they not knowing anything material, their evidence was not committed to writing, and they then took the Oaths. Agreed that the Sheriff of Morris remove Wm. Newman, a prisoner in the common Gaol, who has the smallpox to the hospital in Morristown. Mr Camp has leave of absence on extraordinary occasion. Adjourned till tomorrow morning at 9 o'clock.

1777 July 30 – [Wednesday]. Met pursuant to adjournment. Present – Governor, Hart, Condict, Manning, Elmer. There not being a Quorum, Benjamin Halsey Esqr., one of the Justices of the Peace for the County of Morris, was called in & took his seat on Council. Abraham Ogden presented a Petition to the Council signed by Nicholas Hoffman, Abraham Ogden & Samuel Ogden setting forth: That David Ogden Esq. late of Newark, who on the 5th day of Jany. last went over to Jamaica on Long Island to recover his health, and that the David Ogden has not yet recovered his health so he can return home; praying that "the Sale of the personal Estate of the said David Ogden should be deferred until the health of the said David Ogden will permit him to return to the State of New Jersey, when by complying with the terms of the Act of Grace or such others shall then be thought proper, he may entitle himself to the protection & confidence of the Govt. of New Jersey." The Council taking the above petition into consideration believe that they cannot grant the prayer without suspending the operations of the Act of the Legislature, which has made no such exceptions, but that if said David Ogden can produce sufficient reasons why his present Estate though disposed of agreeable to Law, should be restored to him, application for that purpose must be made to the Legislature of the State, in whom alone is vested the power of relieving him. Albert J. Bogert, William Hammill, Richard Heaton, Abraham Ely, Gillium Outwater, Herman Brays, John Quackenbush, John Duryee appeared before Council and took the Oaths. The Council adjourned to 3 o'clock PM.

Council met pursuant to adjournment. Present as before. Agreed that Garret Lydecker Esqr., be appointed a Commissioner for Bergen County, for the purposes mentioned in an Act of Free & General Pardon & for other purposes therein mentioned, in the room of Teunis Dey Esq, who refused to act, whereupon Garret Lydecker was commissioned accordingly. Cornelius D. Blauvelt and Abraham J. Blauvelt were called to give evidence against Bergen prisoners, they were sworn and their depositions were committed to writing. Adjourned till tomorrow morning 9 o'clock.

1777 July 31 – [Thursday]. Met pursuant to adjournment. Present as before. Collo. Philip Van Courtlandt, who had been ordered to remove several women (being the wives of persons who had gone over to the Enemy) to the South side of Hackensack River, to go into the Enemy's lines made return of the execution of his orders, to wit: "Second River, July 24, 1777 – Sir, at bottom you have a return of the women & children, conveyed to the South side of Hackensack River, according to your Excellency's orders of the 11th Instant, I am, Sir, Your most Humble Servant., Philip V. Cortlandt. Capt. Jos. Pierson's return of the women & children sent to the Enemy's Lines to wit: Mary Kingsland with 2 children; Mary Stages with 1 child; Felia Riker not sent being near her time; Frontie Interest with 1 child; Mary Garrabrants with 3 children; Elizabeth Howet with 1 child; Martha Hicks with 4 children; Mehatabel Houdnot with 1 child; Hannah Weeks with 8 children; Mary Garrabrants with 2 children; Jane Drummond with 2 children; Lydia Sayres; Margaret Nichols with two children; Sara Crawford with 1 child; Abigail Ward with 1 child; LibitieVan Riper, her husband returned & has taken the Oaths. Altie Van Riper, her husband returned & has taken the Oaths. Elizabeth Brown."

John Outwater being called to give evidence against the Bergen prisoners was sworn & his deposition was committed to writing. Ordered that a Warrant be issued to apprehend George Ryerse Esqr., who has long been with the Enemy & has for some time past left them & has returned to his farm. But has not applied to any magistrate for the benefit of the Act of Grace... Ordered that Jost Zobrisci be subpoenaed as a witness. Adam Boyd was examined as a witness against John Demarest & evidence was reduced to writing. Adjourned to 3 o'clock PM.

Met pursuant to adjournment. Present as before. Cornelius Harring was examined as a witness against Capt. John Banta & his evidence commit to writing. Agreed that Garret Vangieson be apprehended & imprisoned in the Common Gaol in Morris County, agreeable to an Act of the Legislature of this State, entitled, An Act for rendering more Effectual two certain acts therein mentioned; in order to induce the enemy to release one or more of such of the good subjects of this State as they have taken and still keep in confinement; the said Vangieson to be kept in said Gaol, till thence delivered by order of the said Governor & Council. Adjourned to 9 o'clock tomorrow morning.

1777 August 1- [Friday]. Met pursuant to adjournment. Present as before. Agreed, that Christiana Depuyster, the wife of William Depuyster, Junr. at present residing near Orange Town, to have permission to remove with her children, servants & effects to the City of New York to her husband. Agreed, that Lieut. Jost Zebrisci, of Paramus have liberty to raise a company of Volunteers in Bergen County, consisting of 30 men under his command, and that he apprehend & send to the Govr. & Council of Safety, wherever they shall sit, all such persons who have gone over to the Enemy since the 4th day of October last, & are since returned without taking the benefit of the Act of Pardon, and without proper Passes from persons duly qualified to grant same, and also to apprehend and & send such persons as may hereafter go to or return from New York, without proper passes during his command of the said detachment, and also to apprehend & send as aforesaid, all persons who have been guilty of plunder, or who shall plunder the inhabitants of the said County during his command, always taking care to send with the prisoners a particular account to prove their offenses, & witnesses who can prove same, or their affidavits in writing taken before a Civil Magistrate. In case the said Jost Zebrisci, declines the above commission, Jacob C. Zebrisci, is hereby authorized to raise and command the above party, and to follow the above directions. [Signed:] Wil. Livingston. The above Company to be in force for one month from the date hereof. Adjourned to 3 o'clock PM.

Met pursuant to adjournment. Present- Governor, Hart, Condict, Halsey, Elmer, Manning. John Earl of Bergen County having been apprehended as a suspicious person & disaffected to the present Government was called in, examined, and took the Oaths. Thomas Welcher of Morris County having lately been with the Enemy on Staten Island, was apprehended, and brought before Council and upon examination & saith that he left the Enemy with an intent to claim & receive the benefit of the Act of Free & General Pardon; and although since he came over his conduct has been very imprudent and suspicious, yet declaring that his true design was to come in and deliver himself up, being fully convinced of his error in going over to the Enemy, and that it was his duty & interest to defend his country in future, was admitted under the Act and given the Oaths. Adjourned till tomorrow morning 9 o'clock.

1777 August 2 – [Saturday]. Met pursuant to adjournment. Present – Governor, Condict, Hart, Halsey, Elmer, Manning. Capt. John Banta appeared before Council & after examination, he took the Oaths, and gave security for his appearance at the next Court of General Sessions of the Peace for Bergen County, and the said John Banta and David Duryee entered into recognizance in the sum of 300 pounds each. Adjourned till Monday 2 o'clock PM.

1777 August 4 – [Monday]. Met pursuant to adjournment. Present – Governor, Elmer, Manning, Halsey, Condict, John Mehelm. Agreed that Hyram Hayward a wounded soldier belonging to the Morris County Militia have the sum of 7 pounds, 10 shillings towards his subsistence. David Bruin who had been committed here by Capt. Wm. Chambers, stationed at Pompton, for passing 2 counterfeit $30 bills made in imitation of the Continental Currency to Abraham Manning of Pompton, was called before the Board & confessed his passing the bills but denied knowing they were counterfeit; stating that they were given him by _____ of New York to purchase a horse. He also confessed he had lately been to Staten Island, Long Island & New York, and returned from the enemy's lines to Bergen County about 3 weeks ago without any permission or passport for either going or returning & declared his willingness to enlist on board the Continental Fleet. Ordered that David Bruin be committed to the Gaol of Morris for passing the counterfeit bills & if acquitted on his trial, that he have the benefit of the Act respecting the other offense, by going on board the Continental Navy; whereupon a Warrant of commitment was made out for him. Andrew Van Buskirk appeared before the Board and confessed that he had sold provisions to the Enemy since he took ye Oaths of the State. Ordered that he be committed to the New Ark Gaol & a Warrant of Commitment was made out for him. Adjourned till tomorrow morning 9 o'clock.

1777 August 5 – [Tuesday]. Met pursuant to adjournment. Present – Governor, Condict, Elmer, Halsey, Manning, Mehelm. David Vanbuskirk a prisoner from Bergen County appeared before the Board and declared his innocence & offered to take the Oaths to the State, and no evidence nor any particular charge appearing against him, he was discharged after taking the Oaths. Adjourned till 3 o'clock PM.

Met pursuant to adjournment. Present as before. Examined a number of the Bergen prisoners & referred them to a further opportunity. [No names given.] Adjourned till tomorrow morning 9 o'clock.

1777 August 6 – [Wednesday]. Met pursuant to adjournment. Present – Governor, Condict, Elmer, Mehelm, Halsey, Manning. Ordered that Saml. Wells & his wife be cited to appear on Friday next at 10 AM, & that Jonathan Dunn be subpoenaed to give evidence against Mrs. Wells. Mr. Yost Zabriska being called a witness against the Bergen prisoners was sworn. Derick Banta, John Degroot, Seba Blinkerhoof, Lawrence Ackerman, Michael Smith & Cornelius Abm. Herring, prisoners from Bergen County, appeared before the Board and on examination declared their innocence and with no evidence against them, offered to take the Oaths, which they did, and were discharged. Yost Zabriska upon Oath charged John Demarest Esqr., Lawrence E. Acreman, Dr. Jas. Vanburen, John Zabriska, Gabriel Van Norden, John Banta, Casparus Westervelt, Cap. Demarest, Cornelius Herring Esqr., John Debarre, Peter J. Herring, John Duryea, David J.

Duryea, Peter Bogert, Cornelius Banta, Simon Simonson, John Powelson, Cornelius Bogert, Samuel Lydecker, Jacob Demot, Peter Degroot, John Degroot, Garret Van Gieson & John Buskirk with being disaffected to the Government of this State. Adjourned until 3 o'clock PM.

Met pursuant to adjournment. Margt. McLean & Joanna Wood being called to give evidence against William Wright & his wife, was sworn & their evidence written down. Adjourned till tomorrow morning.

1777 August 7 – [Thursday]. Council met. Present as before. Dr. James Vanburen & Henry Kingsland prisoners from Bergen County appeared before the Board, produced evidence to the Board that induced them to be discharged upon their taking of the Oaths, entering into recognizance to appear at the next General Quarter Sessions of the Peace to be held for the Bergen County, with Peter Zabriska security for Van Buren & Jas. Zabriska for H. Kingsland. Peter Bogart a prisoner from Bergen upon taking the Oaths was discharged. Mrs. Williams was sworn as a witness against Mr. & Mrs. Wright but her evidence was not material and was not written down. Adjourned to 3 o'clock PM.

Met pursuant to adjournment. Jacob Dey a prisoner from Bergen took the Oaths and was discharged. Mrs. Hannah Wright, wife of William Wright, was brought before the Board and charged on the Oaths of Margaret McClean & Joanna Wood, of an offence against the third section of an Act Entitled An Act to Punish Traitors & Disaffected Persons. Ordered that Hannah Wright be committed to the Gaol of New Ark; whereupon a Warrant for commitment was made out. Mesheck Walker appeared before the Board and was charged upon his own confession of High treason. Ordered that Mesheck Walker be committed to the Gaol in New Ark, whereupon a Warrant was made out. Whereas the Board has received information that John Troop, Peter Saunders & James Moody were recruiting for the Enemy within this State. Ordered that Col. John Munson & _____ do forthwith apprehend & bring forth the said John Troop, Peter Saunders & James Moody. Adjourned till 8 o'clock tomorrow morning.

1777 August 8 – [Friday]. Council met pursuant to adjournment. Present – Governor, Elmer, Condict, Manning, Mehelm, Halsey. The Offices of Lieut. Col. & First & Second Majors of the First Regiment of Foot Militia in Essex County, commanded by Col. Potter, being vacant, the following Gentlemen were appointed to said offices – Moses Jacques for Lieut. Col., Jacob Crane Fist Major, & Ezekiel Woodruff Jr., 2nd Major. Order that the Commissions be made out accordingly. Adjourned till 3 o'clock PM.

Met pursuant to adjournment. Present as before. Henry Shight from Sussex, produced a certificate indicating that he took the Oaths & entered into recognizance with Richard Johnson for his security to appear at the next General Quarter Sessions of the Peace of said County, and in the meantime to be on good behavior. Prisoners from Bergen, John Zabriska and Arent Schuyler, took the Oaths & entered into recognizance for their appearance at the next General Quarter Sessions of the Peace of Bergen County. John Demarest appeared before the Board and entered into recognizance with Peter Zabriska, his surety at 300 pounds, to appear at the next General

Quarter Sessions of the Peace for Essex County at New Ark, and in the meantime to be on good behavior. Adjourned till tomorrow morning 8 o'clock.

1777 August 9 – [Saturday]. Met pursuant to adjournment. Present – Governor, Elmer, Mehelm, Manning, Halsey. A letter was received from Mr. Condict that he was indisposed and couldn't attend and being no Quorum, adjourned till Monday at 3 o'clock.

1777 August 11- [Monday]. Met pursuant to adjournment. Present – Governor, Elmer, Halsey, Manning, Mehelm. There being no Quorum, & a member being wrote for & not expected before Wednesday; adjourned till Wednesday morning 9 o'clock.

1777 August 13 – [Wednesday]. Met pursuant to adjournment. Present – Governor, Elmer, Hart, Mehelm, Manning, Halsey. Mr. Reuben Randle, being apprehended & sent to the Council by Major Sealy, on suspicion of carrying on a correspondence with the Enemy & no evidence of such appearing, he was discharged after taking the Oaths. Adjourned till 3 o'clock PM.

Met pursuant to adjournment. Present as before. Lieut. John Troop of 3rd Battalion of New Jersey Volunteers, in the Enemy's service and being apprehended on an Order by the Governor and the Council of Safety as a Spy or recruiting for the Enemy, was examined. Ordered upon his examination to be sent to General Washington. Ordered that Henry Shoope & Peter Saunders, suspected Spies from the Enemy taken by Lieut. Troop, be remanded to prison in order to determine whether they will take their trial or go on board the Navy of the United States. Adjourned till tomorrow morning 8 o'clock.

1777 August 14 – [Thursday]. Met pursuant to adjournment. Present – Governor, Condict, Elmer, Manning, Mehelm, Halsey, Hart. Silas Drake appeared before the Board by Citation and took the Oaths. Benjamin Tuttle & John Abel prisoners taken near Elizabethtown, belonging to Col. Buskirk's Regiment, were examined. Ordered that they be remanded to prison to determine whether will take their trial or go on board the Navy of the United States. Adjourned till tomorrow morning 3 o'clock PM.

Met pursuant to adjournment. Present as before. Cornelius Herring, John Debarre, John Duryea, Samuel Leydecker & James Campbell, prisoners from Bergen, were brought before the Board, declared their innocence and agreed to take the Oaths, and with no evidence appearing against them, they were discharged upon taking the Oaths. Casparus Westervelt, one of the Bergen prisoners was discharged upon taking the Oaths and entering into recognizance with security for his appearance at the next General Quarter Sessions of the Peace of Bergen County, and in the meantime to be on good behavior. Adjourned till tomorrow morning 9 o'clock.

1777 August 15 – [Friday]. Met pursuant to adjournment. Present – Governor, Condict, Elmer, Manning, Hart, Mehelm, Halsey. Cornelius Banta, a prisoner from Bergen, was brought before Council, examined & upon entering into recognizance with Simon Simonson as security to appear at the next General Quarter Sessions of the Peace, was discharged after taking the Oaths.

David J. Duryea, Simon Simonson, Jacob Demot & Peter Perry, prisoners from Bergen, were discharged upon their taking of the Oaths. Adjourned till 3 o'clock PM.

Met pursuant to adjournment. Present as before. The Board was informed that Walter Rutherford & James Parker, of Hunterdon, who refused to take the Oaths were held over for trial at Trenton, and have also refused to take the Oaths before the said Court. Ordered that Walter Rutherford & James Parker be brought forthwith before ye Governor & the Council of Safety as persons disaffected to this State. Garret Demarest, Cornelius Bogert, John Powlison, Peter J. Herring, John Vanbuskirk, Gabriel Van Norden, Abraham Vanguson & Garret Vanguson, prisoners from Bergen, were brought before the Board & ordered that they be confined as disaffected persons to the State, until an equal number of our subjects are captured and confined by the Enemy in that County, are released or until further orders. Adjourned till 8 o'clock tomorrow morning.

1777 August 16 – [Saturday]. Met pursuant to adjournment. Present – Governor, Manning, Hart, Condict, Elmer, Halsey. Mr. Camp appeared and took his seat. John Bray appeared before the Board, was sworn & his deposition taken in writing. Ordered that Benjamin Pound, Cornelius Boice, Daniel Rangan, Leonard Boice & George Boice, all from Middlesex, be cited to appear before the Council on Tuesday next. Agreed that Ebenezer Bishop, Jacob Rowland, David Jeryard also be cited to appear before the Council on Tuesday next & Ichabod Bunn, Thomas Bloomfield Sr., & Samuel Freeman be cited as evidence & etc. Also Samuel Heard, Michael Long, John Kinsey & Samuel Insley be cited as Evidence; all of Middlesex County. James Smith appeared before the Board and took the Oaths & gave evidence against James Stevens which was committed to writing and filed. Ordered that Mr. Camp pay Col. Morgan the sum of 26 pounds, 18 shillings and 3 pence for apprehending and securing John Troop & others. Agreed that John Munson be appointed Col., Robert Gaston to Lieut. Col, Samuel Sayers to 1st Major & John Start to 2nd Major, of the Western Battalion in Morris County. Abraham Vanguson a prisoner confined in the Common Gaol of Morris, was brought before the Board and confessed he had been three times into the Enemy's lines in New York. Ordered that Abraham Vanguson be confined in Morristown in order to exchange for some one of the Good people of this State now confined in New York. Edward Barnfield appeared before the Board and took & subscribed the Oaths. Adjourned till 3 o'clock PM

Met pursuant to adjournment. Present – Governor, Halsey, Camp, Hart, Elmer, Condict. Abraham Campfield appeared before the Board and took the Oaths. Agreed that Lieut. Jedadiah Mills take John Stewart & bring him before the Board on suspicion of being disaffected to the present Government & that Noadiah Crammer be cited to appear next Monday to give evidence against said Stewart. Adjourned till Monday 9 o'clock.

1777 August 18 – [Monday]. Met pursuant to adjournment. Present – Governor, Hart, Elmer, Condict, Halsey. Pursuant to an order of Saturday last, Gabriel Vanorden, Cornelius Bogert, Garret Demarest, John Vanbuskirk, Garret Vangieson, John Pawlison & Peter J. Harring appeared before the Board & executed their Bond in the amount of 5,000 pounds, dated 18 August 1777, conditioned on each of them to be & remain at the late dwelling house of Nicholas

Houghman, in Morristown or within one mile thereof, and not depart from the limits above, without the Leaves of the Council of Safety & the Bond delivered to Mr. Condict to keep. Adjourned till 3 o'clock PM.

Met pursuant to adjournment. Present as before. Agreeable to Citation, Noadiah Crammer appeared before Council & Gave evidence against John Stewart, which was written down. Sundry prisoners desiring to come before Council were admitted and heard. Also, several of their parents were heard in behalf & relative to the peculiar circumstances of their unhappy offspring. Being there was not a Quorum, no determination could be made. Adjourned till tomorrow morning 8 o'clock.

1777 August 19 – [Tuesday]. Met pursuant to adjournment. Present – Governor, Elmer, Halsey, Hart, Condict. Being there was not a Quorum, adjourned till 3 o'clock PM.

Met pursuant to adjournment. Present - Governor Elmer, Condict, Hart, Mehelm, Halsey. Thos. Bloomfield, Ebenezer Bishop & Samuel Freeman cited to give evidence against Benjamin Pound & others was examined but their evidence not being material, it was not written down. Egbert Saunderson a prisoner from Essex appeared before the Board and with no charge or evidence against him, he took the Oaths and was discharged. Adjourned till tomorrow morning 9 o'clock.

1777 August 20 – [Wednesday]. Met pursuant to adjournment. Present – as before. Abraham Vanguson appeared before the Board and gave Bond with two securities for the sun of 500 pounds, for his continuing within one mile of the Morristown Court House until discharged from his confinement. Ye Bond is committed to ye care of Mr. Condict. Cornelius Vanguson & Isaac Vanguson from Essex taken by Col. Morgan appeared before the Board, took the Oaths and were discharged. David Brown, John Abell, Benjamin Tuttle, Henry Sharpe & Peter Saunders, prisoners who were considering whether to enlist in the Navy or go to trial, were brought before the Board & they declared their willingness to enlist, which they did, and they were ordered to be sent to Philadelphia under guard, to be put on board any of the vessels of war belonging to the United States which they may choose. John Stager & Aaron Clawson, prisoners from Essex, were brought before the Board, took the Oaths and were discharged. Adjourned till 3 o'clock PM.

Met pursuant to adjournment. Present – Governor, Condict, Hart, Mehelm, Elmer, Halsey. The above mentioned prisoners who were permitted to go on board some of the vessels of war, belonging to the United States, signed an enlistment in the words following: "Morristown, August 20, 1777 – We the subscribers do hereby severally promise & agree to and with His Excellency Governor Livingston, to enter ourselves as Mariners on board of some vessel of War belonging to the United States of America, on our arrival at Phila., to serve during the present War, reserving to ourselves the privilege of Election as to the particular vessel, and considering ourselves as Enlisted in the service of the United States from the day of the date hereof, with the reservation afsd; Witness our hands the day & year above written- David Brown, Henry Shupe, Peter Saunderson, Benjamin Tuttle, John Abell; Witness- John Mehelm. A True copy of the Enlistment." Leonard Boice & Daniel Runyan, appeared before the Board by Citation and took the Oaths. Walter Rutherford & James Parker Esqrs, appeared before the Council, by Citation, and after being examined, resolved that Walter Rutherford & Jas. Parker Esqrs be confined as persons disaffected to this State until an equal number of our subjects are held captive are released by the Enemy, or other order taken therein. Adjourned till tomorrow morning.

1777 August 21 – [Thursday]. Met pursuant to adjournment. Present – Governor, Elmer, Halsey, Condict, Hart, Mehelm, Mr. Camp appeared & took his seat. Resolved – The Governor to draw upon the State Treasurer, in favor of Mr. Hart, a sum of 200 pounds being the remainder due of 1,000 pounds made subject of a draught of the Governor, by advice of the Council of Safety, by an Act of the Council & Assembly of this State, Entitled an Act for investing The Governor & a Council consisting of twelve, with certain powers therein mentioned. Adjourned to 3 o'clock PM.

Met pursuant to adjournment, Present as before. Agreed that Capt. Abrm. Harring be directed to enlist a Company of 36 men, and to choose one other commissioned officer, to serve as Volunteers of the Militia of the County of Bergen, for 3 months, unless sooner discharged, as a Guard for the North & East frontier parts of said County & that the said Captain be authorized to purchase provisions for the party when on actual service, or to appoint some proper person to purchase same, transmit proper accounts to the Legislature, or in their recess to the Council of Safety, & that Mr. Camp do furnish Col. Teunis Dey with 35 pounds cash to purchase ammunition for said party & that the sd. Captain do account for the expenditure of such ammunition when the said service is over. Whereas the Company of Militia commanded by Samuel Pinson, has for sometime past done duty in the North Battalion of the Regiment, whereof Philip Van Courtlandt Esqr. is Colonel, and considering that a majority of the members reside in the Southern District, it has proved to be inconvenient to the men, therefore, the said company be for the future joined to & do duty in the South Battalion of the said Regiment. Walter Rutherford & Jas. Parker Esqr. appeared before the Board and executed a Bond of 2,000 pounds, conditioned on them remaining at the Morris County Court House, or within one mile thereof, until further order be taken & the Bond committed to Mr. Condict. The deposition of Wm. Burnet Junr. was presented to the Board setting forth that the Hon. Peter Kemble Esqr. had granted protection under Genl. Howe's proclamation. Ordered that the said Peter Kimble Esqr. be cited to appear before the Board tomorrow morning 9 o'clock. Adjourned till tomorrow morning 8 o'clock.

1777 August 22 – [Friday]. Met pursuant to adjournment. Present – Governor, Elmer, Condict, Hart, Mehelm, Halsey. Agreed that the Governor direct Major Benoni Hathaway to deliver the Field pieces & appurtenances, and also the powder you are to receive for the public use, to the Commanding officer of the Militia stationed along the frontiers near Staten Island, or to his order, & take his receipt or the receipt of the person by him authorized to receive it. The Governor signed the following certificates: To Benjamin Halsey Esqr. – 12 pounds, with 3 pounds, 12 shillings paid to him in June last, 26 days attendance in Council; To John Mehelm – 23 pounds, 8 shillings for 39 days attendance in the Council of Safety. The Council of Safety received a fine of Justice Halsey of 6 pounds for which they are accountable to the treasury, which was a fine sd. Justice received from Samuel Wells of Morris County. Mr. Kimble having been cited to appear before the Board informed the Governor by letter that he was indisposed of body and was unable to attend. Ordered that Justice Halsey calling to his assistance another of the Magistrates of the County of Morris, do wait upon the sd. Peter Kimble and take his recognizance to appear at the next Court of General Quarter Sessions of the Peace, to be held for sd. County & in the meantime to be on his good behavior. Ordered that the Speaker pay Jay Martin $9.00 for 18 days attendance on the Council as DoorKeeper. Benjamin Hatfield being brought before the Board on a charge of trading with the Enemy, confessed the fact & made his election to go on board the Navy of the United States. Ordered that Mr. Hart pay Alexander Carmichael 9 pounds,11 shillings for sundry services performed by order of the Council. Ordered that Mr. Elmer pay Frederick King 3 pounds, 15 shillings for five days riding express for the Governor & Council. Adjourned to Tuesday next to meet at Princetown.

1777 August 26 – [Tuesday]. Princetown - Met pursuant to adjournment. Present – Governor, Elmer, Hart, Manning. There not being a Quorum, adjourned till tomorrow morning 9 o'clock Wednesday.

1777 August 27 - [Wednesday]. Met pursuant to adjournment. Present- Governor, Elmer, Hart, Combs, Scudder, Manning. Ordered, the wives & children (under age) of John Hearn, Ellis Barron, Wm. Smith, Isaac Freeman, and Saml. Moores, late inhabitants of Woodbridge Township, but now with the Enemy, be immediately apprehended & sent over to Staten Island; & that Col. Fredk. Frelinghuysen be directed to carry this order into execution. A number of letters from Col. Fredk. Frelinghuysen requesting an answer were read to the Board by the Governor. It appearing that Hunterdon County is entirely delinquent in furnishing their quota of the detachment of Militia ordered out under Col. Frelinghuysen, the Governor was desired to issue immediate orders to the several Colonels belonging to sd. County, forthwith to furnish & send off their respective quotas of sd. Detachment. Adjourned till 3 o'clock PM.

Met pursuant to adjournment. Present as before. His Excellency having occasion to call a privy Council, the business of which will probably take up a principal part of the afternoon. Adjourned till tomorrow morning 8o'clock.

1777 August 28 – [Thursday]. Met pursuant to adjournment. Present – Governor, Hart, Manning, Combs, Elmer. There not being a Quorum, Enos Kelsey, Esqr., one of the Justices of the Peace for Somerset County was called in and & took his seat in Council. Thomas Flemming employed as Doorkeeper at 5/0p a day. Genl. Sullivan came in & laid before the Board sundry papers found with the prisoners lately taken on Staten Island. James Hetfield of Elizabethtown, who had been taken as a suspicious person, was brought before the Board, examined, and ordered that he remain under guard until further orders. Ordered that Mr. Hart pay Lieut. George Allen the sum of 4 pounds,17 shilling, 6 pence, it being expenses of bringing nine prisoners from Elizabeth Town to Princetown, by order of Col Freilinghousn. Jacob Hetfield was brought before the Board as a person disaffected to the present Government & being examined, took the Oaths and was discharged. Benjm. Barlon, son of Col. Joseph Barlon, taken up & sent under Guard by Genl. Sullivan, was brought before Council. It is said that the said Barton is appointed Capt. In the British Army. Ordered that he be continued under Guard until further Enquiry can be made. Adjourned to 3 o'clock in the Afternoon.

Met pursuant to adjournment. Present as before. James Wells and Richard Churchward, late of Raritan Landing, having been apprehended as disaffected & dangerous persons, were brought before the Board & upon examination acknowledged that they had been in New York with the Enemy, but said that they obliged them so to do, at the time when the British troops left Brunswick. No proof appearing contradictory to their confessions, they took the Oaths and were discharged. Jonathan Clawson, late of Piscataway, was brought before the Board as a disaffected person, who upon being examined, said that some time last winter, being threatened & frightened by the provincials to such a degree to be in fear of his life, he fled into Brunswick for safety, and being there taken sick, he continued till about 3 weeks after the British left Jersey, and then returned home & was soon taken up by Col. Dunn and sent under guard to Elizabeth Town. Cornelius Clowson brought before the Board in like manner and upon examination appeared to be nearly in the same circumstances, having been voluntarily within the enemy's lines for a considerable time & his general character being disaffected to the present Government; ordered that Jonathan Clawson & Cornelius Clowson have it in their election to enlist on board some of the vessels of war belonging to the United States of America, or be confined & take their trial agreeable to the Law of this State. Adjourned till tomorrow morning 8 o'clock.

1777 August 29 – [Friday]. Met pursuant to adjournment. [Not recorded who was present.] John Rynile, Jacob Long & James Medder, late of Northampton County in Pennsylvania, having been apprehended upon Schooley's Mountain in New Jersey, and many suspicious circumstances attending to their conduct, were brought before the Board & being examined. They declared their willingness to enter into the Service of the United States, and promising to enlist with an officer present, were discharged. Michael Brein, who was taken up at the same time and place with the above last named was examined and agreed to enlist in the Continental Army & was thereupon discharged. James Compton of Baskingridge having been apprehended as a disaffected person, was brought before the Board, and upon examination confessed that he had been frightened from home, went over to Staten Island in May last & after continuing there about two months, returned home. He also acknowledged to have been at the taking of Genl. Lee but says the British Light horsemen forced him to go with them for that purpose, threatening to kill him on refusal. Also James Worth of the same place with the sd. Compton, apprehended on like suspicion, was brought before the Board, confessed & was found guilty of going voluntarily into the Enemy's lines upon Staten Island, and after some considerable stay on the said island, returned to the State, and gives no better reason for this his conduct, than the gratifying his curiosity. Benjamin Worth brought in as the two foregoing, and appearing in the same predicament as the others, the Board considered their case & agreed to give each of the three the liberty of entering on board the vessels of War of the United States of America, or take trial for their lives agreeably to Law. Which being made known to the prisoners, they desired time until tomorrow to make their choice, which was granted by the Council, and the prisoners remanded back to the Guard Room. Benjamin Barton of Sussex County (said to be appointed Captn. in the British Service) again brought before the Board, examined & utterly denies his own knowledge of any such appointment, or that he has ever acted inimical to American liberty. Adjourned till 3 PM.

Met pursuant to adjournment. Present as before & Capt. Scudder. Benjamin Barton took the Oaths and entered into Bond with Richard Edsal of Orange County, in New Jersey, & Richard Edsal the 3rd [name probably in error & meant to be Barton] of Sussex, to remain in his home or within two miles of it, till leave obtained to the contrary; and also into recognizance to appear at the next Court of Oyer & Terminer to be held for the County of Sussex. Michael Loffy was brought before the Board & examined, when it appeared that he had lately taken the Oaths before the Board, and being there was no evidence against him, he was discharged. Benjamin Townshend & Levi Townshend were brought before the Board, examined and then remanded to the Guard House. William Quail, a prisoner formerly belonging to the 55th Regt. was ordered to be sent to the board of War. Adjourned till tomorrow morning 8 o'clock.

1777 August 30 – [Saturday]. Met pursuant to adjournment. Present – Governor, Hart, Manning, Kelsey, Scudder, Combes. Cornelius Clawson, James Cumpton, Benjamin Worth & Jonathan Clawson, again appearing before the Board & choosing to take a trial by the Country, were ordered into confinement for that purpose and Mittimus were made out against them, directed to the Sheriff of Morris County. Mr. Henry Waddel & Mr. Joseph Leonard appeared before the Board and took the Oaths and were discharged. Adjourned till 3 o'clock PM.

Met pursuant to adjournment. Present as before. Messrs. James Grover & Thos. Thompson appeared before the Board by Citation, took the Oaths and were discharged. Mittimus was ordered to issue against James Hetfield directed to the Sheriff of Morris County. Benjamin Townshend & Levi Townshend were ordered under Guard to Philadelphia, and there delivered to the Man of War. James Musher & John Martin Sreider were brought before the Board, took the Oaths and were discharged.

1777 September 5 – [Friday]. Governor called a Council of Safety. Present – Governor, Condict, Dick, Manning, Mehelm, Camp. Ezekiel Beech, formerly an inhabitant of Morris County, who joined the Enemy on Staten Island last January & was taken and delivered to this Board, was examined and confessed himself a subject of the King of Great Britain & acknowledged that he had gone to the Enemy last January. Ordered that Ezekiel Beech be committed to the Common Gaol of the County of Morris for High Treason on his own confession. Ordered that the wives of William Lucy and Chevalier Joint and also Betsy Longworth, Charity Longworth, Elizabeth Van Gieson, Elea White, Mary Billington, [Volume 2 – ends abruptly without continuation of the above and picks up in Volume 3 with 22 September 1777.]

[The end of Volume 2]

Council of Safety, State of New Jersey

Volume 3

[Out of Order, No year written] December 12 – Members of the Council of Safety – Silas Condict, Wm. Paterson, Nathl. Scudder, Thos. Elmer, John Hart, Benjin. Manning, Peter Tallman, John Mehelm, Caleb Camp, Jacob Drake, Jonn. Bowen, John Combs, John Buck, Wm. P. Smith, Frederick Frelinghuysen, Edward Fleming.

1777 September 22 – [Monday] - Haddonfield. Pursuant to the power & Authority given in & by an Act of the Council & General Assembly of the State of New Jersey, entitled "An Act of Constituting a Council of Safety," the Council of Safety met. Present – His Excellency Wm. Livingston Esqr, Condict, Paterson, Hart, Camp, Manning, Drake, Buck, Combs. The Governor brought a letter before the Board from Mrs. Catherine Rutherford, setting forth her situation & that of her son & daughter, who are indisposed; and requesting that Mr. Rutherford, her husband, may be released from confinement or that he may be confined on his own farm. Agreed that Mr. Rutherford be permitted to go home and remain there for 10 days, at the expiration of which he must return to confinement in Morristown. Thomas Hooton, of Gloucester County, was ordered before the Board and took the Oaths. Ordered that subpoenas be issued to cite Robert Matox, Henry Thom, George Marpoll, Zechariah Royell & John Bisben to appear before the Board to bear testimony against Northrop Marpoll. Adjourned till tomorrow morning 9 o'clock.

1777 September 23 – [Tuesday]. Met pursuant to adjournment. Present – Governor, Condict, Paterson, Camp, Manning, Buck. The Governor informed the Board that the inhabitants & disaffected persons in Hunterdon, Sussex, etc. are confined in the Common Gaol at Burlington and that there are six men only to perform guard duty over them. The Board advised the Governor to order the Officer of the Guard at this place, commanding him to detach a party of 15 men (inclusive of a Sergeant to command them) from the said Guard and that they go immediately to Burlington to do guard duty over the prisoners. Ordered that the same party take under guard to Burlington, Ezekiel Beech & Northrup Marpoll, & that they be committed to close custody in the Gaol of that place. The Board was informed that George Suydam was at the door seeking admittance before Council and he was admitted. Mr. Suydam gave the Board a copy of a parole, signed by Daniel Bray, Chas. Suydam, William Horn & Wm. Flatt, citizens of this State, who were taken off by the Enemy at the time they left this State, purporting that the above named persons were permitted to pass into Jersey, and to solicit an exchange for Silas Alward, Archd. Alward, Jos. Alward & Jacob Goodwin, now in confinement in Sussex. The Board having taken same under consideration, Agreed that Daniel Bray, Chas. Suydam, Wm. Horn & Wm. Flatt, being in the Civil Line, & Silas Alward, Archd. Alward & Jos. Alward being in the Military Line, cannot be considered as objects of mutual exchange. The Board was willing to observe & act conformably to the established rule of Exchange, viz. Citizen for Citizen & Soldier for Soldier. They will therefore give an equal number of Citizens (of whom they count Jacob Goodwin one) for the persons first above named & they will exchange the 3 Alwards for any 3 persons belonging to Jersey, who have been taken in Arms. The Board consents to exchange Jacob Goodwin for Charles Suydam.

1777 September 25 – [Thursday]. Burlington - Met pursuant to adjournment. Present – Governor, Paterson, Hart, Camp, Mehelm, Tallman, Drake. James Craig of Hunterdon confined in the Gaol of Burlington was ordered before the Board, examined, it reduced to writing, & he was ordered to withdraw. The following persons from Hunterdon County, confined in the Gaol at Burlington, were examined and ordered: Ziba Osmun remanded to Gaol; Elisha Bird, Imlay Drake & Wm Craig were remanded; Lewis Kinney, John Little, John Alias, Joseph Smith & Peter Hiller were remanded to prison; Joseph Cox and George Myers were ordered back to prison. Wm. Brady of Sussex, confined to the Gaol in Burlington, was ordered before the Board, examined, and was remanded to prison. Adjourned till tomorrow 8 o'clock AM.

1777 September 26 – [Friday]. Present as before. James Craig, Joseph Cox, Elisha Bird, Ziba Osmun, George Myers, Imlay Drake, Wm. Craig, Lewis Kinney, John Little and John Hiller, were again called before the Board, they took the Oaths and were dismissed. The above named persons entered into an obligation for the payment of 50 pounds each for the costs and charges of taking them up, conducting them to this place and keeping them under guard. Ordered that Warrants be issued to bring William Smith, Daniel Ellis, Samuel Bullus, John Carty, Thompson Neal, John Neal, Royland Ellis and Saml. Ellis, all of the City of Burlington and persons suspected to be dangerous to the present Government in order that the Oaths may be given. Daniel Ellis and Samuel Bullus appeared before the Board on a Warrant, the Oaths were tendered and refused, and the Council deeming him too dangerous to be allowed to go at large even upon his giving surety for his appearance at the next session of the Peace, etc., ordered that they be committed to close custody in the Gaol of Sussex until the next General Session of the Peace of the County of Burlington. John Carty was brought before the Board on a Warrant, the Oaths were tendered and he refused them, but would be willing & desirous of going with his family into the Enemy's lines, the Council agreed that he have leave to go into the Enemy's lines on Staten Island, and that he set off tomorrow morning with his family. Adjourned till 3 o'clock PM.

Met according to adjournment. Saml. Ellis appeared before the Board and being examined was dismissed for the present. Rowland Ellis appeared before the Board in the forenoon and requested time to consider the Oaths, on his word of honor that he would appear on the hour appointed. Wm. Smith, Thompson Neal & John Neal, persons ordered to be apprehended, could not be found, whereupon ordered that a Warrant be issued to bring Wm. Smith, Thompson Neal, John Neal, & Rowland Ellis before the Board so that the Oaths may be tendered to them. Adjourned to meet at Princeton.

1777 September 30 – [Tuesday]. Princeton - Met pursuant to adjournment. Present – Governor, Condict, Elmer, Paterson, Hart, Combs, Camp, Manning, Drake. Agreed that Dr. Jonn. I. Dayton, Ephraim Mash, and James Morris be ordered to appear before the Board for examination. Agreed that John DeHart Esqr., and John Ross Esqr., of Elizabeth Town, be summoned before the Board on Friday next at 10 o'clock A.M. so that the Oaths may be tendered to them. Daniel Ellis & Samuel Bullus having made application to the Board that they may be admitted to take the Oaths, and they being examined by the Board, took the Oaths and were dismissed. Capt. Arnold gave an account to the Board in the following words, "The Council of Safety to Jacob Arnold Dr – June 1777 – For riding express from Morris Town to Genl.

Newcomb, six days at $3.00 per day - $18.00. Ordered that the above account be paid to Capt. Arnold. John Harry of Salem County was ordered before the Board & examined. The decision in his case was deferred until the arrival of the Salem members, with whom (he says) he is acquainted. A letter from Genl. Dickinson was received and answered. Adjourned till 4 o'clock PM.

Met pursuant to adjournment. Present as before. Agreed that Anna Rapelyie, wife of Richard Rapelyie, who is now on Long Island, be permitted to pass to Staten Island in order to go to her husband; and that she have 10 days for that purpose. James Freeman was ordered before the Board, examined and remanded to prison. Thomas Shoemaker, Mathew Camp, Isaac Ammerman, John Smith, William Paulson, John Kitchen & Joseph Smith, several of the Insurgents taken on their way to join the Enemy in Staten Island, were ordered before the Board, examined and were either returned to or remanded to prison. Adjourned till tomorrow morning at 8 o'clock.

1777 October 1 – [Wednesday]. Met pursuant to adjournment. Present – As before and Mr. Mehelm. Jonathan Palmer appeared before the Board and gave evidence against Elisha Bird, George Myers, William Cragg, Lewis Kinney, Peter Hillier & Emily Drake, which was committed to writing. Ordered that a Warrant be issued to Col. Joseph Beavers to apprehend and bring before the Board the said Elisha Bird, George Myers, William Cragg, Lewis Kinney, Peter Hillier & Emily Drake. Adjourned to 8 o'clock tomorrow morning.

1777 October 2 – [Thursday]. Met pursuant to adjournment. Present – Governor, Mehelm, Elmer, Drake, Camp, Manning, Combs, Condict. Hugh Brown, one of the Insurgents taken on his way to Staten Island, was called before the Board, examined, confessed he had taken a gun from Mr. Parks without leave & carried it along with him till he was taken. He was remanded to the Gaol. Peter Snider, one of the Insurgents, was also examined and confessed that he fired at the Militia before he was taken, and then remanded back to the guard room. Wm. Shoemaker & Thomas Anderson, two of the Insurgents, were examined & confessed that they had deserted from Capt. Henry Lewis's Company in Col. Shrewer's Battalion. Ordered that Wm. Shoemaker & Thos. Anderson be delivered to Lieut. George Reynolds, who was present, to be returned to their Battalion; the said deserters to be kept under guard until Lieut. Reynolds returns from Morristown…then to be delivered to him or his order. James Norris appeared before the Board by Citation to give evidence against Jonathan J. Dayton & others [not named] which was committed to writing. Mr. Scudder and Mr. Paterson attended. Jonn. J. Dayton and Ephraim Marsh, entered into recognizance separately at 300 pounds each, for their appearance at the next Court of Oyer & Terminer & General Gaol Delivery for Essex County, and in the meantime to be on good behavior. Jonn. J. Dayton took the Oaths. Jas. Norris entered into recognizance at 300 pounds, for his appearance at the next Court of Oyer & Terminer & General Gaol Delivery for Essex County, to bear evidence against Jonn. J. Dayton & Ephraim Marsh. Agreed that Maria Elizabeth Leston have leave to go to the City of New York with her children and effects, she being a subject of the State of Holland. Adjourned till Saturday the 4th inst., 10 o'clock AM.

1777 October 4 – [Saturday]. Met pursuant to adjournment. Present – Governor, Condict, Scudder, Paterson, Camp, Elmer. The Governor gave a letter to the Board from Mr. Parker, enclosing a letter from Mr. Cort. Skinner, soliciting an exchange, which was permitted to be sent. Parker also requested permission to return home for 10 days which was unanimously denied. Petition of Mary Williams, wife of Nathaniel Williams, who has gone over to the Enemy's Lines, praying that she & her children may not be sent into the Enemy's lines, but that she may be suffered to continue among her friends, upon which surety as may be deemed proper, was read & ordered to lie on the table for consideration. Agreed that the President draw upon the Treasurer for the sum of 500 pounds in part the sum of 2,000 pounds which he is by law empowered to call for by the Advice of the Council of Safety. It was presented to the President & the Council of Safety that the late Governor Penn of Pennsylvania & Benj. Chew Esqr., late C. Justice of the same State, have been permitted by the Honorable Board of War, to reside at or near the Union in the County of Hunterdon. Agreed that a letter be written to Congress, informing them of the impropriety of suffering disaffected persons to remain on parole in this State, as it is nearly encircled by the Enemy, or if it be suffered, that the above persons be removed from the present situation to some more secure & better affected part of the State; and that the Executive Department of this State, have the disposal of them so far as respects the place of their residence. Adjourned till 3 o'clock PM.

Met pursuant to adjournment. Present – Governor, Condict, Scudder, Paterson, Mehelm, Elmer. Mrs. Leonard, wife of Thos. Leonard, who acted as a Major in the British Service & is now a prisoner of war to the United States, was sent over to New York sometime ago by order of Brig. Genl. Forman and hath lately returned to this State. She complains of indisposition & requests that she may be permitted to tarry in Monmouth County until she is reinstated in her health, and that she be suffered to pass to Easton, to see her husband, and from thence to return to said County there to abide. Agreed that Mrs. Leonard be permitted to pass to Easton, or to any other place in which her husband may be fixed, and to remain with him, and that she go thither without delay. Agreed that a letter be written to the officers of the Guard at Morris, directing him in case of necessity to remove the prisoners under his care to New Town in Sussex. Adjourned till tomorrow 10 o'clock AM.

1777 October 5 – [Sunday]. Met pursuant to adjournment. Present – Governor, Condict, Paterson, Mehelm, Camp, Combs, Drake. Agreed that Aaron Forman, James Ilif, John Mee, John Ink, Hugh Brown, Isaac Lambert, Imlay Drake, George Archer, Thomas Rees, John Alias & Isaac Ammerman, certain insurgents taken in arms on their way to join the Enemy at Staten Island be sent from this place to Morristown and there be committed to custody. Adjourned till tomorrow 10 o'clock AM.

1777 October 6 – [Monday]. Met pursuant to adjournment. Present – Governor, Condict, Paterson, Elmer, Mehelm, Manning, Drake. Governor gave a letter to the Board from Mr. Hooper, D.Q. M. G., at Easton, informing that there are several disaffected persons belonging to Jersey confined in the Gaol at Easton, and requesting that they could be moved to some other part of the State due to the prison being crowded. Agreed, that a letter be written to Mr. Hooper informing him that the Council of Safety will sit at Pitts town some time in the coming week, when his request will be complied with.

1777 October 7 – [Tuesday]. Princeton - Present – Governor, Elmer, Condict, Scudder, Buck, Manning, Combs, Drake. Ordered that a Warrant d be issued to apprehend Isaac Thorn & Jacob Thorn upon the affidavit of Jesse Brooks & Abraham Van Camp. Adjourned till tomorrow 2 o'clock PM.

1777 October 8 – [Wednesday] Met pursuant to adjournment. Present – Governor, Elmer, Scudder, Paterson, Combs, Camp, Drake. Richard Waln (one of the people called Quakers) being convened before the Board, and affirmations to the effect of the Oaths being tendered to him, which he refused to take but willing to go with his family into the Enemy's lines, and he appearing to the Board too dangerous to remain in the State, the Council agreed that he be allowed to go with his family into the Enemy's Lines on Staten Island, in five days from the date thereof. Adjourned till Saturday morning 8 o'clock.

1777 October 11 – [Saturday]. Met pursuant to adjournment. Present – Governor, Paterson, Elmer, Scudder, Mehelm, Drake, Combs, Condict. Capt John Blanchard applied to the Board & informed them that nine pipes of wine, the property of Mr. Hamilton Young & four hogsheads of rum, the property of John Livingston, in whose custody they were committed, have been for some time since by sundry other persons, removed from the place where he had stored them, and either sold or used; and that the sd. Blanchard has not received any consideration whatever for the said liquors; and therefore prays that the Board will issue orders to the persons who have removed, sold, or used the liquors to account for the whole with Blanchard, he at the time proffering ample security that the whole proceeds of the liquors shall come to the State if called for. The Council agreed to order those who took, sold or used the liquors to pay John Blanchard and that Blanchard give a bond with security, if required, that the whole proceeds of the liquor's values shall go to the State whenever called for. Adjourned till 3 o'clock PM.

Met pursuant to adjournment. Present – Governor, Paterson, Elmer, Condict, Scudder, Camp, Drake. Application to the Board from Richard Waln, who had leave to go into the Enemy's lines in five days, states that he could not possibly transact the necessary business relative to his family & private affairs of the same in that time. Council agreed he should have more time and granted him seven days from the date hereof. William Sutton was ordered before the Board, took the Oaths and was dismissed. Adjourned till tomorrow 8 o'clock.

1777 October 12 – [Sunday]. Met pursuant to adjournment. Present – Governor, Elmer, Peterson, Mehelm, Hart, Bowen, Buck. Whereas, Joseph Barton, Patrick Hagerthy & Thomas Russell, who were lately residents in this State, have gone over to the Enemy & not withstanding have left their families behind them. Therefore, it is agreed that Ann Barton, wife of said Joseph Barton, and her children under age, (except Henry & John) & Sarah Hagerthy wife of Patrick Hagerthy, & her children, and _____ Russel, wife of Thomas Russel, be removed to Staten Island, on the South east side of Hackensack River, so they may go into the Enemy lines. Agreed that the officer who shall remove the above persons be directed to make a return to this Board, of his proceedings, and the expenses thereon arising. John Harry was again called before the Board and he took the Oaths and was dismissed. John Harry was required to pay 5 pounds for the cost of taking him up, conducting him to this place and keeping him under guard. Whereas Benjamin Barton did enter into Bond with Richard Edsall of Orange County, & Richard Edsall the 3rd of Sussex County, his sureties, to remain at his house or within two miles of it, until he his told otherwise; and did also enter into recognizance to appear at the next Court of Oyer & Terminer for Sussex County. Whereas an application has been made on behalf of Benjamin Barton to be released from his obligation, as it relates to his remaining at his own house or within 2 miles of it. The Board agreed that he be released of his obligation so far as it relates to his remaining at his own house or within two miles of it. Agreed that Col. Sidney Berry be paid 55 pounds, 18 shillings, 5 pence, the amount of charges for himself and a party of 21 men, in apprehending and securing disaffected persons in sundry parts of the States. Agreed that the Governor be advised to write _____ Meeker of Sussex, directing him to raise a party of 20 men & 2 Sergeants & 2 Corporals, to do guard duty over the prisoners, disaffected persons, etc. at New Town, in Sussex. Adjourned till 8 o'clock AM tomorrow.

1777 October 13 – [Monday]. Met pursuant to adjournment. Present – Governor, Elmer, Bowen, Hart, Buck, Mehelm. Isaac Thorn was called before the Board, examined, ordered he enter into recognizance with security to appear at the next Court of Oyer & Terminer at Morristown. Jacob Thorn was brought before the Board, examined and ordered he be committed to the Morris Jail for High treason. Upon recommendation of Col. Saml. Forman & Lt. Col. Elisha Lawrence of Monmouth, Wm. Montgomery Esqr. was by the Board appointed first Major & John Cook Esqr. Second Major of the 2nd Regiment of Monmouth Militia. Upon affidavit of Aaron Dean against Marmaduke Abbot, charging him with asking a greater price in Continental money than hard money for salt; it was order that Marmaduke Abbot be immediately apprehended and brought before the President & Council of Safety, and a warrant was made out and directed to Chas. Saxton who is to make a return the next Thursday at Pittstown. Ordered that 1 pound, 2 shillings, 6 pence be paid to John Hart Esqr. for hiring Express to send to Judge Smith. Agreed that President apply to Mr. Condict to procure & send to Princeton to Major Kelsy by the return of the wagon who take the prisoners in the care of Capt. Stout, about 150 weight of powder in order that Mr. Kelsy may have the lead now here made up into cartridges. Ordered that Mr. Elmer pay Jacob Berger 115 pounds, 4 shillings, 7 pence in full account for supplying the prisoners taken on their way to Staten Island and the guards while at Princeton---. Ordered that Col. Hyer be given a receipt for 250 weight of Continental bread & flour & two barrels of fish for supplying the above mentioned prisoners & guards. Upon recommendation of Col. Jacob Hyer & Lt. Col. Wm. Scudder of the 3rd Battalion of Middlesex Militia, Robert Dixon was appointed 1st Major & Thos. Egberts, 2nd Major of the sd. Battalion. Council then adjourned to Pittstown to meet on the 15th instant, where they met in the evening and adjourned to the next morning.

1777 October 15 – [Wednesday]. Pittstown - The Council met in the evening & adjourned to next morning.

1777 October 16 – [Thursday]. William P. Smith Esqr. appeared in Council & having taken the Oaths, took his seat at the Board as one of the members of the Council. Present – Governor,

Hart, Elmer, Bowen, Smith, Buck. Agreed that the President write to Majr. Genl. Dickinson to propose to Genl. Skinner that the president & the Council of Safety will release from their confinement – Ja. Parker & Walter Rutherford Esqr., whenever the commanding officer of British Troops in New York shall set at Liberty John Fell Esqr., & Wynant Van Zandt, and that they will also releases Gabriel Van Norden, John Van Buskirk, Garret Vangieson, Garret Demarest, Peter J. Herring, John Paulinson, Cornelius Bogert & Abraham Vangieson now confined in Morristown, for Thos. Banta, Barnabus Verbryske, Isaac Blank. Jacob Wortendyck, John Vanbusson, Jacobus Blauvelt, William Hyer & Abraham Golden now confined in New York; and that Genl. Dickinson be desired to acquaint the President & Council of Safety with whatever answer he may receive from Genl. Skinner on the subject of such application. Also, agreed that Genl. Dickinson be requested to inform the President & Council of Safety of the most proper places for erecting beacons, the material requisite for that purpose, with the best conjecture he can make respecting the expense that may attend the procuring the materials, the erecting and attending the beacons. Adjourned till 3 o'clock in the afternoon.

Met pursuant to adjournment. Present as before. Mr. Marmaduke Abbot appeared before Council by Warrant and not denying the charge of asking for salt more in Continental money than in gold or silver or old money, the Council fined him 6 pounds with the costs of sending for him. The Council then tendered him the Oaths to the State which he refused to take & they gave him till tomorrow at 10 o'clock to find security to appear at the next Court of Quarter Sessions for Burlington County. Mr. Mehelm attended. Mr. Elmer received the above fine of Mr. Abbot. Ordered that Mr. Elmer pay to John Thomson 4 pounds, for two days service with his wagon & horses & expenses bringing the Council of Safety, papers, etc, from Princeton to Pittston. Ordered that Mr. Elmer Jona. Palmer [be paid] 7 pounds 10 pence on acct. for riding express and to John Harris 1 pound 10 pence on acct. for attending as a light Horse. Adjourned till tomorrow morning 9 o'clock.

1777 October 17 – [Friday]. Met pursuant to adjournment. Present – Governor, Elmer, Hart, Mehelm, Smith, Buck, Bowen. Reeder Stout was brought before the Board as a disaffected person & refusing to take the Oaths was ordered to withdraw. Order that Warrants issue to Lieut. Jacob Vanderbelt for apprehending as disaffected persons – William Thatcher, Jas. Thatcher, Thos. Harris, Luther Colvin, William Allen Esqr., William King, Joseph King, John Taylor. Ordered that Mr. Elmer pay Lieut. Cornelius Johnson 3 pounds, 2 shillings, 6 pence in full for himself & five men for apprehending Reeder Stout, Saml. Slater & Henry More. Reeder Stout & Henry More appeared before Council and took the Oaths. Samuel Slater & John Taylor refusing the Oaths were ordered into custody to be exchanged. Marmaduke Abbot entered into recognizance with Jacob Gerhart to appear at the next Court of Quarter Session for Burlington County. Ordered that Mr. Elmer pay Mr. Hillar 3 pounds, a witness under recognizance to appear at the Court of Oyer & Terminer now sitting at Morristown for the trial of the prisoners taken on their way to Staten Island, towards his expenses while attending there. The Electors of Bergen County, not having been able to hold the Election for representatives by reason of the vicinity of the Enemy, at the place and time appointed by Law, the Council directed the Monday, 27th October at the dwelling house of Stephen Bogert near the Pond-church in the said County, for the day & place of the Election & send the receipt by Col. Dey. Thos. Harris took the Oaths and was discharged. Jonas Thatcher, Luther Colvin Junr. were brought before the Board and refused to take the Oaths, were bound in recognizance, with Thos. Harris security in 300 pounds, to appear at the next Court of General Sessions of the Peace at Trenton. Mr. Colvin paid 20/ expenses. Ordered that Mr. Elmer pay Mr. Johnson 4 pounds, 10/. for taking sundry Tories being in full for his Acct. for himself, his Ensign and six men, viz 15/ p day for himself & Ensign & 10/ p day Each of the privates. Adjourned till 9 o'clock tomorrow morning.

1777 October 18 – [Saturday]. Met pursuant to adjournment. Present – The President, Elmer, Smith, Buck. Hart, Bowen, Mehelm. Joseph King was called before Council and the Oaths were tendered but he refused to take them. King appearing to be disaffected to the present Government & too dangerous to be at large, was ordered that he be taken up and kept in safe custody in order to be exchanged. In consequence of a resolution of Congress of 31 July last, recommending it to the Executive Authorities in each state to appoint proper persons in each district to recruit men & apprehend deserters, they agree that several Counties in this State be deemed Districts for the purposes aforesaid, and the persons hereinafter names are appointed in the several Districts for that purpose to wit: Morris County – Alexander Carmichael, William Youngs – To rendezvous at Morristown; Burlington County – John Leak, Capt. Joseph Weaver, Capt. Quigley - To rendezvous at Mount Holly; Cape May County – John Hand, James Willets - To rendezvous at Capt. James Willets; Cumberland County – Azel Pierson, James Ewing, George McGlocklin - To rendezvous at Bridgetown; Bergen County – David Marrinus, Cornelius Erwin - To rendezvous at Pumpton; Monmouth County – Kenell Anderson, Gilbert Longstreet - To rendezvous at Court House at Monmouth; Somerset County – John Baird, Joseph Casterlin, Jacob Flagg - To rendezvous at Court House in Somerset; Sussex County – Isaac Martin, Benj. Cuykindal, Capt. Emmanuel Hover, Wm. Carr - To rendezvous at Court House at Sussex; Gloucester County – Joseph Estell, Wm. Price, Col. Josiah Hilmer, James Tallman - To rendezvous at Woodbury; Salem County – Jas. Sterling, Capt. John Kelly, Maj. Anthony Sharp - To rendezvous at Salem; Essex County – David Ross, James Hedden, Abraham Spier - To rendezvous at Newark; Middlesex County – Robert Nixon, John Webster - To rendezvous at New Brunswick; Hunterdon County – Jesse Hart, Richard Curwine, Jacob Anderson of Lebanon, Samuel Gronendyke - To rendezvous at Flemington. Adjourned to 6 o'clock this afternoon.

6 o'clock PM – Met pursuant to adjournment. Present as before, except Mr. Mehelm. Ordered that Lt. Col. Matthias Shipman be directed to remove from Easton to Sussex Gaol, the following persons, or as many of them as are there confined: John Smith, Isaac Ammerman, Cornelius Bogert, Edward Butler, Philip Force, John Mc Cowen, Wm. Mc Cord, Philip Shults, Aaron Smith, Joseph Pegg, John Klyne, Jacob Shults. Council adjourned to 9 o'clock tomorrow morning.

1777 October 19 – [Sunday]. Met pursuant to adjournment. Present – His Excellency, Wm. Livingston Esqr, President – Hart, Elmer, Bowen, Smith, Buck. Ordered that in case the persons hereinafter named are or shall be charged with or committed for any of the crimes or offences, specified in the first, second or third sections of a certain act entitled – "An Act to punish traitors or disaffected persons, Or are or shall be charged with, or committed for Misprision of Treason, or for any crime of offence specified in the 8th or 9th sections of an act for constituting a Council of Safety, or shall be charged with or command for, any of the Crimes or Offences specified in the 2nd Section, of an act entitled An Act to render Certain Bills of Credit a legal tender within this State, & to prevent the Counterfeiting of the same & other Bills of Credit, or so many of them as have been or shall be So charged or committed, shall be tried for the same in the County of Morris, although the offences they be charged with, or were committed for, were done & perpetrated in any other County. The persons above referred to are viz; Aaron Furman, John Mee, Hugh Brown, George Archer, Isaac Ammerman, Ezekiel Buck, Joseph Cox, George Myers, Lewis Kinney, Ziby Osman, Joseph Smith, Thos. Rees, John Kitchen, Thos. Miles, Saml. Brewer, John Eagle, William Ballum, James Hiff, John Ink, Isaac Lambert, John Alias, Emley Drake, James Craig, John Little, Wm. Craig, Peter Killer, Nicholas Pickel, Jacob Klyne, John Parks, Lot Freeman, John Shannon, John Ellis, Daniel McMullen, Henry Dunfield, Thomas White, Daniel Shannon, James Freeman, Wm. Brady, Frederick Pickles, Thos. Pollock, John Long, Christian Snider, George Labour, Benjn. Hull, James High, Martin Snider, Burnet Banghart, John Smith, Matthew Camp, Joseph Britton, Nathaniel Parker, Thos. Shoemaker, Hugh McDaniel, John Park, Wm. Paul, Phillip Fooes, Phillip Shultz, Aaron Smith, John Klyne, Jacob Bogert, Joseph Pierce, Wm. Newman, Cornelius Clawson, Benjamin Worth, Wm. Shurley, Philip Klyne, Wm. Rice, James Kelly, Wm. Shepherd, Peter Snider, Elias Snider, Cornelius Bogart, Lawrence Flemming, Elias Teelte, David Young, John Ryely, Peter George, Henry Hart, Edward Butler, Wm. Moore, Christian Ruth, Herbert Hendry, Jonathan Robins, George Augustus, Northup Marpoll, John McCowen, Wm. McCord, Joseph Pegg, Jacob Schultz, John Sears, Stout Havens, Richard Margeson, James Worth, Jonathan Clawson. Adjourned to Monday at 9 o'clock AM.

1777 October 20 – [Monday]. Met pursuant to adjournment. Present – Governor, Hart, Buck, Bowen, Elmer, Smith, Mehelm. The Governor gave a letter to Council from Mrs. Gertrude Parker praying for sundry reasons that her husband Mr. Parker might be indulged with the liberty of returning from his place of confinement to his own house 'for one fortnight only.' The Council agreed that Mr. Parker be permitted to return to his own house with liberty to remain there for 14 days, at the expiration of which he must return to his present place of confinement in Morristown. John Clyne of Sussex voluntarily appeared before Council and took the Oaths and was discharged from his confinement in Easton. Ordered that Warrants be issued to apprehend Jeremiah King, Wm. King, Edmund Freeman & Nicholas Pickle, as persons suspected of disaffection to the State. Ordered that Mr. Elmer pay Capt. Arnold six dollars for riding express from Morristown to this place. Adjourned to 9 o'clock tomorrow morning.

1777 October 21 – [Tuesday]. Met pursuant to adjournment. Present – Governor, Hart, Buck, Elmer, Bowen, Mehelm, Manning, Smith. Ordered that a Warrant issue to apprehend Jas. McCord on charge of disaffection to the State. Wm. Craig was called before the Board and ordered to enter into recognizance, with Philip Titus his surety for 300 pounds, for his appearance at the next Court of General Quarter Sessions of the Peace for Hunterdon County, and in the meantime to be of good behavior, and discharged from confinement. Ordered that Warrants be issue to apprehend Levi Ketchum and Thomas Stevenson on suspicion of disaffection to the State. Ordered that Capt. James Morgan be directed to remove out of State into the enemy's lines the following persons, being the wives & children of such as have gone over to the enemy, out of State: Ellinor Nevins & her two children; Elizabeth Cook & her three children; Elizabeth Dial &

her three or four children; Elizabeth Gosling & six children, all of the South Amboy Township; and that Capt. Morgan make a return of his proceedings therein to the Council of Safety. Adjourned till tomorrow morning 9 o'clock.

1777 October 22 – [Wednesday]. Met pursuant to adjournment. Present –Governor, Hart, Buck, Elmer, Smith, Mehelm. On the Representation of John Hooten, Jeremiah Turner, Wm. Drake & Jas. Pyat, late inhabitants of this State, that they were removed out of it in February last by part of the Continental Army belonging to New England, & sent to the town of Hartford in Connecticut, to the vicinity of which they are still confined on their parole. Ordered that the Governor be desired to write to Governor Trumbull, telling him that the Council of Safety is desirous of them set free to return to this State in the penalty of 2,000 pounds – with the condition that they proceed with all convenient speed after their being discharged to this State and abide such order & direction as the Council shall take concerning them. Ordered that a Warrant be issued to apprehend Bartholomew Thatcher. Ordered that the wives of the persons hereafter named appear before the Governor & Council tomorrow at 3 o'clock to show cause why they should not be removed with their children into the Enemy's lines according to Law, and on default of their appearance that they be removed accordingly. Their husband's names are: John Vooght, Christ. Vooght, George Casmer, Peter Young, Conradt Eikler, Michael Dennis, Philip Cyphers, John Mills, Joseph Leo, Jacob Foust. Joseph Slater appeared & took the Oaths and was discharged from confinement. Ordered that Col. Chambers be requested to remove the quantity of 1,256 pounds of lead, and a number of cartouche boxes (now deposited at one Wm. Abbot's) to Princeton and there deliver same into the hands of Major Enos Kelsey; and take his receipt for the lead & etc. to be safely kept for the public use by order of the President & Council of Safety of this State; and Col. Chambers to make a return of his proceedings, and the expense for having it done. Ordered that Mr. Elmer pay Christ. Lawbocker, one dollar for attending as an evidence against Jacob Serooss. William Rittenhouse, Joseph Hart, Bartholomew Thatcher, Abner Rittenhouse, Malachi Bonam, Nathan Pine appeared voluntarily and took the Oaths. Ordered that Mr. Elmer pay to Adam Hope five dollars in full for himself & 4 men to apprehend Jas. McCord, Michael Beedle, Edmund Rittenhouse, Joseph Holdron, Elisha Jolly, Samuel Hall, John Warner, Peter Belles, Hezekiah Waterhouse, John Eyke, Ferris Eyke, Moses Warford, James Warford, Wm. McLean, William Homer, Henry Tronk, Levi Kitchen, Christopher Loop, Wm. Kemple. Dr. George Campbell & William Everet Junr., Stephen Lee, Ferdinand Hulicks & Oakie Voorheis appeared before the Board and took the Oaths. Jas. McCord was brought before the Board and took the Oaths. Ordered that Mr. Elmer pay Daniel Bray 6 pounds,10/ in full for himself, Ensing Cowdrick & 10 men in full for taking John Hill, Henry Waterhouse & sundry others, some of which took the Oaths; and also to pay to Cornelius Johnson, 4 pounds, 15/ in full for himself and 7 men for apprehending sundry disaffected persons. Adjourned till tomorrow morning at 9 o'clock.

1777 October 23 – [Thursday]. Met pursuant to adjournment. Present as before. Ordered that Mr. Elmer pay Capt. Samuel Gronendike 45 pounds, 2 shillings, 3 pence in full of his pay roll for himself, a Sergeant, a Corporal and 10 privates as a guard while the Council sat at Pittstown. Ordered that Mr. Elmer pay Col. Joseph Buvers, 61 pounds, 1 shilling, 1 pence in full for himself, Lt. Col., Major, Adjutant & Quarter Master for assisting in taking up disaffected persons from the

11th September until the 25th. Isaac Robins and Wm. Dealy voluntarily appeared and took the Oaths. Jacob Servess apprehended by Warrant against him on affidavit of Christopher Lowbacker, for selling salt for a greater price in Continental Money than for gold or silver, was brought before Council & confessing to the charge, was fined & he paid same. The wives of sundry persons said to be gone over to the Enemy being cited to appear before Council to show cause why they should not be removed with their children in to the Enemy's lines; eight of them now appeared – the wives of Christopher Vooght, George Casner, Peter Young, Conradt Eikler, Michael Dennis, Philip Cyphers, John Mills, Joseph Lee & Jacob Foust; and Council enquired into their circumstances and situation and determined that it would not be expedient to remove them at this time. Ordered that Col. Bonnel be paid the sum of 30/, in full for this trouble & expenses in citing the women to appear. The Rev. David Sutton requested to appear & took the Oaths. Peter Schultz & Jacob Schultz were discharged from their confinement in Easton upon the Bond of Peter Schultz, their father, to appear before the Council if called upon in two months. Joseph Pegg discharged from the same confinement on entering into recognizance with Peter Schultz to appear at Morris Court the 4th of October next. John Taylor took the Oaths and was discharged. Adjourned till tomorrow morning 9 o'clock.

1777 October 24 – Tuesday [? - Should be a Friday]. Met pursuant to adjournment. Present – Governor, Hart, Elmer, Buck, Smith, Bowen, Manning. John Hill was discharged on taking the Oaths. Henry Waterhouse entered into recognizance with John Hill to appear at the next Court of Quarter Sessions at Trenton. Ordered that 3 pounds be allowed to Wm. Davison, Innholder at Pittstown for the use of a room in his house, as a guard room & providing fire & candle in the same during the sitting of the Council of Safety. John Rockhill Esqr. appeared voluntarily and took the affirmations to the effect of the Oaths. Luther Colvin took the Oaths. Council adjourned to meet at Trenton on Wednesday next the 29th of October instant on 10 o'clock.

1777 October 29 – [Wednesday] – Trenton. Met pursuant to adjournment. There not being a Quorum adjourned to Friday next.

1777 October 31 – [Friday]. Morning, 9oclock. Met pursuant to adjournment. [Nothing further noted.]

1777 November 7 – [Friday - Said Tuesday but should be a Friday]. The Council met at Princeton. Present – Governor, Condict, Elmer, Manning, Camp, Drake. Agreed that Serg. McCue be paid for rations of rum for 9 of the Continental Troops for assisting a detachment of militia in guarding a number of prisoners to Morristown from this place, the sum of 4 pounds, 10/. Agreed that Gabriel Van Norden, John Van Buskirk, Garret Vangieson, Garret Demarest, Peter I. Herring, John Paulinson, Cornelius Bogert & Abraham Vangieson have leave to return to Morristown to their respective places of abode for 14 days including going & returning in order to facilitate their procuring the discharge of Thos. Banta, Barnardus Van Bryck, Isaac Blank, Jacob Wortendyck, John Van Busson, Jacobus Blauvelt, William Hyer & Abraham Golden now confined in New York.

1777 November 10 – [Monday]. Council met at Princeton. Present – Governor, Condict, Camp, Drake, Manning, Speaker, Scudder. Agreed that if John Lawrence, now confined in the Gaol of Burlington County, is committed for any of the crimes in sections 1,2 or 3 in the act to punish traitors … or with Misprision of Treason… or sections 8 7 9 of the act constituting the Council of Safety…or any crimes in section 2 of an act to render certain bills of credit a legal tender in this State, then he is to be tried for the same in the County of Burlington, although the offence he is charged with was in another County.

1777 November 14 – [Friday]. Council met at Princeton. Present – Governor, Manning, Drake, Elmer, Hart, Talman. The Board appointed Wm. Livingston, Jr. Secy, who agreed to serve gratis, while the Assembly sits. Agreed there be paid to Abraham Voorhies, for tending the Council of Safety and riding Express as Light Horseman for six days, the sum of 7 pounds, 17 shilling, 6 pence; To Philip Harder for ditto – 4 pounds, 2 pence; for Conrad Ten Eyck – 1 pound, 10 shillings. Agreed that the President draw on the Treasury for the sum of 500 pounds in favor of Mr. Elmer.

1777 November 15 – [Saturday]. Met at Princeton. Present – Governor, Condict, Elmer, Camp, Buck, Manning, Tallman. Agreed to pay to Jonn. Palmer for attending on the Council of Safety as a Light Horseman and for expenses in attending 30 days at Morristown as a witness against a number of State prisoners apprehended on their way to join the enemy on Staten Island, 60 lbs paid. Agreed that the above Palmer be employed in apprehending & bringing before the Board a certain Nicholas Bickle & Andrew Pickins, who secrete themselves in Hunterdon County and Palmer to be paid 30 pounds for Bickle & 50 pounds for Pickins. Coll. Nicola having referred to the Board Daniel Cornock as a person suspected of being a spy & Council having no cause for such suspicion tendered him the Oaths, which he took, and he was discharged. John Emly and appeared before the Board and took the Affirmations to the effect of the Oaths and was dismissed.

1777 November 17 – [Monday]. Met at Princeton. Present – Governor, Elmer, Condict, Fleming, Hart, Camp, Paterson. The following persons are offered to be exchanged agreeable to the Applications of Wm. Bayard Esqr. to Sir Henry Clinton, New York, October 1, 1777. Prisoners in Morristown – John Van Buskirk, Peter T. Herring, Capt. Garret Demarest, Gabriel Van Norden, John Poulieson, Garret Van Gieson, Cornelius Bogert, Jacobus Peck. Prisoners in New York – Isaac Blanch, Harmanns Tallman, Jacob Warthandicke, Thos. Bantha, Bernardus Van Bryck, Samuel Ver Bryck, John Hays, John Morris. The foregoing Exchange is agreed to on condition that Abraham Van Gieson be substituted in the place of Jacobus Peck, under the head of prisoners in Morristown & David Van Boizon, James Hammerson and Abraham Spear in the place of Harmanns Talman, John Hays & John Morris under the Head of Prisoners in New York. Agreed that Gabriel Van Norden, John Van Buskirk, Gerrit Vanguson, Gerrit Demarest, Peter T. Herring, John Paulison, Cornelius Bogert and Abraham Van Gieson have leave to be absent from the district in which they are confined in Morris County till the first day of December next. Col. Scudder appeared & took his seat at the Board. Whereas James Parker & Walter Rutherford Esqrs. were by order of the Council taken up, admitted to their parole at Morristown, in order to induce the enemy to release or exchange the Hon. John Fell Esqr. & Winant Van Zant now in confinement in New York, and treated with the greatest severity, and whereas that step as been insufficient & such release or exchange has not as yet been effectuated agreeable to this Board, it is ordered that James Parker & Walter Rutherford Esqr be forthwith committed to the Common Gaol in Morristown until Hon. John Fell Esqr and Winant Van Zant are released. The Governor gave the Board a letter from Rev. Caldwell to Maj. Genl. Dickinson dated 22 October last, informing of the most proper place to affix beacons and appoint alarm posts, which appears to this Board to be most expedient to remove the piece of Cannon now lying at Princeton to the mountain that nearly divides the space between Elizabeth and Morristown, to be put under guard of the man who lives where the cannon is to be fixed and a few of his neighbors who ought to be exempted from military duty. It would further be proper to erect a pile on the Hill near where Mr. McGee formerly lived, whence the guard from the mountain may see the fire or smoke and by that know that the guns fired at Elizabeth Town are intended for an alarm and upon that signal to fire the cannon on the Mountain. The Council agreed that Mr. Caldwell be desired to carry the above plan into execution and to transmit an account of his expenses for same. Agreed that the following persons be summoned to attend this Board, to have the Oaths tendered to them: James Clark, Samuel Clark, John Clark, Alexander McDonald, Robert White, John Stockton (son of Joseph), John Heath, Thos. Wilson, Isaac Clark, Benj. Clark, Matthw. Clark, Ezekiel Smith, Wm. McDermott, Andrew Morgan, Thos. Clark, Wm. Clark, Jos. Skelton, Saml. Worth, Josh. Horner, John Hedges, Wm. Bryant.

1777 November 20 – [Thursday]. Met at Princeton. Present – Governor, Camp, Talman, Manning, Drake, Col. Fleming. The Governor gave the Board a letter from Major Meeker respecting the prisoners in Sussex Gaol and the provisions necessary for their support. The Board being of the opinion that there is no necessity for keeping a guard for the above prisoners agreed that Col Symmes direct Major Meeker to discharge the guard and to settle with Meeker the cost of the cattle and flour he has purchased for their support. As for the British prisoners confined in said Gaol, Col. Symmes will acquaint the Commissary of Prisoners with their confinement & procure his directions concerning them. As to deserters from the Continental Army, he will inform the magistrates and endeavor to have them taken to their respective units.

PM – Council met. Present – Governor, Manning, Hart, Col. Fleming, Col. Scudder, Camp, Talman, Col. Drake, Condict. Agreed, instead of exchanging Messrs. Rutherford & Parker for Messrs. Vanzandt & Fell, agreeable to a late resolution of the Board, Mr. Rutherford be exchanged for Mr. Vanzandt and Mr. Parker for Mr. Fell, and that whenever Vanzandt is released from actual imprisonment and on his parole in the City of New York or Long Island, Mr. Rutherford is to be released from actual confinement and remain within a mile of the Court house in Morristown. The same thing with respect to Mr. Parker as to Mr. Fells' release from actual custody, etc. Agreed that the Governor desired to write to the person in Winchester, Virginia, who has custody of Robert James, lately of Monmouth County, and a subject of this State, desiring him to deliver Robert James to either Richard James or Thomas Parker, they having promised to bring him into this State at their or his own expense and to enter into Bond for his appearance before the Council of Safety in a reasonable time after his arrival. Agreed that Warrants be issued for apprehending Joseph Morse, Jr., John Hendricks, Baker Hendricks & John Meeker for trading & carrying provisions to the Enemy on Staten Island.

1777 November 21 – [Friday]. Present – Governor, Condict, Manning, Col. Drake, Elmer, Mr. Speaker. Agreed that the following sums be paid for the persons attending the Council of Safety as Light Horsemen and riding express for four days: To John Voorhies – 4 pounds, 5 shillings, 9 pence; To Sany, Moores – 1 pound; to John Smock – 3 pounds, 12 shillings; to Gerret Terhune – 8 pounds, 5 shillings, 9 pence.

1777 November 24 [26th written, should be the 24th] – Monday. Met at Princeton. Present – Governor, Elmer, Hart, Manning, Col. Fleming, Condict, Col. Drake. Agreed that the Sheriff of Morris County confine Walter Rutherford & James Parker, Esqr., to a private room near the Court House for 3 weeks and then to execute a precept lately delivered to him for their imprisonment, unless he receives further orders. Agreed that Edward Taylor & Jeremiah Taylor of Midditon [Middletown] & George Taylor & Josiah Parker of Shrewsbury be summoned as persons disaffected to the present Government. Agreed that John Van Nest be paid for attending as a witness at the Court of Oyer & Terminer in Morristown 8 days – 6 pounds, 8 shillings, Paid to Benjm. Harris for his expenses attending as a witness 4 days – 3 pounds, 4 shillings, & paid to Joseph Blackford for the same – 3 pounds, 4 shillings. To the Constables attending above their usual term – Joseph Stoutan –1 5 days at 10/. Pday – 7 pounds, 10 shillings; Robert Gould, Jr, 17 days – 8 pounds; 10 shillings, Levi Baldwin, 17 days – 8 pounds, 10 shilling; John Lyon, 18 days – 9 pounds; Ephraim Lindley, 18 days – 9 pounds; and by recommendation of the Court for traveling expenses. Matthias Burnet, Jr, 17 days – 8 pounds, 10 shillings plus traveling expenses in serving subpoenas; John Riggs, 10 days – 5 pounds; to the Cryer, 18 days – 9 pounds; That their be paid to Phillip Young, a wounded soldier of the Militia – 5 pounds, 15 shillings; and to Mr. Condict for the use of John Cooper another wounded soldier – 15 pounds, 2 shillings, & 6 pence. Agreed that the officer who is to conduct John Penry & Benjamin Chew, Esqr. to Wooster be directed to purchase in some of the New England States, for the use of this State, 20,000 flints.

1777 November 26 – [Wednesday]. Met at Princeton. Present – Governor, Elmer, Hart, Manning, Col. Drake, Condict. Governor laid a letter before the Board from Ann Kip petitioning for leave to remove with her family & furniture into New York to her husband, from whence she is a refugee, to Tappen where she is unable any longer to support herself & her children. Agreed that the said Anne Kip be permitted to pass to New York, with her three children & furniture, & three days provisions and that she pass thro' the Guard kept by Capt. Herring who is to inspect the wagons to see that nothing be carried contrary to the interest & meaning hereof; & if she takes benefit of this permission, goes to New York, she is not to return into New Jersey during the present War. Agreed that there be advanced to Col. Chamberlain for purchasing 20,000 flints in New England and for defraying his expenses to Wooster in the Massachusetts Bay, whither he is to conduct Messrs. Penn & Chew, the sum of 200 pounds. Agreed that there to be paid to Col. Ellis Cook for the account of Dr. Jacob Green for attending & administering physic to Wm. Maypowder who was sent by the Board to Morristown as a witness against Northop Marpoll & there taken sick, the sum of 1 pound, 10 shillings, 6 pence for boarding the said witness & keeping his horse 3 pounds, 16/.

1777 November 28 – [Friday]. Met at Princeton. Present – Governor, Elmer, Hart, Condit, Camp, Drake, Fleming. Agreed that to be paid to Col. Cook for the use of Dr. John Powers for attending & dressing the wounds of Thomas Baldwin, a wounded soldier, in Capt. Isaac Halsey's Company of Militia in Col. Ford's Regiment, the sum of 1 pound, 16/.& for the use of the said soldier for the loss of time during his illness and rations the sum of 7 pounds, 18 shillings, 2 pence. Agreed that if John Ackerman, Hendircks Ackerman & Gerret Hopper, inhabitants of Bergen lately deserted from Staten Island, give security for their appearance at the next Court of Oyer & Terminer to be held in Essex County, they to be discharged from the Guard. Patrick Nevens & William Cook appeared before the Board & entered into recognizance (Patrick Nevens with Col Drake his surety & Wm. Cook with Col. Flemming his surety at 300 pounds each) for their appearance at the next Court of Oyer & Terminer and Genl. Gaol Delivery for Hunterdon County & having taken the Oaths, they were discharged. John Ackerman, Hendrick Ackerman & Gerrit Hopper appeared and entered into recognizance with John Outwater as their surety at 300 pounds each for their appearance at the next Court of Oyer & Terminer for Essex County & having taken the Oaths, they were dismissed per the above agreement.

1777 November 30 [31st written, should be 30th]– [Sunday]. Met at Princeton- Present – Governor, Condit, Hart, Manning, Camp, Elmer. Agreed that Lieut. Jacob Boskirk, Lieut. Edward Earle, John Hammel, a Surgeon, & John Brown, a Commissary, in the Service of his Brittanic Majesty, who all went from this State (of which they were subjects) since the passing of the Treason Law in this State, to join the British Army & were lately taken prisoners in Staten Island by a detachment of the militia commanded by Maj. Gen. Dickinson, be committed to Trenton jail for High Treason.

1777 December 1 – [Monday]. Met at Princeton. Present – Governor, Manning, Elmer, Col. Fleming, Col. Drake, Mr. Speaker. The Board received information regarding the lately proposed exchange of 8 Bergen prisoners in Morristown for a like number of our subjects, confined in New York, could not be complied with as Genl. Skinner had no authority to alter the exchange agreed to by Genl. Jones and the latter being absent, but that he would release any 5 of the 9 prisoners confined in New York for the 5 of those confined in Morristown. Agreed that John Van Boskirk, Peter T. Herring Esqr., Capt. Gerret Demarest, John Paulinson & Garret Van Gieson be set at liberty upon the release of Isaac Blanch, Jacob Vertondyck, Thos. Bantha, Barnardus Van Brycke & Samuel Ver Bryck.

1777 December 3 – [Wednesday]. Met at Princeton. Present – Governor, Condit, Mr. Speaker, Manning, Col. Drake, Elmer. John & Baker Hendricks appeared before the Board and entered into recognizance with Col. Dayton as their surety at 300 pounds each for their appearance at the next Court of Oyer & Terminer for Essex County and were discharged from the Guards.

PM-The Council met. Present – Governor, Hart, Condit, Camp, Col. Flemming, Linn, Col. Drake. Agreed that Edward Taylor give Bond of 100 pounds to stay within a mile of the College of Princeton & not depart beyond those limits without leave of the Council & that he be set free when Thos. Canfield, a prisoner at New York shall be discharged by the Enemy and allowed to go home. Agreed that Mr. Taylor notwithstanding his Bond, have leave to appear at the next Court of Oyer & Terminer for Monmouth County according to his recognizance.

1777 December 5 – [Friday]. Met at Princeton. Present – Governor, Col. Scudder, Col. Frelinhuysen, Manning, Col. Drake, Elmer, Mr. Speaker. Agreed that Major Mauritius Goetshius be authorized to raise a Company of 60 men, with 1 lieutenant & an Ensign for the defense of the northern parts of Bergen County & to prevent the depredations of the Enemy & disaffected persons, and the illicit trade & intercourse carried on between Bergen County & New York & that they continue in service for 3 months unless sooner discharged. Agreed that John Aker, John Blinkerhoof, John Smith & Jacob De Groot, who have gone over to the Enemy have permission to return to this State upon the condition of their bringing with them Peter Westervelt, Jacob Westervelt, John Westervelt, Henry Vervalier and Jacob Ferdon, now prisoners in New York.

PM – The Council met at Princeton. Present – Governor, Hart, Camp, Manning, Col. Henning, Col. Drake. Agreed that John Honeyman be committed to Trenton Gaol for High Treason. Agreed that John Meeker enter into recognizance with Thos. Saffen his surety in 300 pounds each, to appear at the next Court of Oyer & Terminer for Essex County. Agreed that Jacob, Joseph, Reuben & Joatham Randolph into recognizance in the like sum to appear at the next Court of Quarter Sessions for Middlesex County.

1777 December 8 – [Monday]. The Council met at Princeton. Present – Governor, Camp, Manning, Col. Drake, Elmer, Mr. Speaker. The following prisoners under Guard from Maj. Potter at Woodbridge, to wit: Ellenor Worth, Charles Friend, John Willis, Walter Noakes, Michael Condin & William Fleming were brought before the Board. Agreed that the first four be committed to the Guard in this place and the two latter be dismissed.

1777 December 8 – [Monday the 8th written but being all new members present was probably Saturday or Sunday]. The Council met at Princeton. Present – Governor, Smith, Cooper, Condict, Imlay, Linn. Jacob Bogert, Samuel Demerest, Henrick Zobriski, Cornelius Ackerman, Isaac Stagg & John Ackerman having been apprehended for going & returned out of the Enemy's lines without passport required by Law, it was agreed that they have 5 days to consider whether they will enlist in one of our Battalions during the War. Mr. Smith & Mr. Cooper left the Board & Col Drake, Col. Fleming & Mr. Camp took their seats. Agreed that _____ Worth apprehended coming out & going into the Enemy's lines without the license required by law enter into recognizance with surety to appear at the next Court of General Quarter Sessions of the Peace for Hunterdon County. Agreed that there be paid to Israel Freeman for coming with his wagon & two horses from Woodbridge with Guards & five prisoners to the Council of Safety and returning to Woodbridge – 4 pounds, 11 shillings, 6 pence. And to Capt. Manning's order for his expenses & of the Guard which was sent in pursuit of a man coming from Staten Island in a clandestine manner – 5 pounds, 1 shilling, 9 pence.

1777 December 9 – [Tuesday]. The Council met at Princeton. Present – Governor, Condict, Manning, Camp, Elmer, Mr. Speaker, Col. Drake. Agreed that the Governor direct Col. Seely commanding at Elizabeth Town to remove the cattle from Rahway-Neck and such other places where from their proximity to the Enemy, they may be in danger of being carried off by them, to places of greater security, (the owners of such cattle refusing to do it, on notice given to them for that purpose) and that the removal of such cattle be effected with little damage to the proprietors as circumstances will allow.... Ordered that Asher Woodruff, Ezekiel Woodruff & William Higgins, be summoned to appear before the Board & give their evidence to support certain facts alleged by them relating to the conduct of Genl. Dickinson, while he commanded at Elizabeth Town.

1777 December 10 – [Wednesday]. The Council met at Princeton. Present – Governor, Cooper, Elmer, Linn, Condict, Imlay, Mehelm, Col. Fleming, Hart, Manning, Camp, Col. Drake. Agreed that at all future meetings of the Council of Safety such members as live nearest the place of meeting shall attend. Agreed that the Council sit at this place immediately after the adjournment of the Assembly till the business arising in this neighborhood is finished & then adjourn to Ringoes & from thence to Springfield, County of Essex. That the following members do meet at this place – Smith, Mehelm, Hart, Linn, Manning & Imlay. That the following members meet at Ringoes: Hart, Mehelm, Drake, Smith, Linn, Tallman. And, that the following members meet at Springfield-Smith, Condict, Camp, Col. Flemming, Col. Drake, & Manning. Agreed that 5 pounds, 4 shillings, 9 pence be paid to Jonathan Palmer in part of what is due to Wm. Niller for attending as a witness in Morris County (Palmer having Niller's order).

1777 December 12 – [Friday]. The Council met at Princeton. Present – Governor, Mr. Speaker, Camp, Manning, Mehelm, Elmer, Col. Fleming, Smith. Application to the Board for payment of money due to the Militia in Gloucester County under the command of Col. Ellis. Agreed that Col. Ellis be informed by letter that the Legislature directed the Delegates to obtain from Congress $120,000 dollars for paying the debt due to the Militia of this State and that the proportion of $16,000 dollars, when obtained, be given to Thos. Carpenter for the payment of the Militia of Gloucester & Salem. A Letter from Asher Holmes Esqr. was read setting forth that a Flag of Truce from New York had just arrived in Shrewsbury River for the families, servants & effects of Mrs. Antil, Mrs. Moore, Mrs. Johnston, Mrs. Miller and Mrs. Kippen. A permission also under the hand of Major Gen. Robinson for the wife of Elisha Laurence to pass to Shrewsbury was laid before the Board. Agreed that Mrs. Antil, Mrs. Moore, Mrs. Johnston, Mrs. Miller & Mrs. Kippen be permitted to pass to New York with their families, servants and effects excepting the property of those whose husbands have joined the Enemy since October 1776.

PM - Present – Governor, Smith, Mr. Speaker, Manning, Mehelm, Imlay. Ordered that there be paid to Cornelius Vanderveer for his services in attending the Council of Safety as a Light Horseman the sum of 5 pounds, 15 shillings, 6 pence. Agreed that Johnn. Dey for leaving the State & going over to the Enemy, since the Treason Act & returning into the State without permission, have his choice whether to enlist into one of the four Battalions of this State raised for the Continental Service or be committed to Trenton Gaol. Agreed that there be paid to John Bennet for Attending the Council of Safety as a Light Horseman - 7 pounds. Agreed that Matthew Wrench for the same crime as above, be in like manner committed to Trenton Jail. Agreed that John Richmond enter into recognizance with surety in 300 pounds each to appear at the next Court of Oyer & Terminer for Hunterdon County. Adjourned till tomorrow morning 9 o'clock.

1777 December 13 – [Saturday]. The Council met at Princeton pursuant to adjournment. Present – Governor, Mr. Speaker, Manning, Mehelm, Imlay, Smith, Mehelm. In consideration of Mr. Rutherford's & Mr. Parker's indisposition, it was agreed that they be enlarged from their present confinement until February 1st next, upon the terms of their obligation of having the district of one mile from the Court House in Morris Town & that they be committed to jail, unless the Council of Safety shall order to the contrary. Agreed that the wife of John Havens have leave to go into the enemy's lines. In reference to the previous order to Col. Seely to remove to safety the cattle from the nearness of the Enemy, it is further agreed, that he also remove sheep, hogs & cows that give no milk that are in danger, and he must be guided by his own judgment as to the places of safety for them. Adjourned till Tuesday morning 8 o'clock.

1777 December 16 – [Tuesday]. The Council met at Princeton. Present- Governor, Smith, Mehelm, Imlay, Mr. Speaker. There not being a Quorum, the Board adjourned till tomorrow morning.

1777 December 17 – [Wednesday]. The Council met at Princeton. Present, as before. The Board adjourned till tomorrow for want of a Quorum.

1777 December 18 – [Thursday]. Met pursuant to adjournment. Present, as before. The Board adjourned till tomorrow morning 9 o'clock for want of a Quorum.

1777 December 19 – [Friday]. Met pursuant to adjournment. Present – Governor, Smith, Mehelm, Imlay, Mr. Speaker. There not being a sufficient number of members to enter upon business that required a vote of the Board, those present proceeded as Magistrates to the examination of certain persons who were by an order of 17 November summoned to appear to take the Oaths. [None named.] Alexander McDonald came before the Board by a Warrant, took the Oaths and was dismissed. Mr. Manning appeared and took his seat. Ezekiel Smith was brought before the to take the Affirmations to the effect of the Oaths, desired leave to consider the matter till tomorrow morning, and request was granted. Adjourned till 3 o'clock PM

Met pursuant to adjournment – Present as before. Agreed, that there to be paid to Frederick Ten Eyck – 4 pounds, 18 shillings, 9 pence for attending the Council of Safety as a Light Horseman and to William Van Dyne – 3 pounds, 12 shillings, 3 pence for the same services & Tunis Hoogland, who present his account - 3 pounds, 12 shillings, 6 pence for the same services plus riding Express. Mathew Clark came before the Board by Warrant, took the Affirmations, and was dismissed. The following persons of the people called Quakers were brought before the Board- Joseph Horner, Isaac Clark, Benjm. Clark, Wm. Clark, John Clark, Thos. Clark & Robert White, who each refused to take the Affirmations & also refused to become bound by surety in order to appear in the next Court of Quarter Sessions of the Peace to be held in & for Middlesex County. Agreed that they all have Warrants of Commitment for their imprisonment. Thos. Wilson appeared, and having taken the Oaths, was dismissed.

1777 December 20 – [Saturday]. Met pursuant to adjournment. Present – Governor, Manning, Mr. Speaker, Smith, HoMehelm, Imlay. John Honeyman having entered into recognizance with Jacob Hyer, his surety, in 300 pounds each, to appear in the next Court of Quarter Sessions of the Peace to be held in & for Hunterdon County, was discharged from the Guard. Mathew Wrench & Charles Friend went before the Board & on failure of security required, were ordered to be sent to Flemington. John Willis apprehended on his way to the Enemy was also sent to Flemington. Isaac Clarke, Benjm. Clarke, William Clarke, John Clarke, Thos. Clarke & Robert White came before the Board & on passing their Words to be forthcoming on Wednesday next, they were dismissed. John Hedger having entered into recognizance with John Scot, his surety, in 300 pounds each, to appear in the next Court of Quarter Sessions of the Peace to be held in & for Somerset County, & in the meantime to be of good behavior, was dismissed. Adjourned till 3 o'clock PM.

Met pursuant to adjournment. Present as before. Ezekiel Smith entered into recognizance with Jonathan Dear, his surety, in 300 pounds each, to appear in the next Court of Quarter Sessions of the Peace to be held in & for Middlesex County, and was dismissed. Sarah Barrow was brought before the Board for going into the enemy's lines & returning to the State without license by Law. Agreed that she be immediately sent back to her husband in New York and remain there during the present War. Priscilla Stewart was brought before the Board for the like offence & entered into recognizance with Peter Teple, her surety, to appear next Friday at the Court of Oyer & Terminer for Hunterdon County. Lewis Freeman entered into recognizance with David Frazey, his surety, in 300 pounds each, to appear in the next Court of Oyer & Terminer for Hunterdon County. Joseph Skelton was brought before the Board and refused to take the Affirmations but having entered into recognizance with Jacob Hyer, his surety, in 300 pounds each, to appear in the next Court of Quarter Sessions of the Peace to be held in & for Middlesex County, was discharged. Ordered that Maj. Potter be directed to remove to Staten Island, Sarah Barron & the wife of William Smith, the wife of John Heard & the wife of Samuel Moore, as well as the wives of such other persons as have returned from the enemy's lines without leave, after having been removed into the same by order of the Council of Safety, & to make return of what he shall have done in the premises with all convenient speed. Agreed that there be paid to Matthew Freeman for himself & Guard of three prisoners from Woodbridge, with a wagon & 2 horses and a spare horse, the sum of 11 pounds. Ordered that in case the persons hereinafter named are or shall be charged with or committed for any of the crimes or offences, specified in the 1st, 2nd, or 3rd sections of a certain act entitled – "An Act to punish traitors or disaffected persons, Or are or shall be charged with, or committed for Misprision of Treason, or for any crime of offence specified in the 8th or 9th sections of an act for constituting a Council of Safety, or shall be charged with or command for, any of the Crimes or Offences specified in the 2nd Section, of an act entitled An Act to render Certain Bills of Credit a legal tender within this State, & to prevent the Counterfeiting of the same & other Bills of Credit", or so many of them as have been or shall be so charged or committed, shall be tried for the same in the County of Hunterdon, although' the offences they be charged with, or shall be committed for, were done & perpetrated in any other County. The persons in the above order referred to are: Lewis Freeman, William Cook, Pricilla

Stewart, John Richmond, John Brown, Matthew Wrench, John Dey, Jacob Bogert, John Honeyman, Charles Friend, Patrick Navins, Saml. Demarest, Hendrick Zabriski, Cornelius Ackerman, Isaac Stagg, John Ackerman, John Willis. Adjourned till Monday morning 9 o'clock.

1777 December 22 – [Monday]. Met pursuant to adjournment. Present – Governor, Mehelm, Smith, Imlay, Manning, Mr. Speaker. Richard Stockton Esqr. was called before the Board and took the Oaths and was dismissed. Agreed that there be paid to Capt. Moore, for himself & the use of 24 men of his Co., for their services in attending the Council of Safety, as a Guard, from the 26th Aug to the 3rd of September, the sum of 18 pounds, 5 shillings, 4 pence. That Moore also to be paid 6 pounds, 7 shillings, 6 pence for removing the wife of Thos. Russel to Staten Island; and also be allowed his expenses in going to Morristown & Philadelphia with prisoners the sum of 8 pounds, 15/. Agreed that Lieut. Bergen be paid for himself & 13 men employed as Guard for the Council of Safety and the security of prisoners the sum of 39 pounds, 16 shillings, 4 pence; and the sum of 28 pounds. For Bounty money for the said Guard and for furnishing them with wood, candles, & sundry other articles, the sum of 14 pounds, 11shillings, 6 pence. Agreed to pay Andrew McMackin the sum of 12 pounds, 7 shillings, 6 pence for making cartridges for the Council of Safety. Ordered that Jonathan Baldwin take charge of the balls & cartridges now in the hands of Andrew McMackin. Agreed that Col. Ellis be authorized to remove any cattle, sheep, & hogs (excepting milch cows) from any place where he thinks them in danger of falling into Enemy's hands, move them to greater security, upon the owners refusing to do it, first giving them notice, who may take care of them at their expense. Agreed that prisoners taken with Richard Stockton & now confined at Carlile be treated as prisoners of War. John Holton, William Drake, Jeremiah Turner & Jas. Pyatt having taken the Oaths were discharged. Adjourned till tomorrow morning 9 o'clock.

1777 December 23 – [Tuesday]. Met pursuant to adjournment. Present – Governor, Manning, Imlay, Mehelm, Smith, Mr. Speaker. Agreed that the Governor, the president, draw on the Treasurer in favor of Mr. Imlay the sum of 1,000 pounds for the use of the Council of Safety. Agreed that Mrs. Lott be paid 40 shillings for firewood & candles provided for the Council of Safety. Adjourned to meet at Ringoes next Wednesday afternoon.

1777 December 24 – [Wednesday] Ringoes - Met pursuant to adjournment. Present – Governor, Mr. Smith, Col. Drake. There being no Quorum, adjourned till tomorrow morning 9 o'clock.

1777 December 25 – [Thursday]. Met pursuant to adjournment. Present – Governor, Smith, Mehelm, Drake, Mr. Speaker. There being no Quorum, adjourned till tomorrow morning.

1777 December 26 – [Friday] - Ringoes. Met pursuant to adjournment. Present as before. There being no Quorum, adjourned till tomorrow morning 9 o'clock.

1777 December 27 – [Saturday] - Ringoes. Met pursuant to adjournment. Present as before. There being no Quorum, adjourned till tomorrow morning.

1777 December 28 – [Sunday] – Ringoes. Met pursuant to adjournment. Present as before. There being no Quorum, adjourned till tomorrow morning 8 o'clock.

1777 December 29 – [Monday]. Met pursuant to adjournment. Present as before. There being no Quorum, adjourned till tomorrow morning.

1777 December 30 – [Tuesday] – Ringoes. Met pursuant to adjournment. Present as before. AM – Mr. Condit & Mr. Linn appeared & took their seats on the Board. Present – Governor, Condict, Linn, Mehelm, Smith, Col. Drake, Mr. Speaker. Agreed that there be paid to Abraham Brokau for attending & riding express for the Council of Safety – 9 pounds, 16 shillings. 3 pence. Adjourned till tomorrow morning 9 o'clock.

1777 December 31 – [Wednesday]. Met pursuant to adjournment. Present as before. The petition of Wm. Bowen indicating that he was desirous of making camp kettles & other necessaries wanted in the Continental Army & praying for an exemption of military duty, while thus engaged ... having taken same into consideration, agreed that it does not appear that Bowen is under any such agreement and his petition cannot be granted, but if he appears before them next Thursday at Springfield and shows them a contract for such, his petition will be taken under consideration. Mr. Speaker having entered at this place (before a Quorum had met) paid the following sums: To John Bennet – 1 pound, 16 shillings, 3 pence; John Voorhise – 7 pounds, 1 shilling, 9 pence; Jarod Saxton – 7 pounds, 10 shillings for riding express for the Council of Safety. The Board agreed at this present meeting to the several payments above. Agreed to be paid to Silas Condit Esqr. for the use of a wounded soldier in Col. Munster's Battalion – 10 pounds. The petition of a number of inhabitants of Hopewell Township, praying exemption for Jacob Osborn, from two tours of military duty, he being a weaver by trade & much wanted in the neighborhood, which was being laid before the Board to take into consideration. Agreed that the above petition cannot be complied with. Agreed that there be paid to John Hart Esqr. for the use of Mary Morshan, the widow of Aaron Morshan, lately belonging to the company of Militia commanded by Capt. Benjamin Van Cleve, who was killed on Long Island, the month of August 1776, in an engagement with the British Troops & which said widow is left with 3 small children in low circumstances, the sum of 15 pounds. Agreed that a Warrant issue for apprehending & bringing before the Board to take the Oaths, John Schenk, late of Poghkeepsie in the State of New York. Adjourned to 3 o'clock PM.

Met pursuant to adjournment. Joseph Lewis made application for himself & several men in his employ in the Commissary Department for exemption from military duty in the militia. Agreed that said Lewis being a Commissary of Issues be exempted and that Nathan Turner, a butcher in his employ, Nathan Howell employed in his store, & Alphus Hughs employed as a Clerk be exempted while in his employ. Agreed to pay to Col. Chambers for use of Valentine Eut – 2 pounds, 10/ for drawing 14 hundred weight of lead from Amwell to Princeton. Agreed that Pricilla Harrison have permission to go to her husband in Philadelphia on condition of not returning into this State during the War. Agreed that Walter Rutherford & Jas. Parkers Esqrs. be discharged from their confinement in Morristown and to return to their places of abode, and to stay there & within one mile of the place until February 1st next & then be committed to &

confined in prison until Honorable John Fell, Esqr. shall be released form his confinement in New York, on condition of liberating the said Jas. Parker & Wynant Van Zant on the condition of liberating Walter Rutherford. Adjourned till tomorrow morning 9 o'clock.

1778 January 1 – [Thursday]. Present – Governor, Mr. Speaker, Smith, Condict, Linn, Col. Drake. Agreed that the Governor draw on the treasury for the sum of 300 pounds for use by the Council of Safety. Ordered that the several sums agreed to be paid to the Constables & Cryer of Morris agreeable to the order of 24 Nov. 1777, be paid [by] Silas Condit, Esqr for the use of the said Constables & Cryer amounting in the whole to 69 pounds. It appearing that the sick in the hospital at Princeton are greatly suffering for want of firewood, and when the Commissary is able to procure wood cutters (which is effected with great difficulty), he has no assurance of them remaining in his service by reason of their being liable to be called out in the Militia, causing him be unsupplied. Resolved that Burgoon Updicke, Peter Updicke, Robert Yates, Hendrick Lane, Lawrence Updicke, David Molisson, William Downey & Peter Archer be exempted from Military duty for the above purpose for 30 days from this date & that on their producing certificates from the Commissary of Hospitals of their having been so employed, they be excused in their next tour of duty for the number of days they were so employed. Agreed that the Constables for their extraordinary duties in attending the Court of Oyer & Terminer at Fleming Town, Hunterdon County be paid the following sums: Rubon Runyon – 8 days – 4 pounds; Andrew McClearly - 9 days – 4 pounds 10 shillings; Joseph Ross – 9 days – 4 pounds 10 shillings; Wm Shoudon – 6 days – 3 pounds; Thos. Reider – 6 days – 3 pounds; Saml. Hulick – 6 days – 3 pounds; Wm. Coolback – 10 days – 5 pounds; John Campbell – 10 days – 5 pounds. John Shenck was brought before the Board by Warrant & having entered into recognizance with John P. Shenck, his surety, in 300 pounds each to appear at the next Court of General Quarter Session of the Peace to be held in & for Somerset County, was dismissed. Agreed that Jonas Stryker be paid 5 pounds, 4 shillings, 9 pence for his services as a Light Horseman for the Council of Safety. Adjourned to meet at Springfield, next Tuesday morning 9 o'clock.

1778 January 7 – [Wednesday]. Springfield. Present – Governor, Col. Flemming, Crane, Smith, Col. Drake, Condit. Agreed to pay Samuel Meeker for sundry expenses for furnishing provisions and other necessaries to the Guard for the prisoners in Sussex Gaol – 104 pounds, 1 shilling, 10 pence. Adjourned till 3 o'clock PM.

Met pursuant to adjournment. Present as before, with Mr. Manning. Major Dally applied to the Board to have a number of men employed by him as teamsters and woodcutters in the Continental Service exempted from serving in the Militia during the time they shall be so employed. Agreed that such exemptions tend to drain the State of Militia but by employing them in the Continental Service does not fall within the Act of the Safety Council and therefore cannot be complied with. Rune & John Runyon applied for leave to go into the Enemy's lines to procure the Will of their father, who went over to & died among the Enemy. Agreed that they have permission to enquire by letter concerning the said Will, and if there is any probability of procuring it, then the matter will be considered. Adjourned till tomorrow morning 9 o'clock.

1778 January 8 – [Thursday]. Met pursuant to adjournment. Present – Governor, Col. Drake, Col. Fleming, Condit, Smith, Manning. Agreed that Col. Seely be paid for the use of Philip Harder for riding Express for him the sum of 6 pounds, 2 shillings, 6 pence. Agreed that John Hunt be paid for riding Express from Annwell [Amwell] to Springfield – 27/6. The Governor laid a letter before the Board from Genl. Washington urging the expediency of removing the cattle & forage that lay near the Enemy, out of their reach. Agreed that the Governor direct Col. Ellis to remove all the horned cattle, sheep, hogs, and all cows which do not give milk from the vicinity of the Jersey Shore in Burlington, Salem and Gloucester Counties that may be within reach of the enemy's foraging parties…and that the General be advised that the powers of the Council of Safety do not include requisition of having the forage removed & it is recommended that he use his own authority in having it accomplished. Agreed to pay Brid. Gen. Winds for expenses accrued by order of the Safety Council – 63 pounds, 5 shillings, 2 pence. Ordered that in addition to the orders already given Mr. Caldwell in reference to the erection of Beacons for the purpose of giving an alarm of an invasion, that he be further directed to have one set up at Morristown and another at Longhill, and one or two to the north of New Ark and that he be requested to appoint proper persons to take the care of & attend them & that the person so provided, shall be exempted, when known, from military duty. Adjourned to meet at Morristown tomorrow.

1778 January 9 – [Friday] Morristown. Present – Governor, Smith, Col. Drake, Condit, Col. Fleming, Manning. Agreed that Alexr. Edwards & John Yalter, millers, & Joseph Smith & Wm. Reynolds, coopers, employed in the Mill in Nottingham Township, and Daniel Edwards & Patrick Puecell, millers & Charles Crossley, Paterson Doyle & Samuel Crossley, coopers, employed at the Mill near Bordentown & John McCartney & Richard Glue, millers, at Mount Holly (which mills are employed in furnishing the Army of the United States with flour) be exempted from military duty for 30 days from this date, provided they continue in such employment. Agreed that the Governor write Mr. Emely for the sum of 500 pounds in part of the order which he has on the Treasury for 1,000 pounds. Adjourned till tomorrow morning 9 o'clock.

1778 January 10 – [Saturday]. Met pursuant to adjournment. Present – Governor, Condict, Manning, Col. Drake, Smith, Col. Flemming. Agreed that a Warrant be issued to apprehend and bring before the Board Archibald Kennedy, Esqr., that an enquiry be made into his past conduct, and the Oaths be tendered to him. Agreed that the following persons: Joseph Morse, Joseph Morse, Jr., Esther Morse, Joshua Wyants & Johiah ….Morse, and Anthony Morse, for aiding & assisting in attempting to carry beef to the Enemy on Staten Island, be brought before the Board to answer the offense. On Application of Joseph Lewis, agreed that Wm. Jones employed by him as a Clerk in the Commissary Department be exempted from serving in the Militia for 30 days from the date thereof. Adjourned till Monday morning 9 o'clock.

1778 January 12 – [Monday]. Met pursuant to adjournment. Present – Governor, Condict, Manning, Col. Drake, Smith, Col. Fleming. A Petition present from inhabitants of Woodbridge Township, which having been considered, it is ordered that Major Potter do permit the wives of Wm. Smith & Philip Goss, who are with the Enemy, to stay among us upon Mrs. Smith's giving security to remove to her father's family & there to continue till the further order of the Board (the order of the 20 December 1777 to the contrary not withstanding) and that in all other respects the said order of 20 December be carried into immediate execution. Ordered that the following persons (prisoners here): Enoch Allen, James Wells, Abraham Man, John Edeson & Wm. Reed be brought before Council to hear & consider their respective circumstances agreeable to their petition. The said prisoners cases being considered, it is ordered that Enoch Allen be discharged on his enlistment in one of the New Jersey Regiments, that James Wells do either enlist, or give security for his appearance at the Court of Quarter Sessions for Middlesex County, that Abraham Man do either enlist, or give security for his appearance at the Court of Quarter Sessions for Essex County, and that John Edeson & Wm. Reed remain in custody until the further order of this Board. Adjourned to 9 o'clock tomorrow morning.

1778 January 13 – [Tuesday] - Met pursuant to adjournment. Present – Governor, Condit, Manning, Col. Drake, Col. Flemming, Smith, Linn. Captn. Archibald Kennedy pursuant to Warrant was brought before the Board, heard, & sundry affidavits transmitted to the Council on his conduct being read & considered, resolved that Capt. Kennedy be permitted to return to his own home and do attend this Board in 14 days from this date and that in the meantime a letter be sent to Genl. Washington respecting the nature of Capt. Kennedy's parole & that copies of the affidavits re: his conduct be also transmitted with the letter. Jehiel Morse was brought before the Board by Warrant, examined with it committed to writing, and was delivered to the custody of the Guard. George Michaldeed appeared before the Board & was examined upon Oath relative to a hogshead of flaxseed given to his care by Anthony Morse, to be conveyed to Staten Island, & his disposition committed to writing, he was dismissed. Adjourned till tomorrow morning 9 o'clock.

1778 January 14-[Wednesday]. Met pursuant to adjournment. Present – Governor, Col. Fleming, Condit, Smith, Linn, Col. Drake. Samuel Lawrence appeared before the Board, and having given a Bond for 100 pounds for his appearance at the next Court of Oyer & Terminer in Essex County, to give testimony for the State against Joseph Morse, Junr. Anthony Morse and Esther Marsh were thereupon dismissed. A letter from Col. Seely was read & answered. Agreed that the following persons have permission to go to their husbands in the Enemy's lines: Lydia Gorman, wife of John Gorman, with her four children, and Sarah Copinger, wife of Wm. Copinger & her three children. A letter from Rev. Caldwell was read & answered. Azariah Clark & Abraham Badgley entered into recognizance for 100 pounds each for their appearance at the next Court of Oyer & Terminer of Essex County, as witnesses in behalf of the State against Joseph Morse, Junr., Anthony Morse, and Esther Marsh. Agreed that Henry Insley be paid 4 pounds, 14 shillings, 3 pence for riding express in the service of the State. Adjourned till 3 o'clock PM.

Met pursuant to adjournment. Present as before. Benjamin Wynants & Robert Clark appeared before the Board & having given Bond of 100 pounds each for the appearance of George Michaeldeed at the next Court of Oyer & Terminer in Essex County, were then discharged. Joshua Winants entered into recognizance with Benjamin Wynants & Robert Clark, his surety for 300 pounds each, for his appearance at the next Court of Oyer & Terminer, Essex County. Anthony Morse in like manner gave bond with Benjamin Wynants his surety at 300 pounds to appear at the same Court. Agreed that David Star be paid 4 pounds, 1 shilling, 3 pence for expenses for attending the Council of Safety as an Express [Rider]. Benj. Wynants entered into bond in the sum of 100 pounds for the appearance of Jehiel Marsh at the above mentioned Court in order to give evidence against Joseph Morse, Jr., Anthony Morse & Esther Marsh, for the State. Agreed that Esther Marsh be committed to the Gaol in this place for High Treason. Agreed that Azariah Clark be paid for his time & trouble in taking up & securing a number of persons detected in trading with the Enemy – 12 pounds, 7 shilling, 6 pence. And that Abraham Badgley paid the sum of 3 pounds for assisting Azariah Clark. Ordered that a Warrant be issued to apprehend and bring Joseph Morse, Jr. before the Board. Governor received by Express the sum of 500 pounds which the Board directed him to draw from Mr. Emely, the said money was by him delivered to Mr. Condict as Treasurer of the Board. Jacob Wood, John Gibeson & Hezekiah Gibeson three of the Green coat new levies, deserted from the Enemy, have permission to consider till tomorrow morning whether they will enlist into our service or be committed for High Treason. Jas. Wells & Abraham Man were ordered before the Board & on refusing to enlist into the Continental Army, it was ordered that they be remanded to prison until they find security for their appearance at the next Court of Oyer & Terminer in Essex County. Adjourned till tomorrow morning.

1778 January 15 – [Thursday]. Met pursuant to adjournment. Present – Governor, Col. Fleming, Condict, Smith, Linn, Col. Drake. Agreed that Col. Drake be refunded $3.00 which he paid to an express while at Ringoes, for bringing papers from Trenton. Agreed that Enoch Allen be exempted from paying for the rations which he drew while a State prisoner in Morristown Gaol. Upon Application, agreed that John Yatter & Alexander Edwards, millers, and Joseph Smith & William Reynolds, coopers, employed at the mill in Nottingham Township; Daniel Edwards & Patrick Puessel, millers, & Chas. Crossley, Paterson Doyle & Samuel Crossley, coopers, employed at the Mill near Borden Town, & John Mc Cartney & Richard Glue, millers, at Mount Holly, who were by a former resolution of the Board exempted from serving in the Militia for 30 days from 9 January are further exempted to the 9th of March next. A letter from Jonathan Elmer, Esqr. was read & answered. Adjourned till tomorrow morning 9 o'clock.

1778 January 16 – [Friday]. Met pursuant to adjournment. Present as before. Ordered that a Warrant be issued for apprehending and bringing Ezekiel Beech before the Board. Agreed that Edward Taylor's Bond to the State of New Jersey & the Bond of Richd. Jones & Thos. Parker be delivered into the hands of Silas Condict, Esqr. Agreed that Honorable Silas Condit Esqr. repay to Col Drake the sum of 147 pounds, 17 shillings, 11 pence advanced by him to the Board while at Ringoes Tavern – January 1st, 1778. A letter from Rev. McWhorter respecting the New Modelling the Militia was laid before the Board, whereupon agreed that the plan contained in the above letter be laid before & recommended by this Board to the Legislature at their next sitting… In addition to the Exchange agreed to on December 1st 1777, it is further agreed that Gabriel Van Norden & Cornelius Bogert now prisoners in Morristown be added to the list & be set at liberty upon the release of David Van Borson and John Hays, now prisoners in New York, and that the said Gabriel Van Norden have leave to be absent a reasonable time for negotiating the proposed exchange. Due to the infirmity of Peter T. Herring, it is agree that he be discharged from his parole until the further orders of the Board concerning him & the Gabriel Van Norden & Gerrit Demarest have permission to attend him home, the latter of whom to return to this place with all convenient speed. Agreed that the Governor be desired by advertisement to recommend to the

Magistrates to execute with all diligence an Act of the Legislature passed on the 11 December last, entitled " An Act for regulating & limiting the price of sundry articles of produce, manufacture & trade" on pain of their being prosecuted for neglect of duty in the premises with the utmost rigor of Law. Ordered that Mrs. Hannah Higgins for coming from the Enemy's lines into this State without the License required by Law give security for her appearance at the next Court of Quarter Sessions of the Peace to be held in Morris County. Adjourned till tomorrow morning.

1778 January 17 – [Saturday]. Present as before. Agreed that Mr. Kinney be paid 40/ for providing Council of Safety with firewood, candles & etc. while they sat at his house. Adjourned till Monday morning 9 o'clock.

1778 January 19 – [Monday]. Met pursuant to adjournment. Present – Governor, Col. Fleming, Condict, Smith, Col. Drake, Linn. Joseph Morse, Jun. was brought by Warrant before the Board and it appearing that he had been into the Enemy's lines & returned into this State without permission, it was agreed that he be committed for trial to the Morristown Gaol. Agreed that John Crane be paid $4.00 for his time & expenses in bringing Joseph Morse, Jun. before the Council. Agreed that Wm. Van Cleaf have an order upon Mr. Baldwin in Princeton for 5,000 cartridges for the use of the Monmouth County Militia. Adjourned till tomorrow morning.

1778 January 20 – [Tuesday]. Met pursuant to adjournment. Agreed that Deborah Ogden, wife of John Ogden, (who is with the enemy) have leave to go to her husband together with her child & wearing apparel. Andrew Mills appeared before the Board, took the Oaths and was discharged. Frederick Cole was brought before the Board and examined on sundry matters and it was ordered that he be committed to close custody until he give security for his appearance at the next Court of General Quarter Sessions of the Peace for Morris County. Agreed that Harman Rosin for going into the Enemy's lines since the Treason Law & returning to the State as a spy, have five days to consider whether he will enlist in our service or be committed for his trial. Agreed that a Warrant be issue to apprehend and bring before the Board Enoch & Peter Vreelandt to answer to what shall be objected to them on behalf of the State. John Francisco brought before the Board denied the facts alleged against him & was remanded to the Guard till the Witnesses arrived who are to support the charge. Richard Lewis for traveling the country without a passport was sent to the Board, and he took the Oaths and was dismissed. Ezekiel Beech being cited before the Board to take the Oaths & he refused, and requested to go into the enemy's lines. Agreed that he have leave to go and that he depart the State for that purpose in 3 days from this date by way of Elizabeth Town to Staten Island and that the commanding officer at Elizabeth Town be directed to send him over to the island. Agreed that Mr. Condit pay Major Crane for the use of Col. Seely – 5 pounds for ten quires of paper purchased by him for the Council of Safety. Elisha Parker & Joseph Moore were examined, which was written down & sworn to, and they gave Bond for their appearance in behalf of the State against Joseph Morse, Jun. at the next Court of Oyer & Terminer in Morris County. Agreed to pay to Elisha Parker, 20 shillings, for attending the Council as a witness against Joseph Morse, Jr. & that Joseph Moore be paid the like sum for the like service. Agreed to pay to Jos. Catalin 8 pounds for serving a Warrant for this Board for Joseph Morse, Junr., and that he be paid for the use of David Smaley

& Clarkson Manning the sum of $2.00 each for assisting, and also that he be paid for the two men employed in carrying the said Morse to Major Crane the sum of 20 shillings each. The Governor laid a letter before the Board for their opinion from Col. Seely setting forth that some tea & sugar was sent to Mrs. Boudinot from her friends at New York and begging his direction in the premises. Agreed that the said Tea & Sugar be delivered to Mrs. Boudinot. Adjourned till tomorrow morning.

1778 January 21 – [Wednesday]. Met pursuant to adjournment. Present – Governor, Col. Fleming, Linn, Smith, Camp, Condit. Leonard Davenport was sent before the Board and denied the facts against him. Agreed that he be remanded to custody, as was Abraham Cole, until the evidences appear against them to support the charge. Austin Wright appeared before the Board having entered into recognizance with Abraham Cole, his surety, at 300 pounds each, for his appearance at the next Court of General Quarter Sessions of the Peace for Morris County, and was then dismissed. William Weaver was brought before the Board, and denying the facts against him, he was remanded for further evidence. David & Henry Van Orden for joining the enemy since the Treason Act & returning to the State, were ordered into custody & given five days allowed to consider whether to enlist into our service during the War or to be tried for High Treason. Ordered that Abraham Smyth remain under Guard for further evidence. Frederick Cole appeared before the Board & entered into recognizance with John Davenport, his surety at 300 pounds each, for his appearance at the next Court of General Quarter Sessions of the Peace for Morris County, and in taking the Oaths, he was then dismissed. Abraham Man in like manner entered into Bond with David Man his surety at 300 pounds each, for his appearance at the next Court of Oyer & Terminer for Essex County, & he too took the Oaths and was then discharged from the Guard. Adjourned till tomorrow morning.

1778 January 22 – [Thursday]. Present as before. Ordered that Hon. Silas Condit pay George King $5 for serving a Warrant (issued from this Board) upon Capt. Kennedy & bringing him before the Council of Safety. Agreed that Mr. Condict pay to Abraham Canfield 40 shillings for going on a Message to Mr. Hart for the Council of Safety. John Folkenier being sent before the Board by Major Groetchius, as having been forced out of the Enemy's lines into this State, Ordered that he be delivered into the custody of the Guard until further proof can be had concerning him. Adjourned till tomorrow morning.

1778 January 23 – [Friday]. Met pursuant to adjournment. Upon the request of the Attorney General, it was agreed that the Monmouth [prisoners] now confined in Sussex Gaol be removed to Freehold for their trial & that the Sheriff of Sussex be directed to send them thither under sufficient guard. Agreed that a Warrant be issued for apprehending & bringing before the Board, Daniel Layton and also Joseph Smith, for refusing to comply with an Act of the Legislature lately passed for regulating the prices of produce, manufacture, and trade. Moses Kilburne appeared before the Board & entered into Bond for his appearance at the next Court of General Quarter Sessions of the Peace for Morris County, as a witness in behalf of the State against Fredk. Cole & others. [Unnamed.] Agreed that a subpoena be issued for Wm. Loocey to appear before the Board to give evidence against Joseph Smith. Agreed that a subpoena be issued to Kessiah Bayles to appear at 10 o'clock tomorrow morning on behalf of Daniel Layton at the suit of Peter Morris.

Agreed that Jas. Serring be paid 9 pounds, 2 pence for going for the Council of Safety to Head Quarters. Abraham Cole, Abraham Smyth, Leonard Davenport & Wm. Weaver appeared before the Board & having entered into recognizance with John Davenport, & John Cole, their sureties, at 300 pounds each, and were then discharged.

1778 January 24 – [Saturday]. Met pursuant to adjournment. Present as before. David & Henry Van Order having enlisted into the first Battalion of this State during the War were discharged from the Guard. Ordered that Benjamin Pitney be summoned to attend this Board on Tuesday morning next at 10 o'clock. Agreed that the Governor draw upon Mr. Jonathan Baldwin for 500 pounds weight of bullets of different sizes, if so many can be spared, if not, to make up the difference in lead to be run into bullets at this place. David Layton pursuant to a Warrant was brought before the Board, and it appearing that he had taken a higher price for grain than allowed; agreed that he be fined for the said offence and that the proportion belonging to the Overseer of the Poor, amounting to 3 pounds, be paid into the hands of Silas Condit, Esqr., to be by paid to the said Overseer. Adjourned till Monday morning 9 o'clock.

1778 January 26 – [Monday]. Met pursuant to adjournment. Present as before. It being presented to the Board that Mrs. Hoffman had propagated through the Country an intended invasion of the enemy into this State, it was agreed that she be sent for before the Board to answer for her conduct in the premises. Joseph Smyth pursuant to a Warrant was brought before the Board & it being proved to them that he had spoken contemptuously of a Law lately passed for the regulating of prices of produce, etc.; it was agreed that he give Bond for his appearance at the next Court of General Quarter Sessions of the Peace for Morris County, which he did with John Symth, his surety, at 300 pounds each & was dismissed. Agreed that there be paid to Cyrus Beckwith 43 pounds, 17 shillings, 11 pence, for transporting into the enemy's lines Mrs. Barton, Mrs. Haggarthe & their families. Agreed that John Smyth refund to the Widow Pearson the over plus of money over & above what the Law allows for wheat, lately purchased by the said Mrs. Pearson from him, and that he produce her receipt for such disbursement within two days from this time. Enoch & Isaac Vreeland appeared before the Board & they took & subscribed the Oaths. Adjourned till tomorrow Morning 9 o'clock.

[The end of Volume 3]

Council of Safety, State of New Jersey

Volume 4

Members of the Council of Safety – Silas Condict, Wm. Paterson, Theo Elmer, John Hart, Benj. Manning, Mr. Cooper, Mr. Imlay, Peter Tallman, Mr. Linn, John Mehelm, Caleb Camp, Jacob Drake, Jonathan Bowen, John Buck, Wm. P. Smith, Edw. Fleming, Mr. Crane, Mr. Fennemore, Mr. Cook, Mr. Keasby.

1778 January 27 – [Tuesday] - Morristown. Present – Governor, Smith, Condit, Linn, Camp, Col. Fleming. Benjamin Pitney was called before the Board, & it was proved upon Oath, that he spoke disrespectfully of an Act of Legislature regulating the prices of produce, etc. and it was agreed that he be bound for his appearance at the next Court of General Quarter Sessions of the Peace for Morris County, with Jas. Puff Locey, is surety at 300 pounds each- Agreed that Pitney be fined 6 pounds for breach of he law and $4.50 which was the price of the shoes he sold. Adjourned till tomorrow morning.

1778 January 28 – [Wednesday]. Met pursuant to adjournment. Present as before. Agreed that Mrs. Spencer (wife of Col. Oliver Spencer) be summoned to the Board. Agreed that Mrs. Hannah Ward, for going into the enemy's lines and returning to this State without permission, give Bond for her appearance at the next Court of General Quarter Sessions of the Peace for Morris County, and that in the meantime she stay within one mile of the Sussex County Court House. Hannah Ward appeared before the Board and entered into recognizance with James Crane, her surety at 300 pounds each, was then discharged. Jas. Wells appeared before the Board and having entered into recognizance with Richard Churchwards, his surety, at 300 pounds each, was dismissed. Thos. Van Camp was brought before the Board & it appearing that he asked more than allowed for flour and made a distinction between hard money & Continental money by undervaluing the latter; agreed that he forfeit flour and be fined 6 pounds for the first offence, & fined 6 pounds for the latter offence. Wm. Page being in like manner was brought before the Board where he asked more for beef than allowed; agreed he be fined 6 pounds and forfeit said beef. Joseph Morse Junr. brought before the Board & having entered into recognizance with William Pearson, his surety, 300 pounds each, for his appearance at the next Court of Oyer & Terminer for Essex County, was discharged from prison. Adjourned till tomorrow morning.

1778 January 29 – [Thursday]. Met at Morristown. Present as before. John Folkiner ordered before the Board & gave his parole in writing to the President & Council of Safety to remain within 3 miles of the Court House in Morristown & was discharged. Agreed that Jane Foster have leave to remove to the Enemy's lines. Agreed that Elias Marsh, John Thomson, Morris Thorpe & Robert Izalton, be committed to close confinement in the Gaol at New Ark, & that Mittimusses be issued to Col. Seely for that purpose. Caleb Avins being charged before the Council for going into the Enemy's lines & returning without the license, declared his willingness to enlist & did enlist in one of the New Jersey Divisions, and he was discharged. Adjourned till tomorrow morning.

1778 January 30 – [Friday]. Met pursuant to adjournment. Mrs. Hoffman (wife of Nicholas Hoffman) appeared before the Board & entered into recognizance with Abraham Ogden her surety, 1,000 pounds each, for her appearance at the next Court of Oyer & Terminer for Essex County; and it was agreed that she stay within 1 mile of the Morris Town Court House until the above mentioned Court sits & that in default, she be committed to prison as a person disaffected to & having dangerous designs against the present Government. It being represented to the Board by Isaac Blank, Jacob Wortendyck & John Morris, late prisoners in New York, are set at liberty and also agreed that Peter T. Herring, Gabriel Van Norden & Cornelius Bogert, prisoners in Morristown be also set at liberty; and that Gerrit Demarest, Gerrit Vangieson, John Paulese & John Van Buskirk, the remaining prisoners at Morristown, who are being held to obtain the release of a like number of prisoners in New York, have the liberty to return to their homes for one month; in order to procure the release of Thos. Bantha, Bernardus Verbryck, Samuel Verbryck & John Hays; & and they are to return to Morristown if such exchange is not obtained by that time; but if it is; then they are discharged from their Bond & may return at home; and also that Abraham Van Gieson be liberated on the like parole with David Van Bursen whenever the nature of Van Bursen's people shall make it known to this Board; & also that Abraham Van Gieson, have also leave to go home for a month. Adjourned till tomorrow morning.

1778 January 31 – [Saturday]. Met pursuant to adjournment. Present as before. Agreed that Mr. William Livingston, Jr. be allowed at the rate of 30 shillings per day for his past services in attending the Council of Safety as their Secretary. Ordered that Mr. Condict advance to Wm. Livingston, Jr., for attending the Council of Safety for 50 days, the sum of 75 pounds. Agreed to pay Rev. Jones for firewood & candles provided to the Council of Safety, during their sitting at his house, the sum of 4 pounds. Ordered that Benoni Hathaway be paid for repairing carriages & moving field pieces by order of the Council, the sum of 4 pounds, 18 shillings, 3 pence. Jacob FitzRandolph appeared before the Board and it appears that he had been providing the enemy with provisions & that he was disaffected & had dangerous designs against the Government; and it was agreed that he be committed for High Treason to the Morristown Gaol and that a Warrant of commitment be issued for that purpose. Agreed that Mr. Condit pay Isaac Clark for bringing in the above Fitz Randolph before the Board; 1 pound, 17 shillings, 6 pence. Agreed that for the like offence as above for Thos. Vancamp & Wm. Pace also be committed to the Morristown Gaol. The Board being informed by Genl. George Washington, by letter of the 20th inst., that he considers Capt. Archibald Kennedy as a State prisoner & therefore he does not think that he has any right to interfere in the matter; & the Board conceiving that Capt. Kennedy is disaffected to the present Government, and his residence at his present place of abode dangerous to the State; it was ordered that he remove within 8 days into the County of Sussex & there remain within one mile of the Court House in Newtown till further order of the Board. Ordered that Mr. Condit pay Caleb Howell for his expenses in transacting business for the Council, in the sum of 3 pounds, 15 shillings, 5 pence. Agreed that David Ogden be paid for is expenses in attending the Council of Safety as a Light Horseman – 2 pounds, 9 shillings, 9 pence. Agreed that the Governor have two Light Horsemen to attend him till meeting of the Assembly, as well as a Guard to his person, as for the purpose of being employed as expresses. Upon application of Joseph Lewis, it was agreed that that Wm. Jones, employed by him in the Commissary Dept., be exempted from Militia Duty during his continuance in that employment. Adjourned till meeting of the Legislature.

1778 February 15 – [Sunday]. Council of Safety met at Trenton. Present – Governor, Mr. Speaker, Condit, Imlay, Camp, Manning. Agreed that Capt. Tucker be directed to order a detachment of the Hunterdon militia of 16 men, with a trusty officer to attend the President & the Council of Safety & Guard the prisoners in the Trenton Gaol. Agreed that Jacob Fitz Randolph discharged from Morris County Sheriff's custody, upon entering into a Bond with surety, 2,000 pounds, and to remain at the house of Hartshorn FitzRandolph at Mondham [Mendham] or within 1 mile thereof until farther order of the Council of Safety. Agreed that Sarah Man have leave to go into the Enemy's lines to her husband, with three children, to wit: David, Thomas, & Mathias, & that Elizabeth Cadington have the like permission wither her five children, to wit: Margaret, Violet, Moses, Isaia & Elizabeth.

1778 February 17 – [Tuesday]. Council of Safety met at Trenton. Present – Governor, Crane, Cooper, Condit, Imlay, Manning, Tallman, Hart. Agreed that Major Hoagland be directed to immediately impress wagons, horses, teams, carriages & drivers & cause them to be transported to this place, the pork at Isaac Reckless,' & at Mr. Talman's, and at John Tomlinson's in the possession of Col. Knot, belonging to the public, and it to be delivered to Jas. Paton at Trenton.

1778 February 18 – [Wednesday]. Council of Safety met at Princeton. Present – Governor, Manning, Condit, Col. Fleming, Elmer, Imlay, Tallman, Drake, Camp. Agreed that Peter Gordon be authorized to impress wagons & teams and suitable drivers to transport provisions from this place to the Continental Army & in case of the need to apply to any Militia Officer to afford him the necessary aid for that purpose. Agreed that a Warrant be issued for John Dixon of Bottle Hill to appear before the Council of Safety.

1778 February 25 – [Wednesday]. Council of Safety met at Trenton. Present – Governor, Condit, Linn, Cooper, Crane, Elmer. John Dixon was brought before the Board by Warrant & spoke contemptuously of the Law regulating prices for produce, manufacture & trade. Agreed that he give Bond, with Daniel Bedford, his surety, at 300 pounds each, for his appearance at the next Court of General Sessions for the Peace of Morris County, and was then dismissed. Ordered that Warrants for apprehending & bringing before the Board John Thomson & Elias Marsh. Mathias Isilton & Norris Thorpe appeared before the Board, it appearing they attempted to go over to the Enemy's lines without permission; it was agreed that they be committed to the Gaol for their trial. The following persons – Jacob Londy, Elijah Londy, Henry Widdonfield & Henry Parker of the people called Quakers, were taken up on the suspicion that they were going into the Enemy's lines, but upon examination that suspicion was found to be ill-founded, and they were discharged from the Guard & had permission to go home.

1778 February 26 – [Thursday]. The Council met. Present – Governor, Cooper, Imlay, Condit, Elmer, Imlay [?]. Agreed that Mr. Pettit be paid 1 pound, 2 shillings, 6 pence for an Express at Princeton. Agreed that Col. Reed be desired to send the following prisoners to the Council of Safety, to wit: William Lippincott, Stacy Atkinson, Wm. Corstron, John Osborne, Nathaniel Smith, Thomas & Nicholas Rice, who were taken up for trading with the Enemy.

PM. The Council met. Present – Governor, Crane, Manning, Elmer, Col. Drake, Linn. Ebert Mount brought before the Board & it appearing that he had enlisted into the Service of the Enemy since the Treason Law was passed; he was given time to consider whether he will enlist into our Service or be committed to Gaol for his trial. Four deserters from the British Army were in like manner brought before the Board & it was agreed that they be delivered to Gen. Pulaski and that they be allowed $60 for four stand of arms brought with them from the Enemy. Adjourned till tomorrow morning.

1778 February 27 – [Friday]. Council met pursuant to adjournment. Present – Governor, Elmer, Col. Drake, Manning, Crane, Buck, Condit. Agreed for Mr. Condit to pay Mr. Liddle 25 pounds, 2 shillings, 1 pound for sundry expenses while in service & and on express by order of Gen. Dickinson. And, also to pay John Goldsmith 3 pounds by order of Council. Agreed that Mary Kerder, a woman from Sussex County, whose husband is with the Enemy, have permission, together with her daughter, to go to Staten Island. Agreed that Mr. Wm. Vandyke be paid 7 pounds, 11 shillings, 3 pence for his trouble & expenses in bringing four deserters from Staten Island to this place from Elizabeth Town. Mr. Buck left his seat at the Board & Mr. Camp took his place. Evert Mount appeared before the Board, enlisted into our service, took the Oaths and was dismissed. Agreed to pay Jas. Paxton the following suns by him for hiring expresses – William Rosin – 3pounds, 7 shillings, 6 pence; William Roscow – 2 pounds, 5 shillings; Richard Bordon – 1 pound 10 shillings. An Application was made to the Board by Jas. Paxton to have the following persons employed in the Commissary Dept in this Town, excused from military duty in the Militia and it was taken into consideration. Agreed that one cooper be exempted from his next tour. The persons alluded to in the above are 1 cooper, 1 commissary clerk, 1 clerk of the scales, & superintendent of the bake houses & 1 commissary.

1778 February 28 – [Saturday]. Council of Safety met at Trenton. Present – Governor, Condict, Col. Fleming, Cooper, Crane, Elmer, Buck. The following subjects – Nathaniel Smith, Thos. Watts & Nicholas Rice, subjects pf Pennsylvania, brought before the Board on suspicion of trading with the Enemy, were examined, and the Council being of the opinion that the charge was not supported, they were dismissed. William Lippincott, an inhabitant of Philadelphia apprehended on his way to the Enemy without a passport is ordered committed to Burlington Gaol for trial. Stacy Atkinson being taken up on his way to Philadelphia with beef destined for that place was ordered to be committed in like manner; as was John Osgood for carrying flour to the Enemy in Philadelphia. Agreed that Col. Bowes Reed be directed to send to this place under a proper Guard, all the prisoners in Burlington Gaol committed for or charged with trading with the Enemy or going into Enemy lines without passports, together with their names. Agreed that the Governor issue an order for impressing a competent number of wagons for transporting provisions purchased by the Board of War of Pennsylvania to the Gallies who are in great want of provisions and unable on account to proceed on their intended cruise from this place towards Philadelphia to prevent design of the Enemy up the Delaware.

1778 March 1 – [Sunday]. Council of Safety met. Present – Governor, Condit, Elmer, Manning, Cooper, Camp. Thos. Hand, Patrick McNelly, & John Baylis deserting from the Enemy were brought before the Board, examined, and were sent to Head Quarters.

1778 March 2 – [Monday]. Council of Safety met at Trenton. Present – Governor, Cooper, Condit, Crane, Elmer, Buck. Agreed that the Governor write to a person in Fredericktown in Virginia, who has the custody of Wm. Wooley, lately of Monmouth County and a subject of this State, desiring Mr. Wooley to be delivered to Richard Bell, he having promised to bring Wooley into this State and to enter into Bond for his appearing before Council in a reasonable time after his arrival in State. The following persons: Thos. Eldridge, John Pearson, Moses Pippit, Wm. Mattock, Samuel Skill, Thos. Bishop, Peter Becket, Stephen Becket, Wm. Lippincott, Saml. Hackney, Joab Eldridge, Ezekiel Cox, Benjamin Nailor, John George, Simeon Collins, Richd. McGennis, George French, John Brock, John Home, John Becket, John Lodge, Andrew Sweeton, and Richard Wright, were sent prisoners from Burlington to the Council of Safety upon suspicion of having been trading with the Enemy. The former ten confessed that they went into the Enemy's line with provisions & the latter that they had been in like manner into Philadelphia and had returned into this State without license by Law. Ordered that they all be committed to Burlington Gaol for their trial. Agreed that the delinquents above named be tried in Burlington County.

1778 March 3 – [Tuesday]. Council of Safety met at Trenton. Present – Governor, Elmer, Buck, Crane, Cooper, Tallman. Agreeable to a recommendation by the Court of Oyer & Terminer & General Gaol Delivery holden at Freehold in the County of Monmouth – January 1, 1778. Agreed to pay the following constables at the said Court – Jas. Wilson – 12 days, 12 pounds; Joseph Coward 12 days, 12 pounds; Jas. Tapscott 10 days, 10 pounds; Zeph. Morris 12 days, 12 pounds; George Harrison –Cryer – 12 days, 6 pounds. Nathaniel Middleton being called before the Board, took the Affirmations to the Effect of the Oaths, and was dismissed. Agreed that Council purchase of Col. Sullivan one ton of Continental powder for use in this state. Agreed that the 160 weight of the said powder & 100 pounds of musket bullets in the hands of Mr. Baldwin in Princeton be delivered to Mr. Hendrick Van Brunt for the use of the Monmouth Militia.

1778 March 7 – [Saturday]. Council of Safety met at Trenton. Present – Governor, Crane, Elmer, Col. Fleming, Imlay, Manning. Elias Marsh, John Thompson, Norris Thorpe & Matthias Iselstin were brought before the Board, took the Oaths, and were discharged; the latter two at the same time entered into recognizance in 300 pounds each for their appearance at the Supreme Court to be held in Middlesex County. Conrad Fredericks was brought before the Board for going into the Enemy's lines and he entered into a Bond with Abm. W. Depuyster in 300 pounds each for his appearance in the Court of Oyer & Terminer for the County of Essex. Gerrit Demarest, Gerrit Van Gieson, John Paulese & John Van Boskirk, who were in the Morristown Gaol to procure an exchange of a like number of prisoners in New York, having had permission by this Board on January 30th last, to go to their homes for one month to negotiate the exchange aforesaid & were to return to Morristown Gaol in that time if the exchange was not effected. And the Board having received advice that they had respectively returned according to their respective engagements (except Boskirk who is taken ill) & were desirous of having further time allowed them for the purpose aforesaid. Agreed, that they have the time extended for one month more, under that same conditions as set forth. Agreed that Abm. Van Gieson have leave in like manner to go home for a month.

1778 March 9 – [Monday]. Council of Safety met at Trenton. Present – Governor, Crane, Elmer, Buck, Elmer, Col. Fleming, Col. Drake. Agreed to purchase from Mr. Collins a half a ream of is printing paper for use by the Council of Safety and that Col. Drake pay for same. Agreed that the powder purchased from Col. Sullivan for use in this State, except the 160 pounds delivered to Hendrick Van Brunt, and the 180 wt. thereof to be sent to the County of Cumberland, to be deposited in Morris County under the care of Genl. Winds, who is to make a return of it to the Governor & also the said powder to Genl. Winds for use of the Militia. Agreed that a company of 60 men, 1 lieut. & an ensign (that Major Goetchius by order of Dec. 5th last was authorized to raise for defense of Bergen County & which were to stay in service for three months from that date) be continued in service 3 months longer unless sooner discharged, or that the like number be raised & continued for that time, & Major Goetchius be authorized to raise four Light Horsemen out of his company of Infantry, who are to be allowed the same pay & rations as the other Light Horsemen of this State.

1778 March 10 – [Tuesday]. Council of Safety met at Trenton. Present – Governor, Buck, Manning, Col. Fleming, Camp, Col. Drake. Samuel Titus was called before the Board and it being proved that he had asked for 5 pounds of butter more than the law allows, it was agreed that he be fined the sum of 6 pounds for the breach of the law in so doing & forfeit the sum of 13/9 the price asked for the butter. Samuel Tucker appeared before the Board & having taken the Oaths, was dismissed. Ordered that Mr. Condit pay to Thos. Philipse for the use of Henry Post, the sum of 10 pounds, 14 shillings, 3 pence for his time & trouble in attending the Council as a Light Horseman from Feb 22nd to March 4th.

1778 March 11 –[Wednesday]. Present as before. Woolingston Redman appearing before the Board pursuant to a Warrant for having sold 200 wt. of flour at a higher price than the law directs, agreed that he be fined the sum of 6 pounds & also the sum of 3 pounds.6 being the price he demanded. Agreed that the Governor publish an advertisement directing the farmers in the neighborhood of this place to bring their provisions into the town, without fear of having their wagons, horses and cattle taken from them, for the Service of the Army.

1778 March 13 – [Friday]. Council of Safety met at Trenton. Present – Governor, Manning, Condit, Tallman, Elmer, Col. Drake. Ordered that Mr. Condit pay Jas. Serrings & others [not named] the sum of 40 pounds, 11 shillings, 7 pence for attending the Council as Light Horsemen. Agreed that 200 weight of lead made into ball & 500 flints be delivered to Newcomb Thomson for use of the Cumberland County Militia.

1778 March 17 – [Tuesday]. Council of Safety met at Trenton. Present – Governor, Condit, Manning, Buck, Col. Flemming, Camp, Mr. Speaker. Agreed that there be paid to Jonathan Dear for the use of Andrew McMackin, 6 pounds, 16 shilling, 6 pence for casting musket balls for the use of the State and his expenses for attending to same. Edward Steward was brought before the Board upon the suspicion of coming into this State as a spy from the Enemy, but there is not enough evidence to convict him; agreed that he be remanded until further testimony can be developed. John Paradise was brought before the Board for going into the Enemy lines & returning to this State without a passport. Agreed that he have 5 days to decide whether he will enlist into a Battalion of this State in the Continental service & in the meantime he be committed to the Guard in this place. Agreed that Col Hathaway receive from Mr. Ogden, at Boontown, 20,000 flints sent or to be sent into this State by Archibald Mercer from Boston (first paying Ogden at Boontown for the cartage) & to be accountable for them when properly called upon. Agreed that Major Asher Holmes be paid 120 pounds – for the use of the wives, widows & children, of the Militia inhabitants of Monmouth County, who have been either taken prisoners by the Enemy or killed in battle & who are proper objects of public charity, and is to be distributed among them at discretion. The prisoners & killed are: James Hibbits, Peter Yateman, Saml. Hanzey, John Bowes, Abraham Merlat, Nathan Maxin, Joseph Davis, Wm. Norris, Wm. Cole, Alexr. Clark, Lambert Johnston & Obidiah Stillwel. Agreed that there be paid to Major Alfred Holmes for monies expended by him in paying sundry expenses on the public service – 4 pounds, 9 shillings, 9 pence. Agreed that Mr. Manning be paid the sum of 11 pounds, 10/ for the use of Reuben Potter for his expenses of removing the wife of Ellis Barron, the wife of Samuel Moores, & the wife of Moses Write from Woodbridge to Elizabeth Town, to be sent over to Staten Island with a flag of truce. Agreed that John Buck be paid 7 pounds, 10/ for the use of Newcomb Thompson for conveying military stores from Princeton to Cumberland County. Agreed that John Hart be paid 32 pounds for the use of constables for their services in attending the Court of Oyer & Terminer, at Flemingtown, Hunterdon County. Agreed that John Hart Esqr. be paid 2 pounds, 16 shilling, 10 pence for the use of Elijah Stout for his services attending the Court in Flemingtown. Agreed that John Hart Esqr. be paid 10 pounds for the use of John Paral, for the expenses attending the cure of a wound which he received on 26 January while engaged in the Militia in Col. Chambers Battalion, in an action with the Enemy. Agreed that John Hart Esqr. be paid 5 pounds, 15 shilling, 6 pence for the use of James Blooks the amount of monies paid to the Doctor for the cure of a wound received from the Enemy while on military duty.

1778 March 18 – [Wednesday]. Council of Safety met at Trenton. Present – Governor, Tallman, Col. Fleming, Mr. Speaker, Manning, Buck, Imlay. Agreed that Stephen Burrows & William Heburn, his journeyman, (or any journeyman in his employ) be exempted from militia duty during the time they shall be engaged in repairing the saddles & accoutrements of the First Regiment of Virginia Cavalry, commanded by Col. Bland & that the exemption is for no longer than for the above stated business. Agreed that Alexander Edwards Miller, employed at Wm. Lewis' Mill & Joseph Smith & Jacob Davenport, coopers, engaged at the same place, be excused from serving in the Militia for one month from this date. Agreed that Thomas Hunt & John Bellerjan & Samuel Tucker, Junr., employed in making & mending boots for the Cavalry by Wm. Tucker, be excused from militia duty during the time they shall be engaged in that work. Agreed that Joseph Holingshead be paid for providing 76 prisoners in Burlington & the Guard for them, with victuals, wood, & other necessaries during September last, & for his time & expenses for same – 82 pounds.2/.

1778 March 20 – [Friday]. Council of Safety met at Trenton. Present, as before. A Memorial presented to the Treasury Board by Thos. Leaming, in reference to the amount of salt taken from him by the Commissary Hugg & by them to the Governor & the Executive Council of this State being read & Mr. Leaming opened the case. The Council thought it proper to defer the hearing till depositions were taken on the part of the public.

1778 March 21 – [Saturday]. Council of Safety met at Princeton. Present – Governor, Buck, Manning, Tallman, Col. Fleming, Col. Drake. Agreed that the Governor write a letter to the person in Reading, Pennsylvania, who has custody of Jacob Bogert, lately of Bergen County and a subject of this State, desiring him to deliver Bogert to Hendrick Bogert & Samuel Campbell, having promised to bring him into this State, & to enter into Bond at 300 pounds of this State aforesaid, for his appearance before the President & Council of Safety, in a reasonable time after his arrival.

1778 March 22 – [Sunday]. The Council met. Present – Governor, Col. Fleming, Manning, Camp, Buck, Col. Drake. Ordered that in virtue of a resolution of the Council of Safety & Assembly, Watres Smith appointed to impress six strong wagons on timber wheels, with six horses each & 18 waggons with four horses each & a sufficient number of drivers for removing cannon to the neighborhood of Trenton & removing stores & ammunition to Pittston, & common stores, rigging & sails to convenient places out of the enemy's reach which common stores, ammunition, rigging & sails belong to the Navy Board of Pennsylvania, to be continued to Service for any term not exceeding 6 days, provided that the said Navy Board of Pennsylvania engage to pay the owners of the said carriages, wagons & teams so impressed & the said drivers, the like wages, as they are allowed when in the service of the Continent, & also make the said Watres Smith a reasonable compensation for his trouble as Wagon Master. John Paradise was discharged from custody upon entering into recognizance wit George Anthony in 300 pounds to appear at the next Court of Oyer & Terminer for Hunterdon County.

1778 March 24 – [Tuesday]. Council of Safety met at Trenton. Present – Governor, Buck, Camp, Crane, Col. Flemming, Condict, Imlay. Agreed that the Governor write a letter advising Brig. Genl. Winds will succeed Col. Seely in the post at Elizabeth Town. Upon application of Benjamin Smith, agreed that Benj. Smith & David Van C[N?]orden, his apprentices, & Lott Dunborr & Wm. Yard his journeymen, employed in working for the Continental Light Horse, stationed in this town, be exempted from serving their respective tours of duty in the Militia for two weeks from this date. Agreed that the powder purchased by the Council of Safety for the use in this State, and lodged in this town, be removed into Burlington County & put under the care of Mr. John Tomkin & that person who carries the powder call at Mr. Imlays's for the lead at his house, to be deposited with the powder at Mr. Tomkin's & that Mr. Tomkin be desired to make up into cartridges the said powder as far as the lead will permit; & to deliver them out as occasion may require to the commanding officer for the time being in the Western parts of the State.

1778 March 25 – [Wednesday]. Council of Safety met at Trenton. Present – Buck, Imlay, Cooper, Linn, Col. Fleming, Condict, Crane, Tallman, Col. Drake, Camp. The Governor being absent & the majority of the Council of Safety present, they proceeded (pursuant to the authority given them in the 21st section of the act entitled "An Act for constituting a Council of Safety) to the choice of a president for the time being. Hon. John Stevens, Esqr. was unanimously appointed to the chair and he too his seat. The following persons- Wm. Rawson, Saml. Courzens, John Sweeton & Joshua Clever, subjects of this State; Jas. Besley, Michael Mains & Joseph Dain, citizens of Delaware State; & Abraham Williams lately of Virginia; were sent from Cumberland before the Board. The Council examined them & reduced it to writing & being informed that they had been previously examined by the Atty. General, agreed that before they were proceeded against, a letter be sent to Mr. Patterson for information of what he knows about them. Samuel Davis Junr, Christopher Guron, Seth Brook & Josiah Lawrence being in like manner brought before the Board in order that they might be moved out of the reach of the Enemy & it appearing that they were under sentence of the law for diverse crimes & misdemeanors – Council thought it best to leave them in the custody of the Sheriff until the law has been duly executed upon them. Agreed that Mr. Condict pay Wm. Low, 6 pounds, 16 shillings, 9 pence in compensation for his time & expenses in bringing the above persons from Cumberland before the Council of Safety.

1778 March 26 – [Thursday]. Council of Safety met at Trenton. Present – Governor, Crane, Imlay, Elmer, Buck, Cooper, Col. Fleming, Condict. The following prisoners from Gloucester – Jacob Shoulder, Jacob Mouse, Isaac Zane, Saml. & Wm. Hewling, Thos. & Jacob Jones, Wm. Davenport, Thos. Smith, Gunrod Shoemaker, Daniel Murray & Blakey Hurltey and a Negro man belonging to John Cox, appeared before the Board - Their several confessions before Justice Hugg having been read & they being examined thereupon & it being too late to enter upon their respective cases, the Council adjourned till tomorrow morning 9 o'clock.

1778 March 27 – [Friday]. Council of Safety met at Trenton. Present – Governor, Elmer, Condict, Col. Fleming, Buck, Imlay. The Council having received the proofs from the Attorney General respecting the prisoners brought before the Board on the 25th, came to the following decision- That William Rawson & Samuel Cousens for going into the Enemy's lines & furnishing them with provisions & returning into this State contrary to law, have five days to consider whether they will enlist into the Continental Army or be committed for trial. That Joshua Clever & John Sweeton be dismissed on taking the Oaths. That Michael Main, James Besley & Joseph Dain, subjects of Delaware State, be sent to head quarters to be at the disposal of Genl. Washington. The Council resumed the consideration of the prisoners from Gloucester from last evening, when the following resolutions were agreed to; that William Hewling & Thos. Jones be committed to Gaol for trial; that Jacob Shoulder, Jacob Mouse, Isaac Zane & Saml. Hewling have 5 days to determine, for going into the Enemy's lines & returning into this State contrary to law, whether they will enlist into the Continental Army or be committed for trial; that Jacob Jones, Gunrod Shoemaker, William Davenport, Thos. Smith and a Negro man belonging to John Cox be discharged; the former four on taking the Oaths; and that Daniel Murray & Blakey Hurltey, suspected of being Spies from the Enemy, & also endeavoring to pass Counterfeit money found upon them, to be sent to head quarters. Joshua Clever, John Sweeton, Jacob Jones, Gunrod Shoemaker & Thos. Smith were called in & having taken the Oaths were discharged. William Davenport was called in, who took the Affirmations to the effect of the Oaths, and was dismissed. James Stealman appeared before the Board & entered into recognizance at 100 pounds to appear at the next Court of Oyer & Terminer for Essex County, and to give evidence for the State against Wm. Hewling & Thos. Jones. Agreed that Mr. Condict pay to Mr. Buck for the use of John Soullard, for the expenses of bringing the prisoners from Cumberland before the Council – 17 pounds, 7shillings. Agreed to the recommendation of the Justices of the Court of Oyer & Terminer held at Crosswicks, in & for Burlington County, March 1, 1778. Resolved that the Constables hereinafter named be paid for their services to the Court – John Hodgkinson, 9 days-

5.8.0 & for his serving 4 subpoenas @ 14 miles each – 1.10.0; Thos. Powell, 9 days – 5.8.0 & for his serving 4 subpoenas @ 14 miles each – 1.10.0; John Smith, 9 days- 5.8.0 & serving serving 3 subpoenas @ 8 miles each – 0.15.0.; John Singleton, 9 days; Richard Cox, 9 days – 5.8.0; Joseph Mingin, 9 days – 5.8.0 & serving 4 subpoenas 14 miles each – 1.10.0. Agreed that Mr. Condict pay Peter Schenck for the use of Asher Holmes for money paid to him to an Express going from Morris Town & New German Town to the Speaker of the Assembly, at the request of the Attorney General, the sum of 6pounds, 8 shilling, 2 pence. Agreed that Mr. Condict pay Peter Schenck 5 pounds, 8 shilling, 9 pence, for the use of Asher Holmes, being money laid out by him for bringing ammunition from Elizabeth Town to Freehold for use of the Monmouth Militia. Agreed that Bartholomew Fort, a cooper, employed at making casks, at George Bergen's Mill, be excused from serving in the Militia for the space of one month from this date.

1778 April 1 – [Wednesday]. Council of Safety met at Trenton. Present – Mr. Vice President, Imlay, Buck, Elmer, Cooper, Condict. William McCollum, Capt. of the *Carolina* Paquet & Hugh Smith, mate of the same, together with five sailors, taken by John Brooks, Commander of the Sloop *Scorpion*, from Salem in New England, were brought before the Board, and it was agreed that Capt. McCollam & Hugh Smith be put on parole to remain in this town until further orders & that the sailors be committed to the Guard. Agreed that the president draw on Capt. Tucker for 150 cartridges for the use of Capt. Quigly's Guard stationed at this place & take his receipt for the same, he promising them within a month. Adjourned till 3 o'clock PM.

Met pursuant to adjournment. Present – Governor, Condict, Manning, Col. Fleming, Elmer, Buck. Agreed that John Drake be paid for the use of Benjamin Blackwell for serving the Council of Safety as a Light Horseman from 2 March 1778 to 1 April 1778 – 17 pounds, 2 shillings, and also for the use of Thos. Philipse for like services from 22 February to 1st of April 1778 – 25 pounds, 9 shillings. And that Benjamin Smith be paid 8 pounds, 4 pence for like services of John Stevens. Agreed that Capt. Leek be paid for his expenses for bringing Capt. McCollam, his mate & men, who were taken by John Brooks, Commander of the sloop *Scorpion* of New England, from Egg Harbour before the Council at Trenton – 25 pounds, 2 shilling. Agreed that Mr. Parker have leave for a fortnight to go to New York to negotiate the exchange of Mr. Fell & to return to Morristown at the end of that time.

1778 April 2 – [Thursday]. Council of Safety met at Trenton. Present – Governor, Condit, Camp, Elmer, Manning, Buck. Agreed that there be advanced to Mr. Tallman 3 pounds being money paid by him to an Express for riding to Haddonfield with a letter to Col. Shreive from Genl. Washington. Order that Mr. Condict pay Wm. Seaman for riding express for the Council & attending them as a Light Horseman from 22 March to 1 April – 18 pounds, 18 shilling, 9 pence. Agreed that the remaining quantity of powder in the hands of Col. Sullivan be removed to Princeton.

1778 April 4 – [Saturday]. Council of Safety met at Trenton. Present – Vice president, Condit, Crane, Col. Fleming, Elmer, Cooper. Saml. Hewling appeared before the Board & gave recognizance for his appearance at the next Supreme Court in Burlington; as did Jacob Mouse, who entered into Bond with Saml. Hewling his surety in 300 pounds each for his like appearance in the same court. Agreed that the prisoners under Guard at this place be removed to Princeton under the care of Capt. Quigly. Ordered that a Warrant be issued to James Ledden, to take Marmaduke Abbot & bring him before the Council on Monday next at Princeton. Peter Vreeland appeared before the Board & gave recognizance with Ricd. Ryerson, his surety, at 300 pounds each, to appear at the next Court of Oyer & Terminer for Bergen County. Agreed that there be paid to Capt. Ward for bringing the above-names Vreeland before Council, the sum of 6 pounds.

1778 April 6 – [Monday]. Council met at Princeton. Present – Governor, Crane, Linn, Buck, Camp, Condict. Agreed that John McArthur have leave to go into the City of Philadelphia on his way to Ireland. Agreed that Wm. McCollam, Capt. Of the "*Carolina*" Paquet, Hugh Smith his mate & Wm. Oliver, Extopher Collan, Wm. Price & John Marton, sailors on board the same – Daniel Murray, Blakely Hurltey, Michael Main, Jas. Besley, Joseph Dain, Asher Horner, John Shever, Jacob Miller, Israel Mills, _____ Martin, Capt. Sloan of the Brig. "*John*", Capt. Maloney of an armed schooner, be sent under Guard to Head Quarters and delivered up to Genl. Washington.

1778 April 7 – [Tuesday]. Council met at Princeton. Present – Governor, Cooper, Tallman, Crane, Elmer, Tallman[twice listed], Manning. Agreed that Capt. Christopher Marsh be paid, for the use of the following persons in his troop of Light Horse, for their several services in riding Express for Genl. Dickenson, from 26th October to the 25th November 1777: Oct 26th - for Joseph Martin for riding express 7 days to Morris, Somerset & Sussex Counties – 5.5.0 & for Oct 30th - riding express from Gen. Dickinson to Gen. Washington – 5 days – 3.15.0; Oct 31st - For Thos. Eaton's express in riding 3 days from Gen. Dickenson to Freehold – 2.5.0; Oct 31st - For Ashabel Freeman for his expenses 3 days riding express form Gen. Dickenson to Gen. Heard & Col. Frelinghuysen & Dunn – 1.10.0, Nov 17th – For Nathaniel Crane for his express services – 2 days – from Gen. Dickenson to Hibernia – 1.10.0; Nov. 23rd – For Elihu Pearson for his expenses in the same service 2.5 days – from Gen. Dickenson to Flemingtown – 1.17.0; Nov 25th – For Wm. Ramsden's expresses 2 days in riding express from Gen. Dickenson to Col. Frelinghuysen – 1.10.0.

Agreed that Nehemiah Dunham Esqr be paid for the use of Peter Barker, George Lupick & Joseph McCafferty for carrying prisoners from Pittstown to Morristown 6 days at 15 shillings a day; also 3 shillings over to the said Barker as Sergeant, 13.13/. Agreed that the following persons be sent to Head Quarters under Guard & delivered to Genl. Washington; Jas. Hudson & Jas. Binly prisoners of War of British Infantry taken at Brandywime; Robert Cannon, George Parker, John Bane, Jas. Peacock, Jas. Cook, British seaman belonging to the transport "*Lord Howe*" Capt. Francis; Jos. Hissock belonging to the brig "*Lord Howe*" Capt. Sloan, Fras. Warrington of the "*Baltic Merchant*" Capt. Geo. Masters; Samuel Weekley & Wm. Wilson belonging to the merchantman brig "*Nancy*" Capt. Dexter; Timothy Hay, mariner on board the "*Carolina*" packet, Capt. McCollom; Edward Stewart, belonging to York, suspected for being a Spy, traveled from Philadelphia to Jersey with merchandise; Abraham Williams, belonging to Philadelphia, who came into Jersey to purchase provisions with intent to carry them into the Enemy's lines; John Martin, taken up by Capt. Parker for deserting from the Light Horse; John Williamson taken up for traveling without a pass, suspected of having deserted from Genl.

Burgoynes'a Army of Prisoners, to make his way to Philadelphia. Agreed that William Heuling, Thos. Jones, Wm. Rawson, Saml. Cousens, Jacob Shoulder & Isaac Zane for carrying provisions into Philadelphia & returning into this State, be committed to Morristown Gaol for their trial with Warrants of commitment issued. Agreed that John King enter into recognizance with William Nutt, his surety, for his appearance at the next Supreme Court in Burlington.

1778 April 8 – [Wednesday]. Council met at Princeton. Present – Governor, Camp, Cooper, Crane, Condict, Elmer. Agreed to pay on account of Josiah Burnet, an Ensign, 8th Co., 1st Regiment of Morris County Militia, who was wounded on the 15th day of September last at Second River, for his present relief the sum of $60.00, and that Dr. Peter Smith deliver an account of the particulars of his bill for administering medicines to him. Agreed that Benjamin Spinning, John Spinning & Nathaniel Bond, three prisoners in the New Ark Gaol, charged with going into the Enemy's lines without passports, be brought before the Council of Safety. Agreed that Gerrit Demarest, Gerrit Van Gieson, John Paulis, John Van Boskirk & Abm. Van Gieson, have leave to go home for a space of six weeks from this time.

1778 April 9 – [Thursday]. Council met at Princeton. Present – Governor, Tallman, Mr. Speaker, Elmer, Buck, Crane. Agreed that Wm. Alger, sent before the Board by Justice Loyd for going into & returning from the Enemy's lines, be committed to the Essex Gaol & that a Warrant of Commitment be issued. Upon petition of Duncan McCall setting forth that he was a deserter from the British Army and had been called to serve in the Militia of this State & had been fined for non-attendance, was craving an exemption from service. Council advised the Governor to direct the officers to excuse him from military duty. Agreed that Mr. Buck be paid for the use of Benoni Dare, for riding express for Gen. Newcomb with orders to several Cols., 4 days at $3.00 per day. Agreed that Samuel Minor be summoned to the Council of Safety.

1778 April 10 – [Friday]. Council met at Princeton. Present – Governor, Buck, Camp, Col. Drake, Crane, Elmer, Tallman, Hoopes, Col. Cook. Samuel Minor was brought before the Board & it appearing that he had attempted by conversation to discourage persons engaged in the American cause. It was agreed that he be fined security for his appearance at the next Court of General Quarter Sessions of the Peace for Middlesex County, which having accordingly given with John Davis, his surety, in 300 pounds each, & he was then dismissed. Ruelof Jacobus, Nicholas Jones, John Schamerhorn, Samuel Berry & David Brown were brought before the Board, took the Oaths and were dismissed. Thos. Jones appeared before the Board & having entered into recognizance with Nicholas Jones as his surety in 300 pounds each for his appearance at the next Court of General Quarter Sessions of the Peace for Bergen County, and was dismissed. Agreed that Capt. John Mead be paid the sum of 5 pounds for bringing the above named persons from Bergen County before the Council. Agreed that John Dennis Esqr be summoned to appear before the Council of Safety of this State.

1778 April 11 – [Saturday]. Council met at Princeton. Present – Governor, Crane, Camp, Manning, Buck, Col. Drake. Agreed that Jacob Weiser be summoned to attend the Board. Agreed that John Richmond, suspected of being a dangerous person, enter into bond with security to remain within one mile of New Germantown in Hunterdon County, until further order of the Council respecting him, with having Jacob Hyer, his surety, in 300 pounds each, was discharged.

1778 April 13 – [Monday]. Council met at Princeton. Present – Governor, Camp, Col. Cook, Manning, Elmer, Buck, Fennimore. Agreed that Henry Bogert & Jacob Lessheir who were taken with provisions intended for the Enemy be committed to Essex Gaol for their trial, & Elias Romyn enter into recognizance to appear against them at the next Court of Oyer & Terminer in Essex County. Agreed that Elias Romyn be paid for his time & expenses in bringing the above persons from Bergen County and as an allowance for returning home be paid 3 pounds, 18 shillings, 6 pence & that Codenis Hoaglandt for assisting in the same service be paid 3 pounds. Agreed that John Barnhill, John Barcalow & Okey Voorhise, employed at the ferry of John Sherard on the Delaware together with Sherard himself, be exempted from doing militia duty until further orders from Council.

1778 April 14 - [Tuesday]. Council met at Princeton. Present – Governor, Manning, Camp, Col. Cook, Tallman, Buck, Col. Drake. Benjamin Spinning, John Spinning & Nathaniel Bond, agreeable to their petition, were brought before the Board. The Council heard their several examinations read & agreed that they be returned to Essex Gaol for trial & that they defray the expenses of the guard in bringing them here & returning them – settled at 10 pounds, 6 pence.

1778 April 15 - [Wednesday]. Council met. Present – Governor, Buck, Fenemore, Camp, Col. Drake, Col. Cook, Tallman. Agreed that Thos. Fenemore Esqr be paid for the use of Saml. Fenemore, 7 pounds, 15 / for riding express by order of Col. Ellis to the following places from 2nd March – to Bordentown, Burlington, Salem, Trenton, Burlington, Long-a-coming & Linneminein.

1778 April 18 – [Saturday]. Council met at Princeton. Present – Governor, Col. Drake, Fenemore, Mr. Speaker, Condict, Tallman, Col. Cook. Agreed that Hannah Gaffin be paid (or to her order) the widow of John Gaffin, a soldier in Capt. Polhemus's Company, 1st NJ Regiment, who died at Crown Point, the 3rd of July 1777, the sum of $30.00. Agreed that Wm. Hewling, Jacob Fitzrandolph & Wm. Pace be tried at the Court now sitting at New Ark, Essex County. Agreed that the following persons – Henry Bogart, Jacob Soyier, Rynere Blanchard, David Rattan, Simeon Van Ripen, Joseph Berry, Benjamin Zobriski, Nancy Arnold, Evert Rickman, Stephanus Torhune, Stephen Berry, James Furlough, Elias Romine, Matthew Reach, Austern Wright, Jas. Wells, John Dey, Jacob Morris, Thos. Jones, Wm. Rawson, Samuel Cousins, Jacob Shoulder, & Isaac Zane be tried at Essex County although the crimes they are charged with were committed in other counties.

1778 April 19 – [Sunday]. Council met. Present – Mr. Speaker, Tallman, Manning, Col. Cook, Col. Drake, Mr. Elmer. Agreed that the Council of Safety meet next Tuesday at Morristown.

1778 April 29 – [Wednesday]. Council met at Morristown. Present – Governor, Smirh, Col. Cook, Condict, Col. Drake. Agreed that Mr. Condict pay Cornelius Stoothoff for his attending the Governor & Council of Safety as a Light Horseman from the 13th to the 24th of April, 6 pounds, 5 shillings, 9 pence; paid to Mr. Wm. Vanduyn for the same services for the same time,

10 pounds, 16 shillings, 2 pence; paid to John Demont for the same services for the same time, 12 pounds, 8 shillings, 9 pence; and to Fredk. Ten Eyck for attending the Govr & Council of Safety as above from 13th to the 29th of April, 11 pounds, 8 shillings, 2 pence. Isaac Conklin appeared before the Board & took the Oaths and was discharged. Adjourned till tomorrow morning 9 o'clock.

1778 April 30 – [Thursday]. Met pursuant to adjournment. Present – Governor, Condict, Smith, Crane, Col. Cook, Col. Drake. Agreed that Mr. Condict pay Stephen Drake, a soldier in Josiah Hall's Company for the loss of his pay and rations from the 1st of April to the 15th of May, in consequence of a wound he received in the 3 months service, 5 pounds, 12 shillings, 6 pence. That there be paid to Edward Tibit upon the same account above 5 pounds, 12 shillings, 6 pence, and 12/, the over amount being the money advanced by him to the doctor. Also, paid to Peter Hill for the same reason the same amount. Also paid to Elias Bedford, a Corporal, in the same Company for his pay & rations during 3 months in consequence of a wound he received at the above mentioned time, 8 pounds, 5/ and also 96/ over being the amount on monies paid by him to the doctor. Agreed that James Burnet be paid for the use of Josiah Burnet, an Ensign, 8th Company, 1st Regiment, 60 pounds, 18 shillings, 1 pence, being the amount of monies expended by him towards the cure of a wound he received on 15 September 1777. Agreed that Mrs. Esther Troup, wife of John Troup, together with her child have leave to pass to her husband in the Enemy's lines, upon the condition that she do not return into this State during the present war, and that she takes with her, her own & her child's wearing apparel. Agreed that the Governor draw upon the Treasurer for 1,000 pounds for the use of the Council of Safety. Adjourned till tomorrow morning 9 o'clock.

1778 May 1 – [Friday]. Met pursuant to adjournment. Present – Governor, Condict, Smith, Crane, Col. Cook, Col. Drake. Agreed that John Faulkinier be discharged from the parole which he gave to the Council on January last. Agreed that Geradus Duyckinck, for selling certain goods to Joseph Lindly, upon his own confession, incur the following fines & forfeitures: For selling 4 yds of silk peeling $16 per yard without certificate – forfeiture of same & fine of 30 pounds; for selling the above at a price higher than limited by law - forfeiture of same & fine of 30 pounds; for selling 3 pounds of red wool at a price without certificate - forfeiture of same & fine of 6 pounds, 7 shillings; for selling the above at a price higher legal price - forfeiture of same & same fine of 6 pounds, 7 shillings. Total – 72 pounds, 15 shillings, less the costs allowed the complainant to be deducted – 3 pounds, 7 shillings, 6 pence; total remaining 69 pounds, 7 shillings, 6 pence. Agreed that Mr. Condict pay Stephen Crane, Esqr. for the use of Michael Magee, a private in Capt. Marsh's troop of Light Horse, who was wounded in an engagement at Elizabeth Town, on the 12 September 1777, the following sums expended by him towards the cure of his wound: To Dr. Wynant's account after deduction, 26 pounds, 6 shillings, 4 pence; to Dr. Dayton's account – 3 pounds; to John Magees's attendance as nurse – 10 pounds.

1778 May 2 – [Saturday]. Council met at Morristown. Present, as before. Agreed that Capt. Smith be summoned to attend the Council at Morristown for charging more for provisions, lodgings & etc than rates affixed by law. Upon the petition of Abraham Odgen, Esqr., for a passport for Mrs. Hoffman to go to the City of New York, it is agreed that the petition cannot be granted until Mrs. Hoffman has answered certain interrogations on behalf of the State, concerning 1,000 pounds said to have been carried by her into the enemy's lines; which sum had been forfeited to the State for which purpose, Mrs. Hoffman, is to attend the Board. Agreed that there be advanced to Capt. Thos. Combs, on account, $60.00 in part payment for money advanced by him to several doctors towards the cure of a wound he received in the service. Adjourned till 3 o'clock Monday afternoon.

1778 May 4 – [Monday]. Met pursuant to adjournment. Present, as before. A letter from Capt. Stryker asking that the Light Horse be exempted from being drafted with the foot, was read & answered. Petition from Hendrick Bennet was read & answered. Agreed that Samuel Smith for selling provisions & etc. at a higher price than allowed, be fined the following with forfeitures: For one supper charged at 5/. – 6 pound, 5 shillings; for one night's lodging at 2/6. – 6 pounds, 2 shillings, 6 pence; ½ gill of bitters at 2/6.- 6 pounds, 2 shillings, 6 pence; Horse hay one night at 5/. - 6 pounds, 5 shillings; 4 quarts of oats at 2/6.- 6 pounds, 2 shillings, 6 pence; one breakfast at 5/. - 6 pounds, 5 shillings; total fine – 37 pounds, 2 shillings, 6 pence. Agreed that 1,000 pounds received this day from the treasury for the Council be delivered in to the hands of Mr. Condict. Adjourned till tomorrow morning.

1778 May 5 – [Tuesday]. Met pursuant to adjournment. Present, as before. Agreed that the horses purchased by Capt. Townshend pursuant to a resolution by both houses of the Legislature for the Continental Service, & rejected by Major Clough & Capt. Harrison, be submitted to the judgment of Messrs. Wilson & Daniel Hunt, to determine whether they are fit for the said service or not. That if they think they come within the description of the Committee of Congress & directions given to Capt. Townshend for purchasing them, they be detained until the opinion of the Legislature shall be known concerning them, except the stallions which are to be disposed of at the risk of the purchaser. Agreed that the following persons be subpoenaed to attend the Council this afternoon, to give evidence in behalf of the United States, relative to the conduct of Gifford Dally in the Dept. of Quarter Master in this place – Malcolm McCurry, Joseph Lewis, Robert Tont, John Pumeroy, Jerod Dey, Elias Van Court & Benj. Lindley. Adjourned till 3 o'clock PM.

Met pursuant to adjournment. John Pumeroy by subpoena appeared before the Board & having sworn upon Mr. Dalley's conduct, which was reduced to writing, he was dismissed, as was John Dey and Elias Van Court, after testimony on the same subject.

1778 May 6 – [Wednesday]. Met pursuant to adjournment. Present, as before. Mr. Dally was called in reference to the matters sworn against him yesterday, he made a defense & was dismissed for the present. Frederick King appeared and gave his evidence against Mr. Dally & was dismissed, as was David Burnet, after his deposition reduced to writing. David Quigg delivered himself to the Governor & Council pursuant to his parole given for that purpose to Thos. Wharton, Esqr., President of the Commonwealth of Pennsylvania, & soliciting a pass to go into the City of New York, he had the Oaths tendered to him, which were refused. Agreed that he give security for his appearance at Court or be committed to the Gaol. Isaac Lyon was called in reference to Mr. Dally's conduct & his deposition taken down & he was thereupon dismissed. Adjourned till 3 o'clock PM.

Met pursuant to adjournment. Agreed that Stephen Ogden be paid 8 pounds, 7 shillings, 6 pence for the amount of Dr. Jones' account as taxed by the Council & paid by Ogden towards the cure of a wound he received in the service. That Capt. John Lindley be paid the sum of 7 pounds, 10 shillings, 6 pence for the amount of what he paid to Dr. Jones for the cure of the wound his son John received in the service. Agreed that Mathias Williamson, Esqr. be summoned to attend the Council at this place Friday next in order to take the Oaths. Agreed that Peter Brunner be appointed Commissioner for disposing of Tory property in Hunterdon County in the place of Azariah Dunham, Esqr., who has resigned, and that a Commission be made out for that purpose. That William Bond be appointed for the same purpose as above in place of John Barber, deceased, for Essex County. And that Nathaniel Hunt be commissioned in place of _____, who resigned. Adjourned till tomorrow morning 8 o'clock.

1778 May 7 – [Thursday]. Met pursuant to adjournment. Present, as before. Agreed that Capt. Kennedy on giving parole to the Governor & Council for his good behavior be released from his confinement at this place & suffered to return to is farm on New Barbadoes Neck – Capt. Kennedy was called in, subscribed his parole & discharged. Agreed that John Sweeney & John Lafferty, accused of harboring Tories & assisting them in going into the enemy, give security for their appearance at Court. Capt. Stoddard appeared before the Board, by Citation, on a complaint exhibited against him by John Hunt respecting the quantity of hay purchased by him from the said Hunt. Capt. Stoddard having produced that proofs respecting the transaction, the Board was of the opinion that the complaint was not supported. Agreed that Col. Christn. Banker be summoned to attend this Board on Saturday next. Caleb Ball was called in & sworn to sundry matters with respect to the Quarter Master & Commissary Department at Succasunny and his disposition reduced to writing and he was dismissed. Agreed that Gerrit Van Geison & Abraham Van Geison have permission to go to New York to procure an exchange for themselves & Gerrit Demarest, John Paulis & John Van Boskirk by negotiating the release of Thos. Bantha, Bernardus Verbyrck, Samuel Verbryck, John Hays & David Van Burson, now confined in New York – That if they fail in this, they return to Morristown on June 1st, agreeable to an order of the Board back on April 8th last. Council was of the opinion on considering the several proofs exhibited against Mr. Dally, that he should be removed from the office of Deputy Quarter Master & his place be filled by a new appointment. Thos. O'Riley, Ebenezer Adams, Barny Cain & John Williams were sent for, they appeared before the Board, their examinations were taken, & they were remanded to prison. Adjourned till tomorrow morning 9 o'clock.

1778 May 8 – [Friday]. Met pursuant to adjournment. Present, as before. Agreed that William Ridley, Capt. of a transport, George Strawbridge, Henry Ozenburg & John Williams, mariners, be detained in this place until the Commissary of Prisoners be notified concerning them. Ordered that in case Henry O'Harry, Simon Sarch, Geo. Bright, Thos. O'Riley, Ebenezer Adams & Barney Cain, are or shall be charged with or committed for any crimes of offences re: traitors and disaffected persons and/or certain bills of credit in this state, they shall be tried for the same in Burlington County although the offenses occurred in other counties. Ordered that William

Turner, an inhabitant of Pennsylvania, who was appointed Lieutenant in a Company of Greens by Genl. Howe, be sent to headquarters to be at the disposal of Genl. Washington. Agreed that John Francisco's finding security for his appearance at the next Court of Oyer & Terminer to be held in and for the County of Bergen, he be discharged from his confinement. That Daniel Bragly, for selling 20 pounds of veal to Samuel Kirkpatrick for 22/6 be fined 6 pounds & forfeit the price he sold for which he sold the veal. Agreed that Wm. Smith, who has made his escape from the enemy & delivered himself up to the Council, be discharged from his imprisonment on his finding security for his appearance at the next Court of Oyer & Terminer for the Bergen County. Genl. Williamson appeared before Council, by summons, took the Oaths and was dismissed. Agreed that the following persons – Jas. Appleby Senr., James Appleby Jr, Jas. Corby & John Burns, upon there respective petitions for a hearing be brought before the Board to hear & determine their several crimes. James Appleby Senr. & Junr. appeared before the Board. Agreed that if they find security for their appearance at the next Court of Oyer & Terminer in Bergen County, that they be discharged from their imprisonment. Jas. Carby appeared before the Board and it appearing that he had been taken up as a suspicious person, & there be no proofs to detain him, agreed that he be discharged from his imprisonment. John Burns was brought before the Board & it appearing that his case would not allow bail, agreed that he be remanded to prison. Agreed that in the Commissary Department in this place, Nathan Howel be dismissed as a supernumerary officer. Adjourned till tomorrow morning.

1778 May 9- [Saturday]. Met pursuant to adjournment. Present as before with Col. Fleming. John Sweeny appeared before the Board & having entered into recognizance with James Buggs, his surety, in 300 pounds each for his appearance at the next Court of Oyer & Terminer for Bergen County, he was dismissed. Agreed that Benjamin Lindsly, Esqr, be appointed Deputy Quarter Master, in this place, in the place of Gifford Dally removed from said office. Agreed that Mr. Condict pay Wm. Livingston Junr for his appearance before Council as their Secretary at Princeton, Trenton, & Morristown, 48 days at 30/. Per day the sum of 72 pounds. Agreed that _____ Wood supposed to be a deserter & apprehended on is way to the enemy, to be sent to Head Quarters to General Washington. Adjourned till 3 o'clock PM.

Met pursuant to adjournment. Present as before. Agreed that Samuel Vance be paid for attending the Council in Morristown as a Light Horseman, 1 pounds, 19 shillings, 11 pence; and that Wm Wick be paid for the same thing at the same place, 5 pounds, 2 shillings, 4 pence 7 like wise, Benj. Freeman, 3 pounds, 6 shillings, 1 pence, and also to Capt. Simmons for like service, 12 pounds, 0 shillings, 9 pence; and for Moses Wick for the same duty; 2 pounds, 0 shillings, 11 pence. Agreed that Daniel Bragly be committed to the Gaol until he pays his fine & forfeiture adjudged on him yesterday. William Templeton appeared before the Board & having entered into recognizance with Walter Anderson, his surety, in 300 pounds each for his appearance at the next Court of Oyer & Terminer in Morristown, he was discharged. Ordered that Catherine Shepard, whose husband is within the enemy's lines, be sent to him & that Major Hays, or the Magistrates in Newark put that order into execution. Christopher Banker appeared before the Board & having been examined with respect to the Forage Master's department at Succassuny, was thereupon dismissed. Agreed that Col. Drake be paid 30/. for the paper furnished by him to the Council.

That Capt. Arnold be allowed 40/. for the use of his room for the Council of Safety. Adjourned to meet at Princeton on the 20th of May.

1778 May 20 – [Wednesday]. The Council of Safety met at Princeton. There not being a quorum, adjourned till tomorrow morning.

1778 May 21 – [Thursday]. Met pursuant to adjournment. Present – Governor, Houston, Camp, Imlay, Hart, Cooper. Agreed that Capt. Williamson conduct the quota of Col. Neilson's Battalion, who have chosen to enter into Capt. Voorhis' Company, in Col. Ogden's Battalion, to the said Battalion now in the neighborhood of Haddonfield & get the commanding officer of the Battalion to certify the receipt of them upon the descriptive list of their entering into the Service and transmit the list with all convenient speed to the Governor. Agreed that William Mariner have permission to call upon Mr. Mercereau or Capt. Morgan for a number of volunteers & to proceed to Flatbush to bring Mr. Baches, Mr. Matthews, Major Moncrieff & as many others as he may think proper. Gerret Van Gieson & Abraham Van Geison appeared before the Board & produced a certificate from Major Genl. Jones that they had applied for themselves & Gerret Demarest, John Paulis & John Van Buskirk to be exchanged for themselves & Thos. Bantha, Bernardus Ver Bryck, Samuel Ver Bryck, John Hays & David Burson, but the same could not be effected, and whereupon it was agreed that they all be permitted to stay at their respective homes until the Council shall order otherwise of them. Adjourned till tomorrow morning.

1778 May 22 – [Friday]. Met pursuant to adjournment. Present as before with Mr. Mehelm. Pursuant to an Act of Assembly entitled "An Act to provide for the Clothing of the New Jersey Regiments in the Service of the United States", directing the commissioners for purchasing clothing to observe the directions of the Council of Safety during the recess of the Legislature, as to the species & quantity to be purchased & manner in which it is to be disposed of and distributed. Agreed that the following directions were given to Major Kelsey, the Commissioner for that purpose: 1. It appears from accounts from the camp that our regiments are more destitute of shirts than of any other article of clothing, he be directed… to the purchasing of linen suitable for that purpose, and in case a sufficient quantity cannot be procured, to buy flax to be manufactured into linen, in this State,…it is conjectured that our Brigade will consist of 1,800 men. 2. That he be directed so to proportion the Linen & Woollen to be purchased, (the latter to be of the coarser sort) as to procure a suitable quantity of each. 3. That he be directed to buy a sufficient quantity of home spun thread to make up that part of the clothing which he cannot purchase ready made. 4. The two houses of the Legislature having entered into a resolve that the Commissioner for purchasing clothing, shall also purchase a quantity of lead for ammunition, tho' the same was omitted to be inserted in the Bill. Agreed that Mr. Kelsey be further directed to purchase on ton of lead. Christopher Curtis, who went over to the enemy before the treason Law was passed, appeared before the Board and took the Oaths and was dismissed. Upon the representation of several inhabitants of Sussex County relative to an expected invasion by the Indians, it was agreed that Genl. Winds be directed not to call any men from Col. Rosecrans Regiment in that County during the next six weeks. Adjourned till 3 o'clock PM.

Met pursuant to adjournment. Present as before. Agreed that Mr. Condict pay to the three Light Horsemen following for attending the Governor from the 9th & 22nd of May per their accounts: To Ebenezer Gregory 10 pounds,18/.; Joseph Breton 9 pounds, 8 shillings, 9 pence; Jonn. Stiles, Junr. 9 pounds, 13 shillings, 9 pence. Adjourned till tomorrow morning.

1778 May 23 – [Saturday]. Princeton – met pursuant to adjournment. Present – Governor, Mehelm, Houston, Hart, Cooper. There not being a Quorum, adjourned till Monday morning. next.

1778 May 24 – [Sunday]. There not being a Quorum, adjourned till tomorrow morning.

1778 May 25 – [Monday]. Present – Governor, Col. Fleming, Mehelm, Houston, Cooper. There not being a Quorum, adjourned till tomorrow morning.

1778 May 26 – [Tuesday]. Met at Princeton pursuant to adjournment. Present – Governor, Mr. Speaker, Cooper, Col. Fleming, Houston, Mehelm. Abel Thomas & James Thomas, inhabitants of Pennsylvania, being sent under Guard to the Board by two magistrates of New Ark, for having been into the enemy's lines in the City of New York & Long Island without passports & suspected of designs injurious to the liberties of America, appeared. The Board upon hearing their defense was satisfied of their innocence & has reason to believe that their journey to the several places was undertaken on a religious account & agreeable to their declared intention to the meeting held at Maiden Creek the 25th of March 1778 of performing a religious visit to the Meeting of Friends in part of the Jerseys & New York governments. The Board therefore discharged the said Abel & James Thomas from their confinement & they were further desirous to visit the meetings of the Friends at Plainfield, Raway, Shrewsbury, Squan, Squan-Kung, Barnaget, Great & Little Egg Harbor and the Capes; and this government being unwilling to obstruct any Society in the exercise of their religion the said Abel & James Thomas were permitted to pass to the nine places last mentioned & then to the State of Pennsylvania. Agreed that Joseph Roberds & David Lyon be paid 9 pounds for their expense in bringing in the persons above named before the Council of Safety from Second River. Adjourned till tomorrow morning.

1778 May 27 – [Wednesday]. Met at Princeton pursuant to adjournment. Present – Governor, Mr. Speaker, Houston, Cooper, Mehelm, Col. Fleming. Agreed that Edward Taylor be discharged from the Bond he gave to the Council sometime in the beginning of December last & have leave to return home for 3 weeks upon entering into another Bond to return within that time to this town & remain here until further order of the Council, unless he shall in the meantime procure the release of John Willett now a prisoner in New York. Adjourned till tomorrow morning.

1778 May 28 – [Thursday]. Met at Princeton pursuant to adjournment. Present – Governor, Cooper, Buck, Imlay, Keasby, Col. Fleming. Agreed that Major Perkins be directed to send all prisoners now in the Burlington Gaol for any crimes to the Governor & Council of Safety at this place. Agreed that Mr. Condict pay Col. Bowes Reed for the money expended by him for guarding a number of prisoners at Burlington Jail and also for the expenses in having them conducted to the Council at Trenton, on the 27th March 1778, 49.5/. as per account. Agreed that there be paid to Edward Keasby Esqr. for the use of Abrm. Richmond for riding express from 1 March from Piles Grove to Trenton & returning back, three days at 30/. Per day, 4 pounds.10/, and, that for the use of Joseph Dickenson for riding express 4 days by order of Col. Hand, from 26 February 1778 the sum of 6 pounds; and also paid the same for the same to David Moores and Daniel Holts. Agreed that Mr. Buck be paid for the use of Webster Newcomb for riding express from the 22 October to the 11th November by order of Genl. Newcomb, 22 Pounds,10/. Adjourned till tomorrow morning.

1778 May 29 – [Friday]. Met at Princeton pursuant to adjournment. Present – Governor, Col. Fleming, Buck, Cooper, Manning, Col. Cook, Condict, Elmer, Imlay. Agreed that John Longstreet, one of the Justices of Peace in Monmouth County, be instructed to tender the Oaths to this State to the following persons – John Taylor Esqr., Joseph Vanmeter, George Taylor Junr., Thos. Thompson, William Lawrence, Josiah Parker, Robert Hartshorne & Ezeck Hartshorne, and that if they refuse to take the same to send them to the Council at this place without giving them a second chance. Agreed that Col. Holmes send the following women to their husbands in the enemy's lines – Mrs. McClease the wife of Cornelius McClease, Mrs. Tilton the wife of John Tilton, Mrs. Tilton the wife of Ezekiel Tilton & Rhody Pew the wife of James Pew. Agreed that Theophilus Elmer Esqr. be paid for the use of Lawrence Johnston for the use of his horse & his extraordinary expenses in riding express for Col. Ellis, 6 pounds, 11 shillings, 3 pence. And, also to Peter Parcel for attending the Governor as a Light Horseman, 5 pounds, 6 shillings, 3 pence. Adjourned till tomorrow morning.

1778 May 30 – [Saturday]. Met at Princeton pursuant to adjournment. Present – Governor, Cooper, Keasby, Col. Fleming, Camp, Buck, Manning, Houston. The Council considered the cases of several prisoners of War & State prisoners sent from Fostertown & not being able to determine where to confine them, they adjourned till tomorrow morning.

1778 May 31 – [Sunday]. Met at Princeton pursuant to adjournment. Present – Governor, Keasby, Buck, Col. Fleming, Manning, Condit, Camp, Houston. Agreed that John Morgan, Robert Compton, Robert Hair, Thos. Egleson, Thos. House, Hugh Queen, Jos. Mansfield, John Gilbert, Cornelius Barn, George Mattox, Gillis Mc Gillis, James Hamilton, Thos. York, Thos. Ewel, Thos. Brooks, John Sproul, John Gevils, Thos. Johnston, Wm. Kaign, Jacob Vago, George Watson, Jas. Downey, John Peel, John McGahon, Jas. McClanagan, John Serterthand, Richd. Clark, John Binley, and John Bougee be sent under Guard to Head Quarters and then Council adjourned till the afternoon.

PM – Met pursuant to adjournment. Present – Governor, Houston, Cooper, Buck, Camp, Manning, Keasby, Condit. Agreed that John Kemble be discharged & give security for his appearance at the next Court of General Quarter Sessions of the Peace, for Burlington County. Agreed that John Clowden & James Livingston be discharged on entering on board a letter of Marque belonging to Mr. Hodge. Agreed that Thomas Canby fined & imprisoned at Burlington be committed to Morris Jail. Adjourned till tomorrow morning.

1778 June 1 – [Monday]. Met at Princeton pursuant to adjournment. Present – Governor, Schenck, Crane, Buck, Condict, Col. Fleming. Agreed that Mr. Buck be paid for the use of Jonn. Beesley for riding express by order of Col. Ellis, 12 days, 18 pounds.

1778 June 2 – [Tuesday]. Council met. Present-Governor, Col. Fleming, Elmer, Col. Cook, Col. Drake, Imlay. Upon the Petition of a number of inhabitants of Monmouth County, setting forth that a number of persons who had been in the enemy's lines, and aiding & assisting to them, and who had plundered a number of inhabitants when the enemy were last at Trenton, have returned to their respective home & been bailed by the Justices & suffered to go at large, praying that an inquiry might be made in the premises. Agreed that Mr. Holmes be directed to furnish the Board, as well with the names of those delinquents who have returned, those of the Magistrates who bailed them out. Adjourned till tomorrow morning.

1778 June 3 – [Wednesday]. Met pursuant to adjournment. Present – Governor, Condit, Keasby, Imlay, Schenk, Col. Cook, Col. Fleming. Agreed to pay Peter Schenk Esqr. for the use of John Vancourt for boarding, attending & taking care of Gershom Vanderhule, a militia soldier belonging to the 1st Regiment, Monmouth Militia, wounded at the battle of Germontown, the 4th of October 1777, from the 16th of October to 18th of November, being 4 weeks & 5 days, at 3 pounds per week, the sum of 14 pounds, 2 shillings, 10 pence. That for the use of Joel Beadle for boarding & attending the above soldier from December 1777 to the 6 January 1778, being 4 weeks & 4 days 20/ per week, 4 pounds, 11 shillings, 6 pence. And for the use of Henry Vanderlink for boarding, nursing & attending the same person from 7th January 1778 being 11 weeks & 3 days, at 20/ per week, at which time he died, the sum of 11 pounds, 8 shillings, 7 pence. That there be paid to Ann Taylor, for boarding & taking care of Joseph Taylor belonging to the Regiment above named, and wounded at the same time, from the 19th October to 9 December, being 9 weeks 2 dollars per week, the sum of 6 pounds, 15/. And for the use of Elizabeth Mains for boarding, attending & taking care of Andrew Main, a militia soldier belonging to the Regiment before named, wounded at the same time, from the 9th October to the 9th April, at 4 pounds per month, the sum of 24 pounds. Agreed that Col. Oakley Hoagland be directed to remove all craft, except ferry boats, between Crosswicks and Burlington on the Jersey shore, to such places where they cannot be used to transport necessaries to the enemy & that such of them as cannot be conveniently removed, as aforesaid, be sunk without loss of time. Upon the Petition of several inhabitants of Sussex County setting forth that Joseph Hancock, Robert Johnston & Ezekiel Younglove, have sometime since left their families & joined the enemy of the United States on Staten Island, & praying that their wives & children may be removed to them to prevent the correspondence which is kept up between them. Agreed that Rachel Hancock, Abigail Johnston & Sarah Younglove, be sent to their husbands in the enemy's lines & that their children who are under age of 12 years have leave to accompany them & that Major Meeker be directed to see to the execution of the order. Adjourned till tomorrow morning.

1778 June 4-[Thursday]. Met pursuant to adjournment. Present – Governor, Mr. Speaker, Buck, Keasby, Manning, Condit, Imlay. Agreed that Mr. Houston be paid for the use of Col. Henry Vandike for sundry expenses in erecting Beacons at or near his farm, 5 pounds, 10 shillings, 8 pence. That John Hart, Esqr. be paid for the use of Nicholas Hoff, a private in Capt. Jacobus

Quick's Company, 2nd Regiment Somerset Militia, who had a thigh broke in the battle of Germantown, for boarding, nursing, attendance and other necessary expenses in consequence of is wound, during the space of 5 months & also for the amount of the Dr.'s bill, 45 pounds, 12 shillings, 6 pence. Agreed that there be paid to Capt. Simmons for the use of Wm. Wilson for riding express by order of the Governor from 30 May to 3 June, 3 pounds,11 shillings, 6 pence. Ordered that Ebenezer Foord be appointed commissioner for disposing of Tory property in the place of Capt. Baker, who resigned in Middlesex County. Adjourned till tomorrow morning.

1778 June 5 – [Friday]. Met at Princeton pursuant to adjournment. Present – Governor, Cooper, Keasby, Imlay, Buck, Condict. The following prisoners – John Kirby, Benj. Allen, Urich West & Jesse Sirran sent before the Board from Gloucester County for joining the enemy & their cases having been taken into consideration; the Council came to the following determination – That they be committed to Freehold jail for their trial & that a Warrant be issued accordingly & to be tried in Monmouth County. Pursuant to a recommendation of the Court of Oyer & Terminer held at New Ark, Essex County, April 1778; agreed that Constables hereinafter named, be allowed the several sums as compensation for their extraordinary services at the said Court and at the same time for their use, be paid to Stephen Crane, Esqr. – The following attending for 7 days at 10/. – Carey Headly, Elias Campbell, Anthony Price, Manning Force, Nathl. Andros, John Tichenor, Thos. Van Riper, John Morris, Wm. King, each at 3 pounds, 10 shillings; Jos. Meeker for 8 days – 4 pounds; Jos. Crane, Wm. Baldwin, Silvenus Baldwin for 9 days each at 4 pounds, 10 shillings; Ebenezer Price and Hendrick Van Bloricum for 6 days – 3 pounds each.

1778 June 6 – [Saturday]. Met at Princeton. Present – Governor, Condict, Col. Drake, Col. Cook, Fenimore, Buck, Imlay. Andrew Lott who went in to the enemy's line, since the Treason law, appeared and gave himself up to the Board & his case having been considered; it was agreed that he enter into recognizance at 300 pounds to appear at the next Court of General Quarter Sessions of he Peace in Morris County, which having done, he was dismissed. Andrew Donaldson, who had gone over to the enemy in December last, appeared before the Board to throw himself on the mercy of his country; whereupon agreed that he be detained under Guard for the present. John Church who had come from the enemy's lines to see his brother was in like manner brought before the Board; the Council thought it proper to detain him also under Guard until further orders. Adjourned till tomorrow,

1778 June 7 – [Sunday]. Met at Princeton pursuant to adjournment. Present – Governor, Condict, Buck, Fenemore, Col. Drake, Elmer. Joseph Fitzrandolph accused of having been trading with the enemy on Staten Island was brought before the Board, examined, and his case taken into consideration; it was agreed that he be sent under Guard to the Court now sitting at Freehold and that John Conner attend with him to give evidence to the said Court respecting the above charge. Ordered that in case Joseph Fitzrandolph is or shall be charged with or committed for any crimes wherever…that he be tried in Monmouth County. Adjourned till tomorrow morning.

1778 June 8 – [Monday]. Council met at Princeton. Present – Governor, Fenemore, Imlay, Elmer, Condict, Col. Drake. Agreed that John Church be dismissed from his confinement at this place. Agreed that the Governor be asked to write to Genl. Washington on the subject of the exchange of prisoners taken on Staten Island by Capt. Fitz Randolph.

1778 June 9 – [Tuesday]. The Council met. Present – Houston, Elmer, Fenemore, Buck, Keasby. John Larking appeared before the Board & it appearing that he escaped from Staten Island & was knowing to the trade carried on at that place by Joseph Fitzrandolph, it was agreed that he be sent to court respecting the above fact, & that $2.00 be advanced to him to pay his expenses. Upon the petition of Elizabeth Boon setting forth that her husband Joseph Boon, was a soldier in Capt. William Shoot's Company of Foot, in the 2nd Jersey Regiment commanded by Wm. Maxwell & had served 9 months in Canada & there died of small pox, leaving a family of small children, she was praying for relief in the premises. Agreed that as the petition is not properly certified, it cannot be complied with at present. Agreed that Mr. Condit pay to John Imlay, Esqr., 20 pounds, 5/ for 162 pounds of lead, which he purchased for the use of the State, by order of Maj. Genl. Dickenson.

1778 June 10 – [Wednesday]. The Council met. Present – Governor, Camp, Condict, Mr. Speaker, Col. Drake, Col. Cook, Manning. Agreed that the Governor write to the person who has custody of James Patterson & David Jeffery, late of Monmouth County, subjects of this State, desiring him to deliver them to Peter Patterson & Thomas Jeffery upon their promising to bring them into this State at their expense & entering into bonds of 500 pounds to produce them to Council in a reasonable time after their arrival in it.

1778 June 11 – [Thursday]. The Council met. Present – Governor, Fenemore, Buck, Houston, Schenk, Col. Drake, Camp. Agreed that Abm. Heyer be paid for money laid by him in supporting a guard of 5 men on duty at Crosswicks, 3 pounds, 3 shillings, 9 pence. Agreed that Lieut. Palmer Roberts be paid 24 pounds, 19 shillings, 4 pence, being his pay & the pay of a party of 12 men under his command for guarding a number of Provision Wagons on 24 February 1778 from Amwell to Head Quarters in consequence of orders from Col. Chambers as per orders & pay roll. And that there be paid to Caleb Camp for the use of Jonas Crane the sum of 3 pounds for riding express for the Court of Oyer & Terminer of Essex County, the distance of 70 miles for Judge Smith.

PM – Present – Governor, Houston, Manning, Crane, Condict, Elmer. Agreed the Governor write to Mr. Yard desiring him to deliver to Mr. Denton the 52 pair of shoes which were put into his possession some time last Spring by order of the Council of Safety.

1778 June 12 – [Friday]. The Council met at Princeton. Present – Governor, Buck, Manning, Imlay, Schenk, Col. Drake, Camp. Agreed to advance to the Treasurer for the payment of Capt. Quigley for the amount of the Bounty Roll of a detachment of the 1st Battalion of Burlington Co Militia, which served the United States in Trenton, under the command of Quigley 54 days, the sum of 120 pounds, 6 shillings, 8 pence. And that there be advanced to the Paymaster for the payment of the said detachment the sum of 150 pounds,18/2. Agreed that Mr. Houston, now appointed Treasurer of this Board, settle with Mr. Condict, the late treasurer, & receive the balance now in Mr. Condict's hands.

1778 June 13 – [Saturday]. The Council met at Princeton. Present – Governor, Mr. Speaker, Elmer, Tallman, Buck, Fenemore. Mr. Edward Taylor having procured the release of John Willet upon parole that whenever required to do so, he shall repair to whatever place any of King of Great Britain's Commanders-in-Chief shall judge expedient, to order him. It was agreed that Mr. Taylor be discharged from his bond & have liberty to return to his place of abode until the said John Willet shall be recalled into the enemy's line; when the said Edward Taylor is to return to Princeton, there to continue within a mile of the College, until he shall be discharged by the Council, or the Executive authority of this State, he pledging his faith & honor, not to do, or say anything contrary to the interest of this State, or the United States & to be subject to all laws of this State, already in being or that may hereafter be made, in like manner as if this parole had never taken place.

1778 June 14 – [Sunday]. The Council met. Present- Governor, Tallman, Buck, Keasby, Fenemore, Elmer. Agreed that upon Andrew Donaldson's entering into recognizance in the sum of 600 pounds – for his appearance at the next Court of Oyer & Terminer in Cumberland County, that he be discharged from his present confinement. Andrew Donaldson, being called in, entered into Bond agreeable to the above order & was dismissed.

1778 June 15 – [Monday]. The Council met at Princeton. Present – Governor, Crane, Tallman, Mr. Speaker, Buck, Schenk, Elmer. Agreed that Jacob Fitz Randolph be removed from Monmouth County Gaol to Morris County Gaol to be confined until the next meeting of the Court of Oyer & Terminer in Middlesex County. Agreed that there be paid to Mr. Hart the sum of 47 pounds, 5 shillings, 4 pence being money advanced by him to Lieut. Henry Young for the pay & Expenses of a Guard at Pittstown the 16 September 1778 [1777].

PM. Present-Buck, Keasby, Cooper, Elmer, Manning, Imlay, Crane. Israel Morris having been sent before the Board on suspicion of being disaffected to the cause of American Independence was offered the Oaths and he refused them, & also refused to become bound for his appearance at the next Court of General Quarter Sessions of the Peace for Hunterdon County. Whereupon, it was agreed that he be committed to Hunterdon Gaol for his trial. Adjourned till tomorrow.

1778 June 16 – [Tuesday]. The Council met at Princeton. Present – Governor, Buck, Elmer, Camp, Col. Drake, Tallman, Crane. Agreed that the Governor write to the person having custody of Danl. Brown & George Johnston, lately of Monmouth County, subjects of this State, desiring him to deliver them to Solomon Wardel & Moses Havens upon their promising to bring them into this State at their expense & entering into Bond of 500 pounds to produce them to the Council or Executive Authority of this State, in a reasonable time after their arrival here. Agreed that there be paid to Jacob Bergen 4 pounds, 8 shillings, 9 pence, paid by him for sundry persons for making cartridges for the use of the State. Samuel Car was called in & examined respecting a certain sum of Continental Currency offered by him to payment of a debt to Henry Desbrow & which he refused to receive & his examination being committed to writing & he was dismissed. Charles Barclay was in like manner examined about the same transaction & dismissed. Agreed that Henry Desbrow & his wife be summoned to appear before the Board on suspicion of disaffection.

1778 June 17 – [Wednesday]. The Council met at Princeton. Present – Governor, Manning, Schenk, Fenemore, Tallman, Col. Drake, Buck. Mrs. Richmond who had been into the enemy's lines appeared before the Board. Agreed that in consideration of her age & infirmities, she be permitted to return to her home. Josiah Grey called before the Board and examined about a trade carried on by our subjects with the enemy & refusing to give satisfaction to the Council in the premises, it was agreed that he be confined for the present. Agreed that there be paid to Capt. Derby for his expenses in bringing the above named Josiah Grey from New Ark before the Council in this place, 6 pounds, 15/. Agreed that the Governor write to Genl. Winds directing him to remove cattle from Woodbridge Neck & such places between Elizabeth Town & Amboy, where they may be in danger of falling into the hands of the enemy, to such place, where they may be out of such danger (the owners of such cattle refusing to do it on notice to them for that purpose) the expenses to be paid by the owners of such cattle so removed; and in executing the order pay proper attention to the public service & do no more damage to the owners of the cattle than the service really requires. Agreed that Col. Neilson be paid 31 pounds, 9 shillings, 9 pence for money expended by him in purchasing lead & cartridge paper for the use of the State as per account & vouchers.

1778 June 18 – [Thursday]. The Council met at Princeton. Present – Governor, Houston, Camp, Fenemore, Schenk, Col. Drake, Tallman. Agreed that John Larkin & John Conner, who were sent to Freehold to give evidence in behalf of the State against Joseph Fitzrandolph, be dismissed. Agreed that the Governor draw upon the Treasury for the sum of 400 pounds for the use of the Council of Safety. Thos. Armstrong taken up yesterday as a suspected person, appeared before the Board & was examined about the cause of suspicion & it appearing that he was innocent, he was dismissed. William Sloan appeared by Citation on a complaint that he had disposed of merchandise at a higher price than regulated by law, the complaint was examined into, and it was agreed that a consideration into the premises be had on tomorrow morning.

1778 June 19 – [Friday]. The Council met at Princeton. Present – Governor, Tallman, Fenemore, Mr. Speaker, Buck, Keasby, Col. Drake, Imlay. A representation having been made to the Board by the Vice President of the State of Pennsylvania, that a robbery had been committed on the property of Gerrit Vansant of Middletown Township, Bucks County, in the State aforesaid, by person belonging to this State & several depositions relating thereto having been read & considered, it was agreed that the Governor write to the Vice president of Pennsylvania, informing him that due attention will be paid to the matter of the said complaint as soon as the Board can examine into the grounds of it more fully than the exigency of public affairs on account of the alarm of the enemy's march through the State will at present admit of. Agreed that Capt. Samuel Stout be paid for the amount of the Bounty Roll, of a detachment of Col. Hyer's Battalion of Middlesex Militia, who were sent as a guard with prisoners from Princeton to Head Quarters, 12 pounds, 9 shillings, 8 pence. That there be paid to Capt. Stout for the amount of a pay roll for the same detachment and for the same duty, 17 pounds, 15 shillings, 2 pence. Agreed that Jonathan Baldwin Esqr. for selling sugar 2.1.24 weight without a certificate, be fined 6 pounds & forfeit the sum of 88 pounds, 13 shillings, 6 pence, the price he sold the sugar at, 94 pounds, 13 shillings, 6 pence, which fine & forfeiture to be paid to Mr. Houston. Agreed that William Sloan be fined the sum of 6 pounds for paying more for the sugar than the law allows, which is in like manner to be paid to Mr. Houston.

[The end of Volume 4]

Council of Safety, State of New Jersey

Volume 5

1778 June 20 – [Saturday]. The Council met at Princeton. Present – Governor, Elmer, Col. Drake, Manning, Keasby, Stephen Crane. Clement Bishop who had been captured by the enemy & retaken by one of our Privateers, was brought before the Board, and he had obtained the office of Prize Master on board one of their Prizes, in order to throw himself into our power, which he did on the first opportunity. It is agreed that he be discharged and permitted to return to his abode. Ordered that Capt. Moore send the following persons – Josiah Grey, John Jones & George Robinson, prisoners, to Morristown if he thinks they might be rescued by the enemy marching through the State. Agreed that Col. Clark be paid for the use of Capt. Leek for his time & expenses in carrying Capt. Harris & three sailors with their baggage from Egg Harbor to the new Mills, being 40 miles & also for procuring wagons & horses, 12 pounds. And that Capt. Leek be paid for bringing Capt. Bishop & two sailors with their baggage from Egg Harbor to Princeton, being 70 miles, 18 pounds. Agreed that Mr. Simmons be paid for the use of Abm. Schenk for his riding express in attending the Governor as a guard from 6th –12th April, 5 pounds, 5 shillings, 6 pence; and for the use of Jacob Van Dike for the same services form the 1st – 12th April, 7 pounds, 7/.; and for the use of John Voorhise for like services, 8 pounds, 2/, as per account, and also to be paid for the use of John Bennet for his expenses as a Light Horseman, 7 pounds, 17 shillings, 3 pence, and for the use of Conred Tincke for his expenses as an express & Light Horseman, from 29 March – 5 April, 7 pounds, 1 shilling, 3 pence.

1778 June 21 – [Sunday]. The Council met. Present – Governor, Camp, Buck, Imlay, Elmer, Col. Drake. Mr. Bach who has his parole given him till it should be known that John Burroughs, a subject of this State, lately captured by the enemy, was confined by them or indulged with the same liberty & it appearing to the Board by letters, that Burroughs was in close confinement in New York, it is agreed that Mr. Bach be discharged from parole & sent under Guard to Morristown Gaol, together with Josiah Grey, John Jones & George Robinson, & that Capt. Moore see this order carried out. Andrew Hodge for speaking contemptuously of the regulating law, was brought before the Board, whereupon, it was agreed that he enter into recognizance in 300 pounds to appear at the next Court of General Sessions of the Peace for Somerset County, which having done, was dismissed. Adjourned to meet at Garritson's Tavern, in the township of Hillsborough, Somerset County, on Wednesday the 24th.

1778 June 24 – [Wednesday]. Council met at Garritson's Tavern pursuant to adjournment. Present – Governor, Camp, Mehelm, Buck, Elmer, Houston. The Governor gave the Board a letter from William P. Smith Esqr. setting forth that Ichabod B. Barnet, who left us sometime ago & went over to the enemy, had returned & thrown himself on the mercy of the country, and due to several favorable circumstances, the magistrates took his recognizance in 1,500 pounds, with two sureties for his appearance at the next Court of Oyer & Terminer in Essex County…Agreed that in addition to the recognizance, the same magistrates take a parole from said Barnet for his remaining at Springfield, or within one mile of the meeting house there, until further orders from the Council, with leave to attend the said Court re: his recognizance. Agreed that Charles Avary & Ezekiel Foster Junr., his apprentice, employed in preparing hides for the Continent be exempted from militia duty until September 1st next as long as they are engaged in the said business. Adjourned till tomorrow morning.

1778 June 25 – [Thursday]. Met pursuant to adjournment. Present – Governor, Camp, Mehelm, Houston, Buck, Elmer. Abel & Thos. Rinear, sent here by the Sheriff of Hunterdon County, through fear of them being rescued by the enemy, appeared before the Board, their several cases examined, and it was agreed that they be sent under guard to Somerset Gaol & that latter be discharged. Agreed that Joseph Roberts be paid for his use & the use of 3 men, who came as a guard from Trenton to here with the above named persons, for their expenses & the expense of the prisoners in coming & returning; 5 pounds, 13/. Agreed that David Nevius be paid for his expenses in attending the Governor as a Light Horseman from 22 May – 24 June 1778, 16 pounds, 7 shillings.

1778 June 26 – [Friday]. The Council met at Hillsborough. Present – Governor, Camp, Mehelm, Houston, Buck, Elmer. Henry Desbrow & wife appeared before the Board by Citation & their several examinations having been taken for their uttering words tending to depreciate the Continental money. Agreed that the said Desbrow be permitted to carry his wife home on the condition of entering into recognizance in 300 pounds, which was done, to appear before the Board tomorrow morning at 10 o'clock, and he was dismissed. Anthony Woodward, who went over to the enemy 2 years ago, & was lately taken by the militia, was brought before the Board and his case considered, it was agreed that he be committed for the present in Morristown Gaol. Agreed that John Totten be advanced $8.00 for defraying the cost of carrying the above Anthony Woodward from this place to Morris town.

1778 June 27 – [Saturday]. The Council met at Hillsborough, pursuant to adjournment. Present – Governor, Camp, Houston, Mehelm, Elmer, Buck. Henry Desbrow pursuant to recognizance went before the Board & was examined & it appeared he was too dangerous to go at large. It was agreed that he be committed to Trenton Gaol as a disaffected person, but he asked to be confined in Somerset Gaol, and Council indulged his request.

1778 June 28 –[Sunday]. The Council met at Hillsborough. Present as before. Adjourned to meet at Kingston on Monday, the 29th inst.

1778 June 29 – [Monday]. The Council met at Kingston, pursuant to adjournment. Present – Governor, Houston, Hart, Elmer, Buck. There not being a Quorum, adjourned till tomorrow morning.

1778 June 30 – [Tuesday]. Met at Kingston, pursuant to adjournment. Present – Governor, Mehelm, Houston, Elmer, Buck, Mr. Speaker. It appeared that John Burrowes was liberated on is parole on Staten Island. Agreed that on Mr. Bache's signing a parole to the same effect, he has on leave to proceed to Elizabeth Town and pass onto Staten Island, as soon as Mr. Burrowes arrives within our lines, and signing a parole similar to that signed by Burrowes before he leaves the enemy. Agreed that Geradus Skillman be paid for attending the Governor & Council as an express rider from 22 May – 30 June 1778, 19 pounds, 5 shillings, 9 pence. And, that he be paid for the use of Abraham Golder for the same service from 22 May-21 June 1778, 13 pounds, 19 shillings, 9 pence. Adjourned to meet at Princeton tomorrow morning.

1778 July 1 – [Wednesday]. Met at Princeton. Present – Governor, Mehelm, Imlay, Buck, Elmer, Houston, Mr. Speaker. On petition of Henry Desbrow lately committed to jail in Somerset, as a disaffected person, it was agreed that on his paying 6 pounds to Justice Van Nest for refusing to take Continental Currency in payment, on taking the Oaths before Van Nest, & entering into recognizance with two sureties in 300 pounds each, he can be discharged from his present confinement and return home if on his good behavior during the war. Agreed that Capt. Moore furnish a guard of 20 men with an officer to convey the British prisoners in this place to Philadelphia & that he send with them a list of their names & their regiments. Adjourned till tomorrow morning.

1778 July 2 – [Thursday]. Met pursuant to adjournment at Princeton. Present – Governor, Imlay, Buck, Mehelm, Elmer, Houston, Mr. Speaker. William McGalvin on a complaint against him, on Oaths of Nicholas Golder, respecting sundry parts of his conduct while the enemy was in this place, was called before the Board. He gave his defense, and was ordered to withdraw. Benjamin Plumb was called in, examined relative to McGalvin, and was dismissed. Agreed that John Covenoven, Philip Young & Henry Blue be subpoenaed to the Board forthwith to give evidence against Wm. McGalvin. Benj. Von Mater being sent before the Board by Col. Moyland, on suspicion of having given intelligence to the enemy. The Council examined into the grounds of the complaint & thinking that Van Mater was guiltless of the charge, it was agreed that he should stay in this town a week from today & might then return to his home. William Hale who went into the enemy's lines since the Treason act, appeared and threw himself on the mercy of the Board, and it was taken into consideration. Agreed that he enter into recognizance in 300 pounds, with Robert Priest his surety, for his appearance at the next Court of Oyer & Terminer for Middlesex County, and he was discharged. Agreed that if the enemy will receive Jacobus Quick, now a prisoner with us in exchange for William Thompson, a prisoner with them, this Board has no objection to it being done. Adjourned until tomorrow morning.

1778 July 3 – [Friday]. Met at Princeton. Present – Governor, Houston, Mehelm, Mr. Speaker, Paterson, Imlay. Philip Young, by Citation, appeared before the Board and gave testimony against Wm. Mc Galvin relative to his conduct while the enemy was in this town, and was dismissed. The Board having considered all proofs against Wm. Mc Galvin, agreed that he should enter into recognizance in 200 pounds, for his appearance at the next Court of Oyer & Terminer for Somerset County. Agreed, that Wm. Seaman be paid for attending Governor & Council as a Light Horseman from 11 May – 21 June 1778, 19 pounds, 5 shillings, 6 pence; and, to John Vandike for the same service from 5 June – 3 July 1778, 8 pounds, 19 shillings, 6 pence; and to Jacob Van Dike, for the same services from 23 June to 3 July 1778, 8 pounds, 19 shillings, 6. Agreed that Mr. Houston advance to the Governor on account 20 pounds.

1778 August 3 – [Monday]. Council met at Morristown. Present – Governor, Camp, Smith, Col. Drake, Col. Fleming, Mr. Cook. Richard James & Thos. Parker, who had consent of the Council to go into Virginia, to procure the liberty of Robert James, a subject of this State, confined there, on their entering a Bond to deliver him to the Council in a reasonable time after entering this State, appeared before the Board & informed them that they procured the release of Robert James, who was ready to wait upon this Council when required. Whereupon, agreed that Richard James & Thos. Parker having complied with their requirement were to have their Bond released to them. Robert James was brought before the Board & examined and it was agreed that he give security for his appearance at the next Court of Oyer & Terminer for Monmouth County, which having done with Richard James, his surety, and he was dismissed. Cornelius Bogert, who had been sentenced to death & pardoned on condition of enlisting in the Continental Army during the War, and having then deserted from the same, was brought before the Board & being examined, he gave information against the following persons who were enlisted at the same time & also deserted from their respective Corps & who were now at their homes- Joseph Britain, John Shannon, James Neigh, Lawrence Fleming, Martin Sneider, Christian Sneider, & Nathaniel Parker. He was then remanded to the Gaol. Agreed that Capt. Morrison for enlisting as substitutes certain convicts whom he knew to have been enlisted in their own right, be summoned to the Board. A petition from the Officer of the New Jersey Brigade setting forth the need for clothing & etc was read and agreed that it be referred to the Legislature. It was brought to the attention of the Board that the Continental Stores in Sussex are exposed to weather & in danger of being embezzled & destroyed. Agreed that the Governor write to John Smyth & Jacob McCollum to inspect into the complaint of neglect, procure affidavits and send them to the Board as soon as possible. Adjourned till tomorrow morning.

1778 August 4 – [Tuesday]. The Council met at Morristown. Present – Governor, Camp, Smith, Col. Drake, Col. Fleming, Col. Cook. Agreed that Joseph Halsey be paid for his expenses & that of 5 men in guarding 6 prisoners from Morristown to Princeton on the 11th of May last, $19.00 and that Mr. Condict advance the money. Ordered that Major Hays be directed to apprehend & deliver to the Magistrates of Essex for examination the following persons – Edmund Leslie, Peter Cadmus, Francis King, Adrain Van Riper, Arent Kingsland, Charles Orsburn, Corse Joralemon son of Cornelius, John Kingsland son of Nathaniel, Isaac Kingsland son of Isaac. Abm. Law, who had been among the enemy & came over to deliver himself up, appeared before the Board and his case taken into consideration. Agreed that recognizance be taken for his appearance at the next Court of General Quarter Sessions of the Peace for Essex County. Agreed that the following persons taken up & sent to this place, on the march of the enemy through the State be sent to Gloucester Jail with a letter to the Justices to take their several examinations – Isaac Lloyd, Samuel Lloyd, Samuel Lippencott, Joseph Myers, Lawrence Cox, David Carter, Jacob Justine, William Kennack and Jessie Serren. Agreed that Uriah West & Anthony Woodward, alias "Little Anthony", be committed to the Gaol in this place for High Treason. Agreed that John O'Hara, a deserter from the enemy, be discharged on his taking the Oaths. Agreed that when Josiah Grey & Peter Hondershute find security for their appearance at the next Court of General Quarter Sessions of the Peace for Essex County, they be discharged. Agreed that John Allwood, Lucas King, Vincent Swim and Joseph Groom, now in prison at this place, be committed to the Monmouth Gaol for their trial & that their commitment be given to the Sheriff of Morris until they are delivered to the Sheriff of Monmouth. Agreed that Thos. Canby sent here from Burlington on the march of the enemy through this State, be remanded to Burlington where he was, in & by virtue of an execution. Agreed that the Sheriff of Essex take charge of Maurice Morisson, now in the Gaol in this place. Adjourned till tomorrow morning.

1778 August 5 – [Wednesday]. Council met pursuant to adjournment. Present – Governor, Camp, Smith, Col. Drake, Col. Fleming, Condict. Agreed that George King be paid for serving process for the Council, $5.00 & Mr. Condict to advance the money. Agreed that William Clark be dismissed of finding security for his appearance at Court and on failure to do so, to be sent to Monmouth in company of the other prisoners ordered there yesterday. The petition of William Smith, confined by Council for High Treason, praying to be admitted to bail on account of his ill health. The Council considered same and agreed that on procuring a certificate from a physician to the truth of the above fact, he be permitted to take private lodgings within a mile of the Morristown Court House. Agreed that Col. Hathaway furnish a Sergeant & five men to guard a number of prisoners from this place to Gloucester & that he direct them to draw rations where they can & to keep an account of their expenses & give it to Council upon his return. Agreed that Capt. Simmons be paid for the use of Joseph Doty for riding in pursuit of Pilots (in behalf of the States) to conduct the French Fleet into the harbor of New York, 4 pounds, 10/. Wm. Smith producing to the Board a certificate from Dr. Van Buren that he had dysentery & fever and his situation was not proper for his recovery & upon entering into Bond of 5,000 pounds with John Blanchard, his surety, he was permitted to take private lodgings in the town. Isaac Bady Esqr. appeared before the Board & on giving recognizance for his appearance at the next Court of Oyer & Terminer for Morris County, he was dismissed.

1778 August 6 – [Thursday]. The Council met at Morris Town. Present – Governor, Condict, Smith, Col. Fleming, Col. Drake, Mr. Camp. Agreed that a warrant be issued to apprehend Gerrit Rappelje as a person suspected of being disaffected & dangerous to this State. Agreed that subpoenas issue to summon John DeGroff & Jaquish Dennis living between Squan & Tom's River at Rapelje's Salt Works, to appear forthwith at Princeton before Silas Condict Esqr. to give evidence against Garret Rappelje on behalf of the State. And, also that subpoenas issue to summon Major John Vliet, Jacob Force, Eve Force his wife, John Marlett, David Davidson & wife, John Mitchel and wife, & William Stevens, Deputy Quarter Master Genl., for the same purpose.

1778 August 18 – [Tuesday]. PM - The Council met at Morristown. Present – Governor, Condict, Smith, Col. Cooke, Col. Drake. There not being a Quorum, adjourned till 8 o'clock tomorrow morning.

1778 August 19 – [Wednesday]. The Council met at Morristown. Present – Governor, Condict, Smith, Col. Cooke, Col. Drake, Mehelm, Col. Hoops. Agreed that the Governor draw of the treasurer for 300 pounds for the Council. Agreed that Mr. Condict pay Abraham Voorhis & Coenradt Ten Eyck for going to the Salt Works near Squan to subpoena witnesses against Gerrit Rapalje, 8 pounds, 9 shillings, 9 pence. Ordered that Noah Hammond & John Whiteacre be subpoenaed as witnesses against Dr. Bullion. Agreed that Herbert Henry, one of the party formerly committed for attempting to join the enemy on Staten Island & escaping by breaking Gaol & now again apprehended with a party who had agreed to take a number of loyal inhabitants & to deliver them to Col. Butler in the enemy's lines), be committed for High Treason. Isaac Thompson was examined as a witness against a number of Tories who had agreed to waylay & captivate a party of men & carry them to Col. Butler & the Indians. Agreed that John Woortman be committed for High Treason for heading the said Tories in the said enterprise. Agree that Abel & Thos. Rynear, two prisoners lately removed from Trenton to Millstone, be carried back & committed to Trenton Gaol. Adjourned till 3 o'clock this afternoon.

The Board met according to adjournment. Ordered that 15,000 flints, now in possession of Major Kelsey in Princeton, be sent for & lodged in the care of Col. Hathaway at this place. Agreed that Mr. Condict pay to Major McDonald 36 pounds, 2 shillings, 9 pence for money expended by him for a guard consisting at different time from 9, 11, 15 men, who escorted 7 Tory prisoners from Sussex to Morristown & 11 pounds, 5/ and to 9 of the said guards for their return expenses. It appearing to the Council that Richd. Waln, who had been sent out of State by the Council, returned to same without permission. Therefore, ordered that Mr. Waln do within 6 days time leave the State, or within the same time appear before the Council or the President thereof at Morristown; & enter into recognizance with surety at 1,000 pounds to appear at the next Court of Oyer & Terminer for Monmouth County. Mr. James Findlass, who lately came from the City of New York into this State without permission, appeared before the Board and was ordered to enter into recognizance with surety to appear at the next Court of Oyer & Terminer for Morris County. Noel Hammond appeared by Citation before the Board & was examined as a witness against Dr. O'Bullion. Adjourned till 9 o'clock tomorrow morning.

1778 August 20 – [Thursday]. The Council met at Morristown according to adjournment. Present – Governor, Condict, Smith, Col. Drake, Mehelm, Col. Cook, Col. Hoops. Jonathan Whiteacre, who had been subpoenaed as a witness against Dr. O'Bullion, appeared before the Board, but knowing nothing of his own knowledge, he referred Council to Wm. Hill & Nathaniel Woodward for information. Ordered that subpoenas be issued immediately for Wm. Hill & Nathaniel Woodward. John Demott & Deich Vreland, who were confined in Morristown Gaol for going & returning from the enemy's lines at New York, appeared and were dismissed from their confinement upon entering into recognizance with John Mead, their surety, to appear at the next Court of Oyer & Terminer for Morris County. Mr. Andrew Gautier, who lately came from New York, appeared before Council & was permitted to enter into recognizance to appear at the next Court of Oyer & Terminer for Morris County. Brig.Genl. Winds having purchased lead pursuant to Council & General Assembly, to an amount larger than the money provided, & the late proprietors thereof wanting their money, it was agreed that Mr. Condict advance him the sum of 300 pounds to enable him to discharge the debt of the purchase. Mr. Gerrit Rapelje, who was confined in Morristown Gaol on suspicion of being disaffected to this state, appeared before the Board. Agreed that Mr. Rapalje be discharged from his confinement upon entering into recognizance with surety, to appear at the next Court of Oyer & Terminer for Sussex County. Adjourned till 3 o'clock this afternoon.

The Council met, according to adjournment. Present as before. Israel Rickey came before the Board & was examined as a witness against Dr. O'Bullion. Peter Appleman came before Council & was permitted to go home upon entering into recognizance to appear at the next Court of Oyer & Terminer for Sussex County. Agreed that the Sheriff deliver Hugh McClean, a prisoner in the Gaol of this town, to Sergeant Hopson sent by Col. Shreve to guard him to Elizabeth Town.; said McClean being a deserter from his Regiment. Agreed that the 300 pounds drawn by the Governor, by order of the Council from the Treasury, & be lodged in the hands of Mr. Condict, the treasurer, which was accordingly done. Adjourned till 9 o'clock tomorrow morning.

1778 August 21 – [Friday]. Met according to adjournment at Morristown. Present – Governor, Smith, Condict, Col. Mehelm, Col. Hoops, Col. Drake, Col. Cook. Wm. Hill & Wm. Boyd agreeable to summons appeared before the Board, were examined concerning Dr. Js. O'Bullion's political conduct, but not knowing anything against the doctor, their affidavits were not taken. Whereas there is a great reason to think that the Slitting-Mill at Boontown carried on by Samuel Ogden Esqr. is the property of Samuel Ogden & several other persons, which other persons are disaffected to the present Government and now with the enemy, and whose personal estate is now forfeited by the law of this State; and whereas all the shares of the profits that have been made by the said Slitting-Mill belong to such disaffected persons are in consequence of the said law forfeited to this State, & there is reason to believe that the said disaffected proprietors have by fraudulent & collusive conveyances transferred their shares in the Slitting-Mill in secret trust for their own uses in order to evade the law & secure their interest therein, & in the profits thereby made, notwithstanding such forfeitures, by means whereof the State is like to be defrauded out of a very considerable sum of money – Therefore, ordered that the Attorney General be directed to file a Bill of Equity against the said Samuel Ogden, for the discovery of all the owners of the said Slitting-Mill and of the neat profits thereby made since the fourth day of June 1777. Ordered that a Warrant be issued to apprehend Dr. James O'Bullion as a person disaffected to the United States of America & dangerous to the welfare of the State. Agreed that John Cole be discharged from his confinement upon entering into recognizance with surety, to appear at the next Court of Oyer & Terminer for Morris County. Agreed that Isaac Goodwin be committed for High Treason for having been taken in arms against the United States of America. Agreed that Matthias Swartfeller be discharged from his confinement on entering into recognizance to appear at the next Court of Oyer & Terminer for Sussex County. Adjourned till 3 o'clock this afternoon.

Met according to adjournment. Present as before. Ordered that Hendrick Banta be committed for High Treason, in aiding & assisting the enemy of the United States of America, by taking up arms against the said States. Mrs. Ludlow applied to the Board in person for permission to go into New York to recover some debts due to her there but was refused. Adjourned till 9 o'clock tomorrow morning.

1778 August 22 – [Saturday]. Council met according to adjournment at Morristown. Present – Governor, Condict, Smith, Col. Hoops, Col. Drake, Col. Mahelm. Agreed that there be paid by Mr. Condict to Nehemiah Mills for going with a guard of 7 men & 10 prisoners to Gloucester & returning with the guard to this place, 10 pounds, 13 shillings, 6 pence. And, to Isaac Hayward for attending the Governor as a Light Horseman, 4 pounds, 11 shillings, 9 pence. Dr. James

O'Bullion came before the Board & upon entering into recognizance with Jos. Annin, his surety, to appear at the next Court of Oyer & Terminer for Morris County, was discharged. Agreed that John Moore, Tice Konkle, Hanadam Konkle, George Moote, Matthias Swartfeller, _____ Kinsberry & Thos. Layton be discharged upon entering into recognizance, with surety, to appear at the next Court of Oyer & Terminer for Sussex County. Agreed that Capt. Symmons be paid for his attendance on the Governor as a Light Horseman from June 22-5 Aug., 23 pounds, 13/. Agreed that there be paid to the Governor for money advanced by him to be paid to the several Light Horsemen for attending as his guard & as expenses, 20 pounds, 6 pence, which the Governor had paid to: Peter Stryker, Saml. Parsons, Benj. Conchlin, Ichabod Grummond, Caleb Woodruff, Nathan Beedle, Timothy Miller. Agreed that the Gaol Guard at Morristown be increased with 12 additional men & that Col. Hathaway be ordered to detach so many men from his Regiment for that purpose. The Council adjourned till 2 o'clock next Tuesday afternoon the 25th inst.

1778 August 25 – [Tuesday]. Council met at Morristown. Present - Governor, Camp, Smith, Mehelm, Col. Cooke, Col. Drake, Condict. _____ Banta, who had been a prisoner in New York, being discharged from his confinement, and returned to New Jersey in exchange for Jacobus Quick, now a State prisoner in the Gaol of this town. Therefore ordered that Quick be released & have permission to go to New York. Richard Waln appearing before the Board pursuant to Citation & entering into recognizance with Mr. Lawrence, his surety, to appear at the next Court of Oyer & Terminer for Monmouth County, was permitted to return to stay with his family agreeable to the prayer of the Petition. Ichabod Barnet, who was bound in a recognizance to appear at the next Court of Oyer & Terminer for Essex County, petitioned the Board to "issue an order for his trial at the Court of Oyer & Terminer now sitting in Middlesex County." Agreed that there was no such necessity at this time and the petition was not granted. Anthony Ludlow, confined in the Gaol in this town, for detaining Henry Brinkerhoff's cattle, appeared before the Board & upon promising to enter into recognizance, with surety, to appear at the next Court of Oyer & Terminer for Morris County, it was agreed that Ludlow be discharged from his confinement on so doing. Ordered that Jacobus Outwater be committed to the Gaol of this town for High Treason. The Council adjourned till 9 o'clock tomorrow morning.

1778 August 26 – [Wednesday]. The council met according to adjournment. Present – Governor, Camp, Condict, Smith, Col. Drake, Col. Cooke, Mehelm. George Hyler, who had lately returned from Staten Island, surrendered himself up to the Council. Agreed that he be dismissed upon entering into recognizance, with surety, to appear at the next Court of Oyer & Terminer for Somerset County. Col. John Starke having preferred an account of the expense of a party of Militia of the West Regiment of Morris County under his command, on a "scout" after a number of disaffected persons, by order of Governor Livingston, amounting to 49 pounds, 16 shillings, 6 pence, to the Council of Safety; and it was agreed that the said account be allowed & that the paymaster be requested to pay same. John McClean, who lately came from Long Island & was confined on suspicion of deserting to the enemy, appeared before the Board & it appearing the said McClean was a lieutenant in the Navy of Pennsylvania & had been taken prisoner by the enemy while in Philadelphia, & had now made his escape from them; it was agreed that he be released from his confinement & permitted to go to Philadelphia. Agreed that Col. Hathaway be authorized to deliver to Genl. Winds or his order, any number of the 15,000 flints belonging to this State & lately lodged in his hands by order of this Board. Agreed that John Smyth Esqr. be paid for his expenses victualling & otherwise providing for a Guard of 15 men who were employed in taking & guarding a number of Tories in Sussex County, 11 pounds, 17 shillings, 6 pence. Agreed that Mr. Condict pay Zophar Lyon 1 pound, 1 shilling, 6 pence for his expenses in riding express on public business for the Governor. Agreed that William Corrent, now in the Gaol of this town on suspicion of assisting the enemies of the United States, be discharged on entering into recognizance, with surety, to appear at the next Court of Oyer & Terminer for Sussex County. Ordered that the following persons – Jas. Findlass, Isaac Godwin, John Cole, Andrew Gautiere, John Demott, Dirck Vreland, Hendrick Bantha, Anthony Ludlow & Jacobus Outwater be tried in Morris County, although their offenses were done in other counties. Agreed that Mr. Condict pay Capt. Henry Luse 66 pounds for his expenses in apprehending a number of Tories in Sussex County with a party of militia under his command. Agreed that Daniel Kinney be paid for his wages & expenses for fetching 15,000 flints from Princeton to this place, 5 pounds, 16 shillings, 3 pence.

1778 September 11 – [Friday]. Met at Princeton. Present – Governor, Cooper, Col. Drake, Imlay, Fenimore, Condict, Elmer. Agreed that Anthony Woodward be offered in Exchange for Peter Imlay. Agreed that Mr. Howard, late Surgeon of the British Light Infantry in New York, be permitted to come & settle in this State, after applying to a magistrate & taking the Oaths with all convenient speed after is arrival in this State.

1778 September 12 – [Saturday]. Met at Princeton. Present – Governor, Cooper, Imlay, Manning, Buck, Condict, Houston. Agreed that Alexander McDonald be permitted to go to New York upon some important business upon parole & not to carry any letters or give any intelligence to the enemy. That Mary, wife of Thos. Hunlock, be permitted to go to New York, with Penelope Van Klyne, her maid, & her two children, upon the condition they not return into this State. Agreed that Col. Henry Vandycke be paid for 184.5 pounds of lead by him furnished to be run into bullets for the militia, at the rate of 2/6 per pound, sum 23 pounds, 1 shilling, 3 pence & for cash paid by him to Oakley Voorhise for 25 days labor in running 200.5 pounds of lead into bullets, sum 6.5/.

1778 September 13 – [Sunday.] Met at Princeton. Present – Governor, Tallman, Imlay, Manning, Houston, Condict, Buck. Agreed that Able & Thos. Rineer, now in confinement in Trenton Gaol, be removed to Burlington County Gaol, which is the county where they reside & that the Sheriff of Hunterdon Co deliver them to Isaac & Joseph English to be carried to Burlington & delivered to the Sheriff there.

1778 September 15 – [Tuesday]. Met at Princeton. Present – Governor, Manning, Hart, Fenemore, Imlay. Agreed that Mr. Condict advance on account 10 pounds to Peter Clinton, a private soldier in Capt. Imlay's Company, 3rd New Jersey Regiment, discharged from the same by Col. Dayton, by reason of a wound received in the service to the United States which rendered him unfit for service on 30 September 1778 as per discharge.

1778 September 17 – [Thursday]. Met at Princeton. Present – Governor, Mr. Speaker, Elmer, Imlay, Schenk, Camp, Fenemore. The petition of Nathaniel Little setting forth that he had been rendered unfit for service from the loss of a leg & for which reason he had a discharge from the Army on the 21st August 1776; praying that this Board would allow him his pay & rations from that time and such other recompense as may be thought reasonable. The Council postponed further consideration of it until some members from Morris County could be consulted respecting this circumstance. A petition from Mary M'Myers setting forth that she had lost a husband in the battle of Germantown, and was left in low circumstances, praying the Board to grant her some relief in the situation. Agreed, that there be paid into the hands of Mr. Manning for her use the sum of $60.00. John Fenemore, John Seal, Jacob Heumel, Thos. Miller & John Ansley who had joined the British Army and deserted from them, appeared before the Board & having severally entered into recognizance for their appearance at Court, they were dismissed.

1778 September 18 – [Friday]. Met at Princeton. Present – Governor, Buck, Imlay, Manning, Fenemore, Camp. Agreed that Archibald Mercer be paid the sum of 145 pounds.10/; for 21,000 flints purchased by him at the request of the Council for the use of the Militia of this State & for expenses in transporting them from Boston to this State. Upon the petition of Sarah Royal, setting forth that she had lost her husband in the service & left in distressing circumstances, Agreed that there be paid to Col. Crips for her use as a temporary relief the sum of $60.00. Agreed to the recommendation of the Court of Oyer & Terminer & General Gaol Delivery, held at New Brunswick, 11 August 1778, that there be paid to Mr. Manning for the use of the following Constables for their extraordinary attendance in Court- for 15 days - 7 pounds, 10/ - to John Witlock, Anthony Denton, John Seaburne, Benj. Ford; for 14 days - 7 pounds – to Stephen Voorhise, Joseph Applegate, George Kelley; for 11 days – 5 pounds, 10/ - Clarke Smith; and for 9 days – 4 pounds, 10/ - Benj. Lucker, Abel Still. Pursuant to the recommendation of the Court of Oyer & Terminer at Freehold, Monmouth County, June 1778, it was agreed that Mr. Schenk be paid for the use of the following Constables for their extraordinary attendance in Court – For 15 days – 15 pounds – to George Harris, Benj. Van Cleaf, Peter Johnston, Wm. Lloyd, Joseph Coward; For 12 days – 12 pounds - Edward Wilburne; and for 11 days- 11 pounds – Zephaniah Morris.

1778 September 19 – [Saturday]. Met at Princeton. Present – Governor, Imlay, Schenk, Elmer, Camp, Mr. Speaker. The petition of David Pinkerton praying permission to go to New York to obtain payment for several articles taken from him by the enemy in their march through the State in December 1776 was read & considered. Agreed, that Mr. Pinkerton be directed to attend this Board before such permission can be granted. The memorial of Elizabeth Boon respecting that she had lost a husband in the service & thereby (with three small children) rendered destitute & helpless, being considered. It was agreed that there be paid to Mr. Keasby for her use, as a temporary relief, the sum of $40.00. Agreed that there be advanced to Capt. Voorhise 11 pounds, 2/ for the pay & bounty of a detachment of 10 men from Col. Neilson's Regiment ordered out by the Court of Oyer & Terminer, lately held for Middlesex County, as a guard for the said Court, & who were on duty for 4 days.

1778 September 22 – [Tuesday]. Met at Princeton. Present – Governor, Crane, Schenk, Keasby, Elmer, Buck, Hart. Agreed that a Warrant be issued for John Hartwick for carrying flour on board of an enemy's Flag, of Truce & that Capt. Briningon, George Neffis & John Halfpenny be subpoenaed as witnesses. Agreed that David Pickerson have leave to go to New York. Agreed that Solomon Wardel & Moses Havens be discharged from their Bond, they having produced to the Board the bodies of Daniel Brown & George Johnston agreeable to the condition thereof, Agreed that Daniel Brown & George Johnston enter into recognizance with Solomon Wardel, 300 pounds each, as their surety for their appearance at the next Court of Oyer & Terminer for Monmouth County.

1778 September 24 – [Thursday]. Met at Princeton. Present – Governor, Condict, Imlay, Drake, Schenk, Hart, Manning, Elmer, Camp, Buck. Agreed that Lieut. Joseph Schenk be paid 5 pounds, 7/ for guarding with an officer & 6 privates, a number of prisoners from Princeton to Morristown in April last. Agreed to pay to Silas Condict Esq. for Nathaniel Little, a soldier in one of the Jersey Battalions, who was taken sick in the Northern Campaign, for his expenses in boarding & surgeons, as several certificates by him produced, the sum of 18 pounds, 14 shillings, 10 pence. Agreed that there be paid to Joseph Holmes for the use of Patience Sayre (the widow of Nathaniel Sayre who died in the service of the United States, a soldier in the 3rd New Jersey Battalion) 11 pounds, 5/ to be applied to the relief of her necessities according to his discretion. Mr. Speaker paid into Mr. Condict's hands, the treasurer, 158 pounds, 17 shillings, 6 pence being the remaining balance of the sum of 200 pounds which Mr. Elmer had received from Lt. Col. Chamberlain, being the sum lately advanced to Lt. Col. Chamberlain by the Council to defray his expenses to the Massachusetts Bay, whither he was ordered to convoy the honorable John Penn & Joseph Chois Esqr. & which order was afterwards countermanded, in consequences of leave obtained by those gentlemen from Congress and to remain in New Jersey. Of the 41 pounds, 2 shillings, 6 pence paid out of the 200 pounds, the sum of 4 pounds, 12 shillings, 6 pence was agreed to be paid to Col. Chamberlain for his expenses in attending the Council of Safety, on the above business, as per his receipt & the sum of 36 pounds, 10/ to Mr. Wm. Livingston Junr for his attendance as Secretary as per his receipt.

1778 September 25 – [Friday]. Met at Princeton. Present – Governor, Keasby, Buck, Imlay, Elmer, Hart, Condict. Agreed that Mr. Sinnickson be paid 4 pounds, 11 shillings, 6 pence for money advanced by him to Capt. Beasley for Capt. Beasley's expenses in taking with a guard of militia, Northrop Marpole, & a sum of 3 pounds, 14/ for the expenses of a detachment of militia of a Captain & 10 privates in bringing a number of prisoners before Council in August 1777. Adjourned till 8 o'clock.

Met pursuant to adjournment. [Not indicated whether the same day or not.] Present – Governor, Buck, Condict, Schenk, Imlay, Manning, Keasby. Agreed that Susanna Morris, wife of Asa Morris, enter into recognizance to appear at the next Court of Oyer & Terminer for Middlesex County; as well as, Joseph D. Camp, who put up 500 pounds for his appearance. Agreed that Joseph Shatwell, the [4th] fourth, be committed for High treason to Morristown Jail.

The same day, PM – Present – Governor, Tallman, Manning, Condict, Fenemore, Imlay. Agreed that Abraham Thorne enter into recognizance for his appearance at the next Court of Oyer & Terminer for Essex County, and that Eva Morris enter into recognizance to appear at the next Court of Quarter Sessions for Middlesex County, for refusing to take the Oaths. Agreed that _____ Finlass have leave to return to this State. Agreed that Abijah Cheesman be committed to Middlesex Gaol for High Treason & passing counterfeit money.

1778 September 26 – [Saturday]. Met at Princeton. Present – Governor, Manning, Tallman, Imlay, Buck, Schenk. Agreed that Robert Waller, Jacob Wilson, Jas. Davis & Jos. Wilson be committed to Morris Gaol for High Treason for having joined the enemy & now returning to the State without leave. Agreed that Sarah Alboy, with her daughter Anne, and one large trunk & two small ones, with her wearing apparel & bed & bedding, have leave to go to New York. That Rachel Wells, wife of James Wells, have also leave to go to New York, having both engaged not to return into this State.

1778 September 28 – [Monday]. Council met at Princeton. Present – Governor, Condict, Elmer, Keasby, Schenk, Hart, Buck. Agreed that Mrs. Reziah Lott be permitted to go to New York. Agreed that there be paid to Wm. Wick, a Light Horseman, for attending the Governor, the sum 17 pounds, 7 shillings, 8 pence; and, to Joseph Briton for the like service, 17 pounds, 4 shillings, 2 pence. Agreed that Mr. Schenk be paid for the use of Nicholas Van Brunt, Sheriff of Monmouth, for his expenses in removing the prisoners from the Monmouth Gaol to that of Morris, at the time of the enemy's march through Monmouth & in fetching back to Monmouth those who were there to be executed, as per his account, 48 pounds.

1778 September 30 – [Wednesday]. Council met at Princeton. Present – Governor, Fennemore, Buck, Imlay, Crane, Manning. Agreed that Mr. Bowen & Mr. Helmo have leave to go to New York being laid under the injunction not to give any information relative to our public affairs.

1778 October 2 – [Friday]. Council met at Princeton. Present – Governor, Schenk, Camp, Manning, Condict, Imlay, Buck. Agreed that Dr. Moses Bloomfield be requested to attend the Board tomorrow at 8 o'clock with a list of the physicians, surgeons, & surgeon's mates attending Princeton & the number of the sick in the hospital there. Agreed that Mr. Condict be paid for the use of Jonn. Stiles Junr. for attending the Governor as a Light horseman, 8 pounds, 19 shillings, 2 pence. Agreed that a Warrant be issued for Wm. Curtis of Shrewsbury for supplying the enemy with provisions.

1778 October 3 – [Saturday]. Council met at Princeton. [The proceedings of the 3rd were not reported.]

1778 October 7 – [Wednesday]. Council met at Princeton. Present – Governor, Crane, Condict, Tallman, Camp, Col. Drake. Agreed that Mr. Condict be paid for the use of the Constables hereinafter named for extraordinary services to the Court of Oyer & Terminer in Morris County in

September last – James Young, Joseph Stouten, John Horton, Levi Baldwin, John Riggs Christopher Mulford, & Ebenezer Hayward, 8 days each, and Samuel Oliver & Isaac Pierson, 7 days each, Joseph Conger & Abraham Mansfield, 5 days…amounting to 60 pounds. 5/. Agreed that Mr. Camp be paid $14.00 by him advanced to Isaac Coxe, Sergeant of the Guard at Haddonfield in part pay for the said Guard… Agreed that Mr. Houston be paid for monies advanced by him to Henry Kennedy, a Light Horseman, in the recess of the Council of Safety, - 19 pounds, 15 shillings, 9 pence. Agreed that the Governor draw on the treasurer for the Council of Safety 450 pounds.

1778 October 8 – [Thursday]. Council met at Princeton. Present – Governor, Hart, Camp, Schenk, Tallman, Col. Drake. Agreed that John Hart Esqr. be paid for the use of Hannah Gaffin, the widow of John Gaffin, late belonging to Capt. Polhemus' Company, 1st New Jersey Regiment, who died in the service at Crown Point, in the month of August 1776, the sum of $60.00 to be by him distributed for the relief of her necessities according to his discretion. And, also that there be paid to Mr. Hart for cash advanced by him to Mrs. Lott, for the use of her room for the Council of Safety, the 30th August 1777, the sum of 15/.

[The end of Council of Safety Minutes]

INDEX

"Baltic Merchant", 89
"Carolina", packet, 89
    paquet, 88
    piquet, 89
"English Tom", 14
"John", brig, 89
"Lord Howe", transport, 89
"Nancy", merchantman brig, 89
"Scorpion", sloop, 88

A

Abbot, Marmaduke, 56, 57, 89
  Mr., 57
  Wm., 60
Abel, John, 44
Abell, John, 46
Ackerman, Cornelius, 66, 70
  Hendricks, 65
  James, 25
  John, 65, 66, 70
  Laurence E., 30
  Lawrence, 42
Acreman, Lawrence E., 42
Adams, Alexander, 29, 31
  Ebenezer, 94
Aker, John, 66
Albertson, Esqr.
  Garrat, 37
Albough, William, 33
Alboy, Anne, 116
  Sarah, 116
Alger, Wm., 90
Alias, John, 52, 54, 59
Allen, Abraham, 39
  Benj., 100
  Enoch, 74, 75
  George, 28
  George, Lieut., 48
  John, 19, 38
  Mary, Mrs., 18
  Mr., 29
  Nathan, 6, 11

Allen, Esqr.
  William, 57
Allison, Robert, 7
Allpaugh, William, 34
Allwood, John, 108
Alward, Archd., 51
  Jos., 51
  Joseph, 30
  Silas, 30, 51
Ammerman, Isaac, 53, 54, 58, 59
Anbel, Andrew, 33
Anderson, David, 39
  Jacob, 58
  John, 13
  Kenell, 58
  Thomas, 53
  Walter, 95
  Wm., 37
Anderson, Esqr.
  Thomas, 32
Andrews, John, 11
Annin, Jos., 112
Ansley, John, 114
Anthony, George, 86
Antil, Mrs., 67
Appleby, Jr.
  James, 95
Appleby, Senr.
  Jas., 95
Applegate, George, 11
  Joseph, 114
Appleman, Peter, 111
Archer, George, 54, 59
  Peter, 72
Arlas, Samuel, 36
Armstrong, Thos., 103
Arnold, Capt., 2, 7, 53, 59, 96
  Jacob, Dr., 53
  Nancy, 91
Arnot, Isaac, 23
Ashton, John, 2
Atkinson, Stacy, 81, 82
Aubal, Senr.
  Michael, 33
Augustus, George, 59

Auled, Jr.
  Matthias, 33
Aupelman, John, 36, 37
  Mathias, 37
Aupleman, Tice, 36
Avary, Charles, 106
Avins, Caleb, 79
Axford, Charles, 2
Ayres, Gershom, 20

B

Babel, Christopher, 36
Bache, Mr., 106
Baches, Mr., 96
Back, Mr., 105
Badcock, Simeon, 12
Badgley, Abraham, 74, 75
Bady, Esqr.
  Isaac, 109
Bainbridge, Edmund, 11
Baird, John, 58
Baird, Esqr.
  Benjamin, 4
Baker, Capt., 100
Baldwin, Jonathan, 70, 78
  Levi, 64, 117
  Mr., 83
  Silvenus, 100
  Thomas, 65
  Wm., 100
Baldwin, Esqr.
  Jonathan, 103
Ball, Caleb, 94
Ballum, William, 59
Bancroft, Daniel, 10
Bane, John, 89
Banghart, Burnet, 59
  George, 37
Bangheart, George, 36
Banker, Christn., Col., 94
  Christopher, 95
Banks, Phebe, 24
  Phoebe, 26
Banta, 112
  Cornelius, 31, 43, 44
  Derick, 31, 42

INDEX

Hendrick, 111
John, 42
John, Capt., 31, 41, 42
Thos., 57, 61
Bantha, Hendrick, 113
Thos., 62, 65, 80, 94, 96
Barber, John, 19, 20, 21, 23, 94
Justice, 30
Barcalow, John, 91
Barclay, Charles, 102
Barker, Peter, 89
Sergeant, 89
Barlon, Benjm., 48
Joseph, Col., 48
Barn, Cornelius, 98
Barnet, Ichabod, 112
Ichabod B., 105
Barnet, Esqr.
Oliver, 35, 36
Barnfield, Edward, 45
Barnhill, John, 91
Barns, Robert, 1
Barron, Ellis, 48, 85
Mrs., 85
Sarah, 69
Barrow, Sarah, 69
Barry, Samuel, 90
Barton, Benjamin, 50, 56
Gilbert, 4
Henry, 55
John, 55
Joseph, 55
Mrs., 78
Bastedo, Lewis, 8, 9
Batey, Elizabeth, 26
Bayard, Esqr.
Wm., 62
Bayles, Kessiah, 77
Baylis, John, 82
Beach, Elisha, 26
Beadle, Joel, 99
Beasley, Capt., 115
Beavers, Col., 3, 37
Joseph, Col., 53

Becket, John, 83
Peter, 83
Stephen, 83
Beckwith, Cyrus, 78
Cyrus, Capt., 31
Bedford, Daniel, 81
Elias, Corp., 92
Bedson, Nathaniel, 38
Beech, Ezekiel, 50, 51, 75, 76
Beedle, Michael, 60
Nathan, 112
Beesley, Jonn., 99
Bell, James, 11
Richard, 83
Bellerjan, John, 85
Belles, Peter, 60
Bennet, Jeremiah, 11
John, 67, 71, 105
Joseph, 11
Theophilus, 11
Thomas, 11
Bergen, Jacob, 102
Lieut., 70
Berger, John, 56
Beron, Michael, 33
Berry, John, 39
Joseph, 91
Sidney, Col., 56
Stephen, 91
Besley, James, 87
Jas., 86
jas., 89
Betson, Thos., 37
Betty, Elizabeth, 24
Bickle, Nicholas, 62
Billington, Mary, 50
Binley, John, 98
Binly, Jas., 89
Bird, Elisha, 52, 53
Bisben, John, 51
Bishop, Capt., 105
Clement, 105
Ebenezer, 45, 46
Thos., 83
Blackford, Joseph, 64
Blackwell, Benjamin, 88

John, 8, 13, 14
Blanch, Isaac, 62, 65
Blanchard, John, Capt., 55
Rynere, 91
Bland, Col., 85
Blank, Isaac, 57, 61, 80
Blauvelt, Abraham J., 40
Cornelius D., 40
Jacobus, 57
Blinkerhoff, John, 66
Blinkerhoof, Seba, 42
Blooks, James, 85
Bloom, Frederick, 29, 31
Bloomfield, Moses, Dr., 116
Thos., 46
Bloomfield, Sr.
Thomas, 45
Blue, Henry, 107
Bodine, Jacob, 33, 35
Bogart, Henry, 91
Jacob, 21, 23
Bogert, Albert J., 40
Cornelious, 31
Cornelius, 43, 45, 57, 58, 59, 61, 62, 75, 80, 108
Hendrick, 86
Henry, 91
Jacob, 59, 66, 70, 86
Peter, 31, 43
Stephen, 58
Boice, Cornelius, 45
George, 45
Leonard, 45, 46
Bolies, Simeon, 29
Bonam, Malachi, 60
Bond, Nathaniel, 90, 91
William, 94
Bonnel, Col., 61
Boon, Elizabeth, 101, 114
Joseph, 101
Booth, William, 35
Borden, Joseph, 10
Bordon, Richard, 82

120

INDEX

Borrows, Stephen, 85
Boskirk, Jacob, Lieut., 65
Boudinot, Col., 26
   Elisha, Esqr., 13
   Mr., 14
   Mrs., 77
Boudinot, Esqr.
   Elisha, 7
   Elias, 14
Bougee, John, 98
Bouton, William, 25
Bowen, 55, 56, 57, 58, 59, 61
   Jonathan, 79
   Jonn., 51
   Mr., 116
   Wm., 71
Bowes, John, 85
Boyd, Adam, 41
   Wm., 111
Boyles, Simeon, 31
Brady, Wm., 52, 59
Bragly, Daniel, 95
Bray, Daniel, 51, 60
   John, 45
Brean, Michael, 35
Brein, Michael, 49
Breton, Joseph, 97
Brewer, George, 1
   Peter, 20
   Saml., 59
Briarley, Col., 21
Bright, Geo., 94
Briningon, Capt., 115
Brinkerhoff, John, Capt., 31
   Seba, 31
Brinkeroff, Henry, 112
Britain, Joseph, 108
Briton, Abraham, 1
   Joseph, 116
   William, 28
Britton, Abraham, 1
   Joseph, 59
   Wm., 29
Brock, John, 83

Brockman, John, 39
Brokau, Abraham, 71
Brook, Seth, 87
Brooks, Jesse, 55
   John, 88
   Thos., 98
Bross, Hendrick, 24
Brower, Aaron Robbins, 7
Brown, Daniel, 115
   Danl., 102
   David, 46, 90
   Elisabeth, 31
   Elizabeth, 40
   George, 7
   Hugh, 53, 54, 59
   John, 65, 70
   John aka "John Lee", 15
   John, Dr., 36
Brown, Esqr.
   Abia, 28
Bruin, David, 42
Brunner, Peter, 94
Bryant, Wm., 63
Bryas, Herman, 40
Buck, 51, 55, 56, 57, 58, 59, 60, 61, 62, 82, 83, 84, 85, 86, 87, 88, 89, 90, 91, 97, 98, 99, 100, 101, 102, 103, 105, 106, 107, 113, 114, 115, 116
   Ezekiel, 59
   John, 51, 79, 85
   Mr., 87, 90, 98
Budd, Joseph, 5
Buganer, John, 32
Buggs, James, 95
Bugner, John, 31
Bullion, Dr., 109
Bullus, Samuel, 52
Bume, Coorad, 33
Bunn, Ichabod, 45
   John, 33
   Laurence, 33
Burdge, Joseph, 13
Burge, Jonathan, 11, 19

Burgoyne, Genl., 89
Burling, Saml., 5
   Samuel, 3, 4, 6
Burnet, David, 93
   James, 92
   Josiah, Ensign, 90, 92
Burnet, Jr.
   Matthias, 64
Burnet, Junr.
   Wm., 47
Burns, John, 95
Burroughs, John, 105
Burrowe's Company, 19
Burrowes, John, 106
Burson, David, 96
Burton, David, 14
Buskirk, Col., 44
   John, 43
Buth, Wm., 33
Butler, Col., 110
   Edward, 58, 59
   John, 2
Buvers, Joseph, Col., 61

C

Cadington, Elizabeth, 81
   Isaia, 81
   Margaret, 81
   Moses, 81
   Violet, 81
Cadmus, Peter, 108
Cadmus, Jr.
   Thos., 29
Cadmus, Junr.
   Thomas, 34
Cahill, Daniel, 39
   Thomas, 35
Cain, Adams, 94
   Barney, 94
Caldwell, 34
   Mr., 63, 73
   Rev., 63, 74
Camp, 1, 7, 8, 9, 10, 11, 12, 13, 15, 16, 17, 18, 19, 20, 21, 22, 23, 24, 25, 26, 27, 28,

INDEX

    29, 30, 34, 35, 36, 37, 39, 45, 47, 50, 51, 52, 53, 54, 61, 62, 63, 65, 66, 67, 77, 81, 82, 84, 86, 88, 89, 90, 91, 96, 98, 101, 103, 105, 106, 108, 109, 112, 114, 115, 116, 117
    Caleb, 1, 51, 79, 101
    Joseph D., 115
    Mathew, 53
    Matthew, 59
    Mr., 6, 18, 28, 31, 34, 36, 40, 66, 117
Camp, Esqr.
    Caleb, 15
Campbell, Capt., 25
    Colin, 3, 4, 6
    David, 33
    Elias, 100
    George, Dr., 60
    James, 31, 44
    John, 72
    Mr., 39
    Samuel, 86
Campfield, Abraham, 45
Campion, Joseph, 13, 14
Canby, Thomas, 98
    Thos., 109
Canfield, Abraham, 77
    Thos., 65
Cannon, Robert, 89
Car, Samuel, 102
Carby, Jas., 95
Carey, Esqr.
    Isaac, 29
Carmichael, Alexander, 48, 58
Carpenter, Thos., 67
Carr, Wm., 58
Carson, John, 11
Carter, David, 108

Cartwright, Solomon, 29
Carty, John, 5, 6, 52
Casmer, George, 60
Casner, George, 61
Casterlin, Joseph, 58
Castner, Abraham, 36
    Coonrad, 37
    Coorad, 37
    Jacob, 36, 37
    James, 36
Castner, Junr.
    John, 36, 37
Castner, Senr.
    John, 36, 37
Catlin, Jos., 76
Chamberlain, Col., 64, 115
    Lt. Col., 115
Chambers, Abijah, 29
    Col., 60, 71, 85
    Wm., Capt., 42
Cheesman, Abijah, 116
Chestnutwood, Sebastian, 30
Chew, Mr., 64
Chew, Esqr.
    Benj., 54
    Benjamin, 64
Chois, Esqr.
    Joseph, 115
Church, John, 100
Churchward, Richard, 49
Churchwards, Richard, 79
Clandening, James, 29
Clark, Alexr., 85
    Azariah, 74, 75
    Benj., 63
    Benjm., 68
    Col., 105
    Elijah, 28
    Isaac, 63, 68, 80
    James, 63
    John, 63, 68
    Lardner, 26
    Mathew, 68
    Matthw., 63
    Richd., 98
    Robert, 23, 74

    Samuel, 63
    Thos., 63, 68
    William, 109
    Wm., 63, 68
Clarke, Anne, 24
    Benjm., 69
    Isaac, 69
    John, 69
    Thos., 69
    William, 69
Clawson, Aaron, 46
    Cornelius, 50, 59
    John, 27
    Jonathan, 49, 50, 59
Cleayton, Cornelius, 11
    John, 6
    Thomas, 11
Cleehaws, Arnold, 33
Clement, Jacob, 21
Clever, Joshua, 86
    Joshua, 87
Clinton, Henry, Sir, 62
    Peter, 113
Clough, Major, 93
Clowden, John, 98
Clowson, Cornelius, 49
Clyne, John, 59
Coble, Joseph, 34
Codmus, Jr.
    Thomas, 27
Cole, Abraham, 77, 78
    Frederick, 76, 77
    Fredk., 77
    Isaac, 113
    John, 78, 111
    Justice, 36, 37
    Wm., 85
Coleman, Jacob, 34
Collins, Elijah, 33
    John, 29
    Jonathan, 31
    Jonn., 32
    Liga, 31
    Mahlon, 33
    Malon, 31
    Mr., 84

INDEX

Simeon, 83
Collver, Joseph, 35
Colven, Thos., 33
Colver, James, 33
    John, 33
    Robert, 33, 35
    Simon, 37
    Thos., 37
    Timothy, 35
Colver, Senr.
    Robert, 33
Colvin, Luther, 57, 61
Colvin, Junr.
    Luther, 58
Combe, 20
Combes, 5, 7, 11, 12, 13, 16, 50
Combs, 9, 10, 15, 17, 19, 20, 21, 22, 27, 48, 51, 53, 54, 55
    John, 1, 51
    Mr., 18
    Thos., Capt., 93
Combs, Esqr.
    John, 14
Compton, James, 49
    Robert, 98
Conchlin, Benj., 112
Conck, George, 36
Condict, 15, 16, 17, 18, 19, 20, 21, 22, 23, 24, 25, 26, 27, 28, 29, 30, 32, 34, 36, 37, 39, 40, 41, 42, 43, 45, 46, 47, 50, 51, 53, 54, 55, 56, 61, 62, 64, 66, 67, 72, 74, 75, 76, 86, 87, 88, 89, 90, 92, 98, 99, 100, 101, 108, 109, 111, 112, 113, 115, 116

    Mr., 44, 64, 71, 75, 77, 80, 87, 88, 91, 93, 95, 97, 110, 111, 116
    Silas, 1, 51, 79
Condict, Esqr.
    David, 7
    Silas, 71, 75, 109, 115
Condin, Michael, 66
Condit, 27, 65, 72, 73, 76, 77, 81, 83, 88, 98, 99
    Mr., 84, 101
    Silas, Hon., 77
Condit, Esqr.
    Silas, 72, 78
Conger, Joseph, 117
Conklin, Isaac, 92
Conner, John, 100
Connolly, Henry, 36
Connor, John, 103
Cook, Col., 65, 90, 91, 92, 98, 99, 100, 101, 108, 110, 111
    Elizabeth, 60
    Ellis, Col., 64
    Jas., 89
    Mr., 79, 108
    William, 65, 69
    Wm., 65
Cook, Esqr.
    John, 56
Cooke, Col., 109, 112
    Greene, 6
    Robert, 4, 35
Coolback, Wm., 72
Cooley, Captain, 9
Coombes, 8, 9, 10
Cooper, 66, 67, 81, 83, 86, 87, 88, 89, 90, 96, 97, 98, 100, 102, 113
    Jacob, 20
    John, 64
    Mr., 66, 79
    William, 10
Coperthwaite, John, 1
Copinger, Sarah, 74

Wm., 74
Corby, Jas., 95
Cornelius, James, 20
Cornock, Daniel, 62
Corp, Joseph, 33
Corrent, William, 113
Corsly, Paul, 35
Corstron, Wm., 81
Cortlandt, Col., 24
Cotterell, John, 13
Coult, Junr.
    Isaac, 32
Council of Safety, Pennsylvania, 14
Courtlandt, Phillip V., 40
Courzens, Saml., 86
Cousens, Saml., 90
    Samuel, 87
Cousins, Samuel, 91
Covenhoven, Garrat, 3
    John, 107
Coward, Joseph, 83, 114
Cowdrick, Ensing, 60
Cowel, Isaac, 33
Cowen, William, 15, 16
Cox, Esekiel, 83
    John, 28, 87
    John, Col., 18
    Joseph, 52, 59
    Lawrence, 108
    Mary, 18
    Richard, 88
Cox, Junr.
    John, 2
Coxe, Isaac, Sergeant, 117
Cragg, William, 53
Craig, Aaron, 36
    Aaron, Dr., 37
    James, 52, 59
    Wm., 52, 59
Cramer, Jeremiah, 33
    Philip, 38
Crammer, Noadiah, 45, 46
Crane, 72, 81, 82, 83, 84,

INDEX

86, 87, 88, 89, 90, 92, 99, 101, 102, 115, 116
Jacob, 43
James, 79
John, 76
Jonas, 101
Jos., 100
Major, 76, 77
Mr., 79
Nathaniel, 89
Stephen, 105
Crane, Esqr.
   Stephen, 92, 100
Crawford, Sara, 40
   Sarah, 31
Crestley, David, 33
Creter, Morrice, 33
Cretor, Morris, 36
Cretsley, Powel, 33
Crips, Adam, 33
   Col., 114
Crissman, Charles, 29
Croley, John, 36
Crooks, Mr., 38
Crosly, David, 35
Crossley, Charles,
   cooper, 73
   Chas, cooper, 75
   Samuel, cooper, 73, 75
Crow, Richard R., 7
Crowel, Rachel, 32
   Richard, 32
Culver, Robert, 36
Cummins, Jacob, 5, 7
Cumpton, Aaron, 19
   James, 19, 50
Curtis, Christopher, 96
   Thomas, 20
   Walter, 20
   Wm., 116
Curwine, Richard, 58
Cuykindal, Benj., 58
Cyphers, Philip, 60, 61

D

Dain, Joseph, 86, 87, 89
Dakey, Gifford, Capt., 26
Dally, Gifford, 93, 95
   Major, 72
   Mr., 94
Dals, Wm., 37
Dancer, Daniel, 13
   Jacob, 13
Dare, Benoni, 90
Davenport, Jacob, cooper, 85
   John, 77, 78
   Leonard, 77, 78
   William, 87
   Wm., 87
Davidson, David, 109
   John, 3
   Mrs., 109
Davis, Jas., 116
   John, 35, 90
   Joseph, 85
Davis, Junr.
   Samuel, 87
Davison, Mary, 3, 4
   Wm., Innholder, 61
Dayton, Col., 19, 65, 113
   Dr., 92
   Jonathan J., 53
   Jonn. I., Dr., 52
De Cond, John, 29
De Groot, Jacob, 66
Dealy, Wm., 61
Dean, Aaron, 56
Dear, Jonathan, 69, 84
Debarre, John, 42, 44
Debauc, John, 31
DeGroff, John, 109
Degroot, John, 42, 43
   Peter, 43
Degrote, Jacob, 31
   John, 31
   Peter, 31
DeHart, Esqr.
   John, 52
Demarest, Cap., 42
   David, 26
   Garret, 45, 57, 61
   Garret, Capt., 62
   Gerret, 96
   Gerret, Capt., 65
   Gerrit, 75, 80, 83, 90, 94
   John, 26, 41, 43
   Saml., 70
Demarest, Esqr.
   John, 42
Demerest, Samuel, 66
Demerest, Esqr.
   John, 30
Demerist, Garret,
   Captain, 31
Demont, John, 92
Demot, Jacob, 43, 45
Demott, John, 110, 113
Dennis, Jaquish, 109
   John, Capt., 15
   Michael, 60, 61
Dennis, Esqr., John, 90
Denny, Thomas, 16
Denny, Esqr.
   Thomas, 17
Denton, Anthony, 114
   Mr., 101
Depuyster, Abm. W., 83
   Christiana, 41
Depuyster, Junr.
   William, 41
Dercberah, Philip, 36
Dermott, Jacob, 31
Desbrow, Henry, 102, 106, 107
   Mrs., 106
Dexter, Capt., 89
Dey, Abraham, 31
   Col., 58
   Jacob, 31, 43
   Jerod, 93
   John, 70, 91, 93
   Johnn., 67
   Teunis, Col., 47
Dey, Esq.
   Teunis, 40
   Thomas, 20
Dey, Esqr.

INDEX

Teunis, 29
Dial, Elizabeth, 60
Dick, 1, 2, 4, 5, 7, 15, 19, 50
  Col., 8
  Coll., 1
  Mr., 18
  Samuel, 1
Dickenson, Gen., 89
  Genl., 89
  Joseph, 98
  Maj. Genl., 101
Dickinson, Gen., 3, 82
  Genl., 53, 57, 67
  Maj. Gen., 63, 65
Dilts, Mw., 29
Dinkinson, Majr. Genl., 57
Dixon, John, 81
  Robert, 56
Doane, Titus, 31
Dobbins, William, 7
Dodd, Isaac, 25
Donaldson, Andrew, 100, 102
Doty, Joseph, 109
Downey, Jas., 98
  William, 72
Doyle, Francis, 8
  Paterson, cooper, 73
  Patrick, cooper, 75
Drake, 51, 52, 53, 54, 55, 61, 62, 63, 65, 81, 115
  Col., 63, 64, 65, 66, 67, 70, 71, 72, 73, 74, 75, 76, 82, 84, 86, 90, 91, 92, 95, 99, 100, 101, 102, 103, 105, 108, 109, 110, 111, 112, 113, 116, 117
  Emily, 53, 59
  Ephraim, 28, 29

Hezekiah, 39
Imlay, 52, 54
Jacob, 18, 51, 79
John, 88
Joseph, 39
Silas, 44
Stephen, 92
William, 70
Wm., 60
Drummond, Jane, 31, 40
  John, 23
  William, 25
Dubois, Peter, 27, 29, 34
Duboise, Peter, 30
Dufford, Jacob, 36
  Stephen, 36
Duggen, Wm., 33
Dumont, Peter, 39
Dunborr, Lott, 86
Dunfield, Henry, 59
Dunham, Esqr.
  Azariah, 94
Dunham, Esr.
  Nehemiah, 89
Dunn, Col., 49, 89
  Jonathan, 42
Duryea, David J., 42, 45
  John, 42, 44
Duryee, David, 42
  John, 40
Durzee, Daniel J., 31
  John [miller], 31
Dusenberry, John, 37
Duyckinck, Geradus, 92
  John, 7
Duycknick, Col., 8

E

Eagle, John, 59
Earl, John, 41
Earle, Edward, Lieut., 65
  John, 30
Eaton, Thos., 89
Eddy, John, 30
Ederson, John, 20
Edeson, John, 74
Edison, John, 27

Edsal, Richard, 50
Edsal, III
  Richard, 50
Edsall, Richard, 56
Edsall, III
  Richard, 56
Edward, Alexander, miller, 75
  Daniel, miller, 75
Edwards, Alexr., miller, 73
  Daniel, miller, 73
Egberts, Thos., 56
Egleson, Thos., 98
Eick, Casper, 35
  Gasper, 33
Eikler, Conradt, 60, 61
Eldridge, Joab, 83
  Thos., 83
Ellis, Col., 67, 70, 73, 91, 98
  Daniel, 4, 6, 52
  John, 59
  Joseph, Col., 17
  Rowland, 52
  Royland, 52
  Saml., 52
  William, Major, 15
Ellis, Esqr.
  Joseph, 16
Ellison, Lewis, 8
  Robert, 5, 6
Elmer, 9, 10, 11, 12, 13, 15, 16, 17, 18, 19, 20, 21, 28, 29, 30, 32, 33, 34, 35, 36, 37, 39, 40, 41, 42, 43, 44, 45, 46, 47, 48, 53, 54, 55, 56, 57, 58, 59, 60, 61, 62, 64, 65, 66, 67, 81, 82, 83, 84, 87, 88, 89, 90, 91, 98, 100, 101,

INDEX

    102, 105, 106, 107, 113, 114, 115, 116
  Mr., 48, 57
  Theo., 79
  Theophilus, 1
  Thos., 51
Elmer, Esqr.
  Jonathan, 75
  Theophilus, 98
Elmore, Theophilus, 15
Ely, Abraham, 40
Emely, Mr., 73, 75
Emley, John, 35, 38
  Samuel, 1
Emley, Junr.
  William, 1
Emly, John, 62
Engellman, Jacob, 36
English, Isaac, 113
  Joseph, 113
Eoff, Junr.
  Jacob, 36, 37
Eoff, Senr.
  Jacob, 37
Erwin, Cornelius, 58
Estell, Joseph, 58
Eut, Valentine, 71
Evert, Jacob, 39
Evert, Junr
  William, 60
Ewel, Thos., 98
Ewing, James, 58
Extopher, Collan, sailor, 89
Eyke, Ferris, 60
  John, 60

F

Farnsworth, Amariah, 12
Farr, Thomas, 4
Faulkinier, John, 92
Fell, Mr., 63, 88
  Peter, 24
Fell, Esqr.
  John, 57
  John, Hon., 62, 63
  John, Honorable, 72
  Peter, 29
Fenemore, 91, 101, 102, 103, 113, 114, 116
  John, 114
  Samuel, 91
Fenemore, Esqr.
  Thos., 91
Fenimore, 100, 113
Fennemore, 116
  Mr., 79
Fennimore, 91
Ferdon, Jacob, 66
Ferriberry, Fredk., 37
Findlass, James, 110
  Jas., 113
Finlass, 116
Fisher, John, 37
Fitcher, George, 31
Fitz,
  Randolph
    Capt., 101
Fitz Randolph, Jacob, 81, 102
FitzRandolph, Hartshorn, 81
  Hartshorne, 26
  Jacob, 80
Fitzrandolph, Jacob, 91
  Joseph, 101, 103
  Jospeh, 100
Flagg, Jacob, 58
Flatt, Wm., 51
Fleming, 62, 65, 88
  Col., 63, 65, 66, 67, 75, 76, 77, 81, 83, 84, 85, 86, 87, 95, 97, 98, 99, 108, 109
  Edw., 79
  Edward, 51
  Lawrence, 108
  William, 66
Flemming, Col., 65, 67, 72, 73, 74, 84
  Lawrence, 59
  Thomas, 48
Flock, Andrew, 33
Flock, Junr.
  Andrew, 33
Flood, Stephen, 13
Folkenier, John, 77
Folkiner, John, 79
Fonger, John, 33
Fooes, Phillip, 59
Foord, Ebenezer, 100
Force, Eve, 109
  Jacob, 109
  Manning, 100
  Philip, 58
Ford, Benj., 114
  Col., 65
Forman, Aaron, 54
  Col., 3
  David, Col., 19
  General, 10
  Jonathan, 1
  Saml., Col., 56
  Ezekiel, 10
Forman, Esqr.
  Thomas, 10
Fort, Bartholomew, cooper, 88
Fossey, John, 36
Foster, Benjamin, 23
  Jacob, 35
  Jane, 79
Foster, Junr.
  Ezekiel, 106
Fouger, John, 36
Foust, Jacob, 60, 61
Fowler, Thomas, 6, 8, 32
  Thos., 30
Francis, Capt., 89
  Richard, 11
Francisco, John, 76
Fransico, John, 95
Frayee, Jacob, 33
Fraze, Frederick, 37
  Hendrick, 34
  Henry, 33
Frazey, David, 69
Fredericks, Conrad, 83
Freelynhuysen, Col., 8
Freeman, Ashabel, 89

INDEX

Benj., 95
Edmund, 59
Isaac, 48
Israel, 66
James, 53, 59
Lewis, 69
Lot, 59
Matthew, 69
Samuel, 45, 46
Freilinghousn, Col., 48
Frelinghuysen, Col., 27, 89
   Frederick, 51
   Fredk., Col., 48
Frelinhuysen, Col., 66
French, George, 83
Friend, Charles, 66, 69, 70
Frieze, Jacob, 35
Fritz, Frederick, 37
   Fredk., 36
Furlough, James, 91
Furman, Aaron, 35, 59
   Aaron, Dr., 38
Fussler, Jacob, 36

G

Gaffin, Hannah, 91
   Hannah, widow, 117
   John, 91, 117
Gamble, Capt., 15
Ganalvant, Mary, 31
Gardner, Jacob, 16, 21
Garrabrants, Mary, 40
Garritson's Tavern, 105
Gaston, Robert, 45
Gates, Martin, 37
Gautier, Andrew, 110
Gautiere, Andrew, 113
George, John, 83
   Peter, 59
Gerhart, Jacob, 57
Gevils, John, 98
Gibeson, Hezekiah, 75
   John, 75
Gilbert, John, 98
Giston, Wm., 37

Glue, Richard, miller, 73, 75
Godwin, Isaac, 113
Goetchius, Major, 84
Gohem, Thomas, 13, 14
Golden, Abraham, 61
Golder, Abraham, 57, 107
   Nicholas, 107
Goldsmith, John, 82
Goodin, Moses, 35
Goodwin, Isaac, 111
   Jacob, 5, 51, 52
   Moses, 33
Gordon, Major, 23
   Peter, 81
Gorman, John, 74
   Lydia, 74
Gosling, Elizabeth, 60
Goss, Philip, 73
Gould, Jr.
   Robert, 64
Governeur, Nicholas, 30
Governor, 1, 2, 4, 5, 6, 7, 8, 9, 11, 12, 13, 14, 15, 16, 17, 18, 19, 20, 21, 22, 23, 24, 25, 26, 27, 28, 29, 30, 32, 33, 34, 35, 36, 37, 39, 40, 41, 42, 43, 44, 45, 46, 47, 48, 50, 52, 53, 54, 55, 56, 57, 59, 60, 61, 62, 63, 64, 65, 66, 67, 68, 69, 70, 71, 72, 73, 74, 75, 76, 77, 78, 81, 82, 83, 84, 85, 86, 87, 88, 89, 90, 91, 92, 94, 96, 97, 98, 99, 100, 102, 103, 105, 106, 107, 108, 109, 110, 111, 112, 113, 114, 115, 116, 117
Grandin, John, 39
Grandine, Daniel, 11, 12
   John, 35
   William, 12

Wm., 11
Green, Adam, 29, 30
   Captain, 5
   Jacob, Dr., 64
   John, 29, 30
   William, 30
Gregory, Ebenezer, 97
Grey, Josiah, 103, 105, 108
Griggs, Daniel, 4
Groetchius, Major, 77
Gronendike, Samuel, Capt., 60
Gronendyke, Samuel, 58
Gronman, Junr.
   Ichabod, 35
Groom, Joseph, 2, 9, 108
   Thomas, 2, 9
Grover, James, 3, 50
   William, 7, 10, 35
   Wm., 11
Grummond, Ichabod, 112
Guisbertson, William, 4
Guron, Christopher, 87
Gustin, Thomas, 33

H

Hackney, Saml., 83
Hagar, David, 37
   Jacob, 35
   John, 38
Hager, Jacob, 33
   John, 33
   Laurence, 33, 35
Hagerthy, Patrick, 55
   Sarah, 55
Haggarthe, Mrs., 78
Haight, Col., 5
   Joseph, 5, 7
Hair, Robert, 98
Hale, William, 107
Halfpenny, John, 115
   William, 13
Hall, 15
   Edward, 35
   Josiah, 92
   Samuel, 60

INDEX

Halsey, 24, 41, 42, 43, 44, 45, 46, 47
   Isaac, Capt., 65
   Joseph, 108
   Justice, 47, 48
Halsey, Esqr.
   Benjamin, 23, 40, 47
Hamilton, James, 98
Hammel, John, Surgeon, 65
Hammill, William, 40
Hammond, Noah, 109
   Noel, 110
Hampton, Mr., 23
Hancock, Joseph, 99
   Rachel, 99
Hand, Col., 98
   Elijah, 9
   John, 58
   Thos., 82
Handinot, Mahitabel, 31
Hann, Jacob, 36
   William, 36
Hannah, James, 29
Hansey, Saml., 85
Harder, Philip, 62, 73
Harley, William, 4
Harring, Abrm., Capt., 47
   Cornelius, 41
   Cornelius, Captain, 31
   Peter J., 45
Harring, Esqr.
   Cornelius, 31
   Peter J., 31
Harris, Benjm., 64
   Capt., 105
   Edmund, 10
   Ephraim Drake, 4
   George, 114
   John, 4, 57
   Mathias, 39
   Thos., 57, 58
Harrison, Capt., 93
   George, 25, 83
   Pricilla, Mrs., 71
   William, 16
   William, Capt., 17
Harrison, Esqr.
   Samuel, 16, 17
Harry, John, 53, 56
Hart, 1, 2, 9, 10, 11, 12, 15, 21, 39, 40, 41, 42, 44, 45, 46, 47, 48, 50, 51, 52, 55, 56, 57, 58, 59, 60, 61, 62, 64, 65, 66, 67, 81, 96, 97, 106, 113, 115, 117
   Henry, 59
   Jesse, 58
   John, 1, 51, 79, 85
   Joseph, 60
   Mr., 48, 77, 102
   Nathaniel, 29, 31
Hart, Esqr.
   John, 15, 56, 71, 85, 99, 117
Hartsaugh, Peter, 39
Hartshorn, Ezek, 4
   Robert, 4
Hartshorne, Essek, 12
   Ezeck, 98
   Robert, 12, 98
Hartwick, John, 115
Harvey, Jacob, 10
   Stephen, 11
Hassen, Felix, 30
Hatfield, Benjamin, 48
Hathaay, Benoni, Major, 47
Hathaway, Benoni, 80
   Col., 85, 109, 110, 112
Havens, John, 34, 68
   Moses, 102, 115
   Stout, 19, 20, 21, 23, 59
Haveris, John, 27
Hay, Timothy, mariner, 89
Hayes, Major, 24, 26, 30
Hayes, Esqr.
   Samuel, 7
Hays, John, 62, 75, 80, 94, 96
   Major, 95, 108
Hayward, Ebenezer, 117
   Hyram, 42
   Isaac, 111
Headly, Carey, 100
Heard, Gen., 3, 5, 7, 9, 17, 18, 21, 89
   General, 16, 22, 23
   John, Mrs., 69
   Samuel, 45
Hearn, John, 48
Heath, John, 63
   Samuel, 4
Heaton, Richard, 40
Hebler, Adam, 23, 24
   John, 31
   William, 31
Heburn, William, 85
Hedden, James, 58
   William, 37
Hedden, Esqr.
   Joseph, 27
Hedger, john, 69
Hedges, John, 63
   Stephen, 12
Helm, Benjamin, 6
   Mr., 5
Helme, Benjamin, 8, 9
Helmo, Mr., 16
Hen, Jacob, 33
   John, 33
   Peter, 36
   Philip, 33
   William, 33
Hen, Junr.
   William, 33
Henchman, Esqr.
   John, 16, 21
Henchman, Esqr. John, 17, 19
Hendershed, Jeremiah, 33
Hendershut, Christopher, 34
Hendricks, Abraham, 3, 4, 5
   Baker, 27, 63, 65
   John, 63, 65

INDEX

Hendrickson, Daniel, 4, 12
Hendry, Doctor, 3
   Herbert, 59
   John, 22
Henning, Col., 66
Henry, Herbert, 109
Herring, Capt., 64
   Cornelius, 44
   Cornelius Abm., 42
   Peter I., 61
   Peter J., 42, 45, 57
   Peter T., 62, 75, 80
Herring, Esqr.
   Cornelius, 42
   Peter T., 65
Heslip, David, 11
Hetfield, Jacob, 48
   James, 48, 50
   Morris, 27
   Smith, 27
Heuling, William, 90
Heumel, Jacob, 114
Hewling, Saml., 87, 88
   William, 87
   Wm., 87, 91
Hewlings, Abraham, 6, 8
   Joseph, 16, 17
   Thomas P., 3, 4, 6
Heyer, Abm., 101
Hibbits, James, 85
Hicks, Martha, 31, 40
Hiff, James, 59
Higgins, Hannah, Mrs., 76
   William, 67
High, James, 59
Hilar, Jacob, 16
   Nicholas, 16
Hile, Jacob, 33
Hill, John, 60, 61
   Peter, 92
   Thomas, 35
   Wm., 110, 111
Hillar, Mr., 57
Hiller, Peter, 52

Hillier, Peter, 53
Hills, Thos., 33
Hilmer, Josiah, Col., 58
Hincksman, Esqr.
   John, 18
Hind, Peter, 37
Hissock, Jos., 89
Hoagland, Major, 81
   Oakley, Col., 99
Hoagland, Esqr.
   Oake, 25
Hoaglandt, Codenis, 91
Hodden, Jr., Esqr
   Joseph, 24
Hodge, Andrew, 105
   Mr., 98
Hodgkinson, John, 87
Hoff, Nicholas, 99
Hoffman, Christian, 39
   Mrs., 78, 92, 93
   Mrs. Nicholas, 80
   Nicholas, 40, 80
   Phillip, 25
Holdron, Joseph, 60
Hole, John, 33
Holingshead, Joseph, 85
Hollman, Elias, 14
Holmes, Alfred, Major, 85
   Asher, 88
   Asher, Major, 85
   Col., 98
   Joseph, 115
   Mr., 99
Holmes, Esqr.
   Asher, 67
Holton, John, 70
Holts, Daniel, 98
Home, John, 83
Homer, William, 60
Hondershute, Peter, 108
Honeyman, John, 66, 69, 70
Honeywell, John, 28, 30
   William, 28
   Wm., 29
Hoogland, Tunis, 68
Hoole, John, 31

Hooper, Gerret, 65
   Mr., 54
Hoopes, 90
Hoops, Col., 109, 110, 111
Hooten, John, 60
Hooton, Thomas, 51
Hope, Adam, 60
Hopkins, John Estaugh, 17, 18, 19
   Mary, 31
   Silas, 32
Horn, William, 51
Horner, Asher, 89
   Joseph, 68
   Josh., 63
Hornor, Joseph, 1
Horthrun, George, 36
Horton, John, 34, 117
Houdnot, Mehatabel, 40
Houghman, Nicholas, 45
House, Thos, 98
Houston, 96, 97, 98, 101, 103, 105, 106, 107, 113
   Mr., 103, 104, 117
Hover, Emmanuel, Capt., 58
   George, 37
How, Lord & General, 3
Howard, Bloomy [female], 39
   Hiram, 24
   Mr., 113
Howe, Genl., 95
Howel, Henry, 7
   Nathan, 95
Howell, Caleb, 80
   Elizabeth, 31
   Nathan, 71
   Sampson, 30
   Simpson, 29
Howes, Genl., 47
Howet, Elizabeth, 40
Howey, Abraham, 32
Hudson, Jas., 89

INDEX

Hugg, Commissary, 85
   Joseph, 16
   Samuel, Capt., 17
Hughes, William, 39
Hughs, Alphus, 71
Hughstus, James, 29
Hulick, Saml., 72
Hulicks, Ferdinand, 60
Hull, Benjn., 59
Hunlock, Mary, 113
   Thos., 113
Hunt, Daniel, 93
   John, 73, 94
   Nathaniel, 94
   Ralph, 29, 30
   Thomas, 85
Huntley, Richard, 1
Hurltey, Blakey, 87
Hurtley, Blakely, , 89
Hyd, Jacob, 34
Hyer, Col., 56, 103
   Jacob, 69
   Jacob, Col., 56
   William, 57, 61
Hyler, George, 112

I

Ilif, James, 54
Imlay, 66, 67, 68, 69, 70,
   81, 83, 85, 86,
   87, 88, 97, 98,
   99, 100, 101,
   102, 103, 105,
   107, 113, 114,
   115, 116
   Capt., 113
   Gilbert, Lieut., 18, 20
   Isaac, 6
   Mr., 70, 79
   Peter, 3, 4, 12, 113
   William, 6
   Wm., 6
Imlay, Esqr.
   John, 10, 101
Ink, John, 54, 59
Inlay, 96
Inman, John, 33, 36

Insley, Henry, 74
   Samuel, 45
Interest, Frontie, 40
Iselstin, Matthias, 83
Isilton, Mathias, 81
Ivins, Moses, 1
Izalton, Robert, 79

J

Jacobus, Ruelof, 90
Jacques, Moses, 43
James, Richard, 63, 108
   Robert, 63, 108
Jeffery, David, 101
   Thomas, 101
Jeffrey, Richard, 9, 10
Jeryard, David, 45
John, Morgan, 2
Johnson, Cornelius, 60
   Cornelius, Lieut., 57
   Daniel, 34
   Eliphelet, 27, 29, 34
   Jonas, 30
   Justice, 39
   Mr., 58
   Richard, 43
Johnston, Abigail, 99
   George, 102, 115
   Lambert, 85
   Lawrence, 14, 98
   Mrs., 67
   Peter, 114
   Robert, 99
   Thos., 98
Joint, Chevalier, 50
Jolley, John, 14
Jolly, Elisha, 60
Jones, Benjamin, 11
   Dr., 94
   Francis, 5
   Genl., 65
   Jacob, 87
   John, 2, 4, 6, 105
   Major Genl., 96
   Nicholas, 90
   Rev., 80
   Richard, 75

   Thos., 87, 90, 91
   Wm., 73, 80
Jonston, Lary, 13
Joralemon, Cornelius, 108
   Corse, 108
   Joseph, Pierce, 23
Justine, Jacob, 108

K

Kaign, Wm., 98
Kain, Junr.
   Christopher, 33
Kam, Christopher, 33
Kann, Christopher, 36
Kay, Isaac, 22
   Isaac, Mr., 16
   Marshall Isaac, 15
Keasby, 97, 98, 99, 100,
   101, 102, 103,
   105, 115, 116
   Mr., 79, 114
Keasby, Esqr.
   Edward, 98
Kelley, George, 114
Kelly, James, 59
   John, 37
   John, Capt., 58
   Joseph, 36, 37
Kellyham, Thos., 38
Kelsey, 50
   Enos, 4
   Enos, Major, 60
   Major, 56, 96, 110
   Mr., 96
Kelsey, Esqr.
   Enos, 48
Kemble, John, 98
   Richard, 26
Kemble, Esqr.
   Peter, Hon., 47
Kemple, Wm., 60
Kendry, Thos., 38
Kennack, William, 108
Kennedy, Archibald, 74
   Archibald, Capt., 80
   Capt., 74, 77, 80, 94

INDEX

Henry, 117
Kennedy, Esqr.
    Archibald, 73
Kerder, Mary, 82
Kerney, Thomas, 11, 12
Ketcham, Saml., 37
Ketchum, Levi, 59
Kilburne, Moses, 77
Killer, Peter, 59
Kimball, Christopher, 37
Kimble, Mr., 47
    Peter, 48
Kimpel, Christian, 33
King, Francis, 108
    Frederick, 25, 93
    George, 77, 109
    Jeremiah, 59
    Jerh., 35
    John, 90
    Joseph, 57, 58
    Lucas, 108
    Mr., 25
    Obadiah, 11
    William, 57
    Wm., 59, 100
King, Junr.
    David, 36, 37
King, Senr.
    David, 36, 37
Kingsland, Aaron, 27, 36
    Arent, 108
    H., 43
    Henry, 30, 43
    Isaac, 108
    John, 108
    Mary, 31, 40
    Nathaniel, 108
Kinney, Daniel, 113
    Lewis, 52, 53, 59
    Mr., 76
    Thomas, Capt., 25
Kinsberry, 112
Kinsey, John, 45
Kip, Ann, 64
Kippen, Mrs., 67
Kirby, John, 100

Kirkendall, Mr., 29
    Samuel, 28
Kirkpatrick, Samuel, 95
Kitchen, John, 53, 59
    Levi, 60
Kite, John, 19
Klyne, Jacob, 59
    John, 58, 59
    Philip, 59
Knot, Col., 81
Knott, Samuel, 11
Konk, George, 33
Konkle, Hanadam, 112
    Tice, 112

L

Labour, George, 59
Laboyteaux, Peter, 34
Lafferty, John, 94
Lake, Timothy, 7, 9, 10
    William, 15
Lambert, Isaac, 54, 59
Lance, Christopher, 30
    George, 30
    Jacob, 30
    Peter, 30
    Wendle, 30
Land, Hendrick, 72
Large, Aaron, 35, 38
    John, 35
    Robert, 35
Larkin, John, 101, 103
Laun, John, 31
Laurance, Daniel, 39
    Elisha, 21
    Wm., Captain, 39
Laurannce, Elisha, 36
Laurence, Adam, Doctr., 33
    Daniel, 8, 9
    Elisha, 67
    John, 4, 5, 8
    John, Doctre., 4
    Jos., 4
    William, 4, 9
Laurence, Esqr.
    Joseph, 4
Laurence, Jr.

    Joseph, 8
Laurence, Senr.
    John, 4, 7
Laurence, Sr.
    John, 3, 4
Law, Abm., 108
Lawbocker, Christ., 60
Lawrence, Elisha, Lt.
    Col., 56
    John, 62
    Josiah, 87
    Mr., 112
    Samuel, 74
    William, 98
Lawrence, Esq.
    John, 2
Lawrence, Esqr.
    John, 3
    Joseph, 3
Lawrence, Jr.
    John, 3
Lawrence, Sr.
    John, 3
Lawrie, Jacob, 3
Layboyteaux, Joseph, 34
Layton, Daniel, 77
    David, 78
    Thos., 112
Leak, John, 58
Leake, Adam, 38
Leaming, Mr., 85
    Thos., 85
Leamon, Joseph, 33
Ledden, James, 89
Lee, Genl., 49
    Giles, 37
    John, 5
    Joseph, 61
    Stephen, 60
Leek, Capt., 88, 105
Lefan, Michael, 33
Leferty, Brian, 34
Leinback, Frederick, 31
Leo, Joseph, 60
Leonard, John, 10
    Joseph, 4, 7, 35

INDEX

Joseph, Mr., 50
   Mrs., 54
   Thos., 54
Leslie, Edmund, 108
Lessheir, Jacob, 91
Lesten, Maria Elizabeth, Mrs., 38
   Michael Henry, 38
Leston, Maria Elizabeth, 53
Letts, Francis, 15
Lever, Henry, 33
Levet, Michael, 36
Lewis, Henry, Capt., 53
   Joseph, 71, 73, 80, 93
   Levi, 23, 24
   Nathaniel, 5
   Peter, 37
   Richard, 76
   Wm., 85
Lewis, Esqr.
   Nathaniel, 25
Leydecker, Samuel, 44
Lick, John, 33
Liddle, Mr., 82
Limbock, Frederick, 29
Linch, William Butler, 13
Lindley, Benj., 93
   Ephraim, 64
   John, Capt., 94
Lindsly, Esqr.
   Benjamin, 95
Linn, 65, 66, 67, 71, 72, 75, 76, 77, 81, 82, 86, 89
   Capt., 74
   Mr., 71, 79
Linnerberry, Nicholas, 36
Lippencott, Samuel, 108
Lippencut, Samuel, 6
Lippincot, Jedediah, 10
Lippincott, William, 9, 11, 81, 82
   Wm., 83
Little, John, 52, 59
   Nathaniel, 114, 115

William, 31, 32
Livingston, Governor, 46, 112
   James, 98
   John, 55
   Wil., 41
   Wil., Governor & President, 23
   William, Esq., Governor, 51
Livingston, Esqr.
   Wm., President, 58
Livingston, Jr.
   William, 80
   Wm., 62, 95
Livingston, Junr.
   Wm., 115
Lloyd, Isaac, 108
   Samuel, 108
   Wm., 114
Locey, Jas. Puff, 79
Lockman, Isaac, 37
Lodge, John, 83
Loffy, Michael, 50
Londy, Elijah, 81
   Jacob, 81
Long, Jacob, 49
   John, 59
   Michael, 45
Longstreet, Gilbert, 58
   John, 98
Longworth, Betsy, 50
   Catharine, 24, 26
   Charity, 50
   Mary, 24, 26
Loocey, Wm., 77
Loop, Christopher, 60
Losan, 16
Lott, Andrew, 100
   Mrs., 70, 117
   Reziah, Mrs, 116
Low, Wm., 87
Lowbacker, Christopher, 61
Loyd, Justice, 90
Lucas, Charles, 3
Luce, Peter, 33

Lucker, Benj., 114
Lucy, William, 50
Ludlow, Anthony, 112, 113
   Mrs., 111
Lugdecker, Samuel, 31
Lum, Jemima, Widdow, 24
Lundy, Jacob, 29, 32
   Reuben, 31, 32, 33
   Samuel, 29, 32
   Thomas, 29, 31, 32
Lupick, George, 89
Luse, Henry, Capt., 113
Lydecker, Samuel, 43
Lydecker, Esqr.
   Garret, 40
Lyon, David, 97
   Isaac, 93
   John, 64
   Zophar, 113

M

M'Myers, Mary, 114
Mackie, Peter, Mr., 25
Maddock, Thomas, aka "English Tom", 14
Magee, Michael, private, 92
Mahelm, Col., 111
Main, Andrew, 99
   Michael, 87, 89
Mains, Elizabeth, 99
   Michael, 86
Maloney, Capt., 89
Man, Abraham, 74, 75, 77
   David, 77, 81
   Mathias, 81
   Sarah, 81
   Thomas, 81
Man, Jr.
   Thomas, 33
Mann, John, 33
   Levi, 37
   Richard, 37

INDEX

Wm., 33
Manning, 1, 2, 4, 5, 7, 8, 9, 10, 15, 16, 17, 18, 19, 20, 21, 22, 23, 24, 25, 26, 39, 40, 41, 42, 43, 44, 45, 48, 50, 51, 53, 55, 59, 61, 62, 63, 64, 65, 66, 67, 68, 69, 70, 73, 74, 81, 82, 84, 85, 86, 88, 89, 91, 98, 99, 101, 102, 103, 105, 113, 114, 115, 116
  Abraham, 42
  Benj., 79
  Benjamin, 1
  Benjin., 51
  Capt., 66
  Clarkson, 77
  Mr., 68, 72, 85, 114
  Nathan, 28, 29
  William, 25
Manning, Esqr.
  Benjamin, 15
Mansfield, Abraham, 117
  Jos., 98
Margeson, Richard, 59
Margison, Richard, 19, 20, 21
Marigson, Richard, 23
Mariner, William, 96
Marlett, John, 109
Marpole, Northrop, 115
Marpoll, George, 51
  Northop, 64
  Northrop, 51
  Northup, 59
Marrinus, David, 58
Marsh, Capt., 92
  Captain, 24
  Christopher, Capt., 89
  Elias, 79, 81, 83

Ephraim, 53
Esther, 74, 75
Jehiel, 75
Martin, 89
  Isaac, 28, 58
  Jay, 48
  John, 15, 16, 89
  Joseph, 89
  Margaret, widow, 29
  Mr., 29
Marton, John, 89
Mash, Ephraim, 52
Massig, Peter, 39
Master, Geo. Capt., 89
Matox, Robert, 51
Matthews, Mr., 96
Mattock, Wm., 83
Mattox, George, 98
Maxin, Nathan, 85
Maxwell, General, 10
  Wm., 101
Maypowder, Wm., 64
Mc Calvin, Wm., 107
Mc Cartney, John, miler, 75
Mc Cowan, John, 58
McArthur, John, 89
McCafferty, Joseph, 89
McCall, Duncan, 90
McCartney, John, miller, 73
McClan, Andrew, 31
McClanagan, Jas., 98
McClean, Andrew, 33
  Hugh, 111
  John, 112
McClearly, Andrew, 72
McClease, Cornelius, 98
  Mrs., 98
McCollam, Capt., 88
  Wm., Captain, 89
McCollom, Jacob, 28
  Mr., 29
McCollum, Capt., 89
  Jacob, 108
  William, 88
McCord, Jas., 59, 60
  Wm., 59

McCowen, John, 59
McCrakan, Wm., 36
McCue, Serg., 61
McCurry, Malcolm, 93
McDaniel, Hugh, 59
McDermott, Wm., 63
McDonald, Alexander, 63, 68, 113
  David, 5
  Major, 110
McDonald, Esqr.
  Daniel, 37
McDonals, Esqr.
  Daniel, 37
McGabon, John, 98
McGalvin, William, 107
McGee, Francis, 30
  Mr., 63
McGennis, Richard, 83
McGillis, Gillis, 98
McGinness, John, 27
McGinnis, John, 34
McGlocklin, George, 58
McKinstey, Mathias, 36
McLean, Margaret, 43
  Margt., 43
  Wm., 60
McMackin, Andrew, 70, 84
McMullen, Daniel, 59
McMurray, William, 12
McNelly, Patrick, 82
McPherson, Nathaniel, 35, 38
McWhorter, Rev., 34, 75
Mead, John, 110
  John, Capt., 90
Meait, Isaac, 14
Medder, James, 49
Mee, John, 4, 54, 59
Meeker, 56
  John, 63, 66
  Jos., 100
  Major, 63, 99
  Mr., 29
  Samuel, 72

INDEX

Samuel, Major, 28
Meelick, Peter, 36
    Philip, 36, 37
Meerakey, Wm., 33
Mehelm, 16, 21, 25, 26,
        27, 33, 34, 35,
        36, 37, 43, 44,
        46, 47, 50, 52,
        53, 54, 55, 56,
        57, 58, 59, 60,
        67, 68, 69, 70,
        71, 97, 105, 106,
        107, 110, 112
    Col., 111
    John, 1, 42, 46, 47, 51,
        79
    Mr., 36, 57, 96
Meldrum, John, 10
Mercer, Archibald, 85,
        114
Mercereau, Mr., 96
Merit, Isaac, 13
Merlet, Abraham, 85
Merrit, Abijah, 37
Michaeldeed, George, 74
Michaldeed, George, 74
Middleton, Nathaniel, 83
Mifflin, Maj. Gen., 26
    Major, 18, 19, 20, 21
Mildrum, John, 5, 9
Miles, Thos., 59
Miller, Alexander
        Edward, 85
    Francis, 25
    Jacob, 89
    Mrs., 67
    Thos., 114
    Timothy, 112
Mills, Andrew, 76
    Israel, 89
    Jedadiah, Lieut., 45
    John, 31, 32, 60, 61
    Nehemiah, 111
Mingin, Joseph, 88
Minor, Samuel, 90
Misener, John, 32

Misner, John, 31
    Peter, 31, 33
Mitchel, John, 109
    Mrs., 109
Molisson, David, 72
Moncrieff, Major, 96
Montgomery, Alexander, 6
Montgomery, Esqr.
    Wm., 56
Moody, James, 43
Moore, Capt., 70, 105, 107
    John, 112
    Joseph, 76
    Mrs., 67
    Samuel, Mrs., 69
    Wm., 59
MooreCapt., 105
Moores, David, 98
    Mrs., 85
    Saml., 48
    Samuel, 85
    Sany., 64
Moote, George, 112
More, Henry, 57
Morehouse, John, 33
Morgan, Andrew, 63
    Benjamin, 28
    Capt., 60, 96
    Col., 45, 46
    James, Capt., 59
    John, 98
Morgan, Esq.
    Benjamin, 24
Morris, Amos, 9
    Asa, 115
    Chief Justice, 25
    Col., 19
    Eva, 116
    Israel, 16, 17, 102
    Jacob, 91
    James, 30, 52
    John, 62, 80, 100
    Peter, 77
    Susanna, 115
    Zeph., 83
    Zephaniah, 114

Morrison, Capt., 108
Morse, 77
    Anthony, 73, 74, 75
    Esther, 73
    Jehiel, 74
    Johiah[?], 73
    Joseph, 73
    Joseph, Junr., 74
Morse, Jr.
    Joseph, 63, 73, 75
Morse, Jun.
    Joseph, 76
Morse, Junr.
    Joseph, 79
Morshan, Aaron, 71
    Mary, widow, 71
Mount, Ebert, 82
    Evert, 82
    George, 7
    Michael, 6
    Moses, 5
Mourisson, Francis, 16
    Henry, 16
Mouse, Jacob, 87, 88
Moyland, Col., 107
Muckleroy, Archibald, 6
    Mr., 5, 6
Mulford, Christopher,
    117
Munson, John, 45
    John, Col., 43
Munster, Col., 71
Murray, Daniel, 87, 89
Mushback, John, 31
Musher, James, 50
Mushpan, John, 29
Myers, George, 52, 53, 59
    Joseph, 108

N

Nadros, Nathl., 100
Nailor, Benjamin, 83
Navins, Patrick, 70
Neal, John, 52
    Thomas, 33, 34
    Thompson, 52
Neffis, George, 115

INDEX

Negro Man, 87
Neigh, James, 108
Neighbour, Leonard, 33
Neighbur, Leonard, 34
Neilson, Capt., 96
    Col., 103, 114
Nevens, Patrick, 65
Nevill, James, 17
Nevins, Ellinor, 60
Nevius, David, 106
Newbolt, William, 2
Newcomb, Gen., 90
    Webster, 98
Newman, William, 19, 21, 23
    Wm., 39, 59
Nichols, Margaret, 31, 40
Nicols, Coll., 62
Niller, Wm., 67
Nisbett, Robt., 37
Nitzer, William, 33, 36
Nixon, Robert, 58
Noakes, Walter, 66
Norris, James, 53
    Robert, 26
    Wm., 85
North, John, 5, 6
    William, 5, 6
Norton, William, 13, 14, 16, 17
Nutt, William, 90
Nuttman, James, 27, 29, 34

O

O'Bullion, Dr., 110, 111
    Ja., Dr., 111
    James, Dr., 111
O'Hara, John, 108
O'Harra, Capt., 23
O'Harry, Henry, 94
O'Riley, Thos., 94
Oart, Christian, 34
Obart, Peter, 15
Odell, Samuel, 6
Odgen, Isaac, 27
Odgen, Esqr.

Abraham, 92
Oest, Christian, 33
Ogden, Abraham, 40, 80
    Col., 96
    David, 80
    Deborah, 76
    Isaac, 24, 25, 36
    John, 27, 76
    Mr., 85
    Samuel, 9, 27, 40
    Stephen, 93
Ogden, Esqr.
    Abraham, 26
    Samuel, 111
Ogden, Esqr.
    David, 40
Oliphan, Jacob, Captain, 5
Oliver, Samuel, 117
    Wm., sailor, 89
Orsburn, Charles, 108
Osborn, Jacob, weaver, 71
Osborne, John, 81
Osgood, John, 82
Osman, Ziby, 59
Osmun, Benaja, 2
    Ziba, 52
Outwater, Gillium, 40
    Jacobus, 112, 113
    John, 41, 65
Ozenburg, Henry, mariner, 94

P

Pace, Daniel, 35
    Michael, 34, 35
    Wm., 35, 80, 91
Page, Wm., 79
Palmer, Elmer Jona., 57
    Jonathan, 53, 67
    Jonn., 62
Pane, Daniel, 33
Paradise, John, 84, 86
Paral, John, 85
Parcel, Peter, 98
Parent, Thomas, 5
Park, John, 59
Parker, Abraham, 7

    Capt., 89
    Elisha, 76
    George, 89
    Gertrude, Mrs., 59
    Henry, 81
    Ja., 57
    James, 35, 45, 62, 63, 64
    James, Esqr., 47
    Jas., 37, 71, 72
    Josiah, 64, 98
    Mr., 54, 63, 68, 88
    Nathaniel, 59, 108
    Peter, 15, 18, 19
    Thomas, 31, 63
    Thos., 33, 75, 108
    William, 19
Parks, John, 59
    Mr., 53
Parry, Adam, 35
Parsons, Saml., 112
Paterson, 2, 4, 5, 7, 8, 9, 10, 11, 12, 13, 25, 26, 27, 28, 29, 30, 32, 33, 34, 35, 36, 37, 51, 52, 53, 54, 55, 62, 107
    Dick, 9
    Matthew, 5
    Mr., 39
    William, 1, 5
    Wm., 51, 79
Paton, Jas., 81
Patre, William, 33
Patterson, James, 101
    Mr., 87
    Peter, 101
    Thomas, Capt., 19
Paul, Wm., 59
Paulese, John, 80, 83
Paulinson, John, 57, 61, 65
Paulis, John, 90, 94, 96
Paulison, John, 31
Paulson, William, 53

INDEX

Pawlison, john, 45
Paxton, Jas., 82
Peacock, Jos., 89
Pearce, Joseph, 21
Pearson, Elihu, 89
   John, 83
   Widow, 78
   William, 79
Peck, Jacobus, 31, 62
   Samuel, 31
Peel, John, 98
Pegg, Joseph, 58, 59, 61
Peirce, James, 19
   Joseph, 19
Penn, Governor, 54
   John, 115
   Mr., 64
Penry, John, 64
Perkins, Major, 97
Perry, Adam, 33
   Peter, 45
Perry, Samuel, 36
Peterson, William B., Dr., 30
Pettit, Charles, 29, 30
   Mr., 81
   Nathl., 30
Pew, James, 98
   Mw., 33
   Rhody, 98
   Stephen, 33
   Thomas, 33
   William, 33
Phar, Thomas, 3
Philips, Ephraim, 6
   Gabriel, 33
   Thomas, 24
Philipse, Thos., 88
Phillips, Gabriel, 34
Philpse, Thos., 84
Pickerson, David, 115
Pickins, Andrew, 62
Pickle, Nicholas, 59
Pickles, Frederick, 59
Pierce, Joseph, 59
Pierson, Azel, 58

Isaac, 117
   Jos., Capt., 40
Pine, Nathan, 60
Pinkerton, David, 114
Pinson, Samuel, 47
Pipit, Moses, 83
Pitney, Benjamin, 78, 79
Pizer, John, 33
Pizor, John, 35
Plumb, Benjamin, 107
Polhemus, Capt., 117
Pollock, Thomas, 4
   Thos., 59
Pope, John, 2
Porter, William, 33
   Wm., 34
Potter, 34
   Col., 43
   Isaac, 4
   Maj., 66, 69
   Major, 73
   Reuben, 85
Poulieson, John, 62
Pound, Benjamin, 45, 46
Powel, Thomas, 14
Powell, Thos., 88
Powelson, John, 43
Powers, John. Dr., 65
Powlison, John, 45
Price, Anthony, 100
   Ebenezer, 100
   Wm., 58
   Wm., sailor, 89
Priest, Robert, 107
Puce, Daniel, 33
   William, 33
Puce, Jr.
   Michael, 33
Puecell, Patrick, miller, 73
Puessel, Patrick, miller, 75
Pulaski, Gen., 82
Pumeroy, John, 93
Putnam, Gen., 2, 4, 7, 13, 15
   General, 1, 18
Pyat, Jas., 60
Pyatt, Jas., 70

Q

Quackenbush, John, 40
Quail, William, 50
Queen, Hugh, 98
Quick, Jacobus, 107, 112
   Jacobus, Capt., 99
Quigg, David, 93
Quigley, Capt., 58, 101
Quigly, Capt., 88, 89
Quimby, Josiah, 25

R

Ramsden, Wm., 89
Randle, Reuben, 44
Randolph, Col., 7
   Jacob, 66
   Joatham, 66
   Joseph, 66
   Mr., 3
   Reuben, 66
Rangan, Daniel, 45
Rapalje, Garret, 17, 18
   George, 18
   Gerge, 17
   Gerrit, 109
   Mr., 110
Rapelje, Gerrit, 110
Rapelyie, Anna, 53
   Richard, 53
Rappelje, Gerrit, 109
Rattan, David, 91
Rawson, William, 87
   Wm., 86, 90, 91
Reach, Matthew, 91
Reckless, Isaac, 81
Redman, Woolingston, 84
Reed, Asher, 31
   Aza, 32
   Bowes, Col., 8, 13, 82, 97
   Col., 81
   Joseph, 28, 29
   Wm., 74
Rees, Thomas, 54
   Thos., 59
Reider, Thos., 72

INDEX

Rerick, Conrad, 36
   Coonrad, 33
Reynold, Thos., Col., 7
Reynolds, George, Lieut., 53
   William, cooper, 75
   Wm., cooper, 73
Reynolds, Esqr.
   Thomas, 5
Rhinehart, Adam, 33
Rice, Nicholas, 81, 82
   Thomas, 81
   Wm., 59
Richmond, Abrm., 98
   John, 67, 70, 90
   Mrs., 103
Rickey, Israel, 111
Rickman, Evert, 91
Riddle, John, 10
Ridley, William, Capt., 94
Riggs, John, 64, 117
Riker, Felia, 40
Rinear, Abel, 106
   Thos., 106
Rineer, Able, 113
   Thos., 113
Rittenhouse, Abner, 60
   Edmund, 60
   William, 60
Robbins, Richard, 6
Roberds, Joseph, 97
Roberts, Jacob, 17
   Joseph, 106
   Palmer, Lt., 101
   Silas, 16
Robins, Isaac, 61
   Jonathan, 59
   Richard, 8, 9, 30, 32
Robinson, George, 105
   John, 27, 29, 34
   Major Genl., 67
Rockhill, John, 35
Rockhill, Esqr.
   John, 61
Rocloffson, Laurence, 33, 35
Rocloff, 36
Rodney, Elizabeth, 39
   Howard, 39
Rogers, Abner, 1
   Isaac, 1
Roloffson, Rocloff, 33
Romine, Elias, 91
Romyn, Elias, 91
Rosbrook, Robert, 30
Roscow, William, 82
Rose, Jacob, 33
Rosecrans, Col., 96
Rosin, Herman, 76
   William, 82
Ross, David, 58
   Joseph, 72
Ross, Esqr.
   John, 52
Rossell, Zachary, Mr., 17
Rotor, Jacob, 1
Rowland, Jacob, 45
Royal, Sarah, 114
Royell, Zechariah, 51
Rozel, Zachary, & wife, 16
Runyon, Daniel, 46
   John, 72
   Rubon, 72
   Rune, 72
Russel, Thomas, 55, 70
Russell, Thomas, 55
Ruth, Christian, 59
Rutherford, Catherine, Mrs., 51
   Mr., 51, 63, 68
   Walter, 37, 45, 62, 63, 64, 71, 72
   Walter, Esqr., 47
Rutherford, Esqr.
   Walter, 57, 63
Ryely, john, 59
Ryerse, Esqr.
   George, 41
Ryerson, Ricd., 89
Rynear, Abel, 110
   Thos., 110
Rynile, John, 49

S

Saffen, Thos., 66
Safrene, David, 33
   Frederick, 33
Safrene, Senr.
   Frederick, 33
Sagar, John, 33
Sager, Henry, 33
Saltar, Joseph, 4
Salter, Joseph, 3
Sands, Mr., 11
   Wm., 10
Sarch, Simon, 94
Saunders, Peter, 43, 44, 46
Saunderson, Egbert, 46
   Peter, 46
Savage, Mr., 3, 6
Saxton, Chas., 56
   Jarod, 71
Sayer, Lydia, 31
Sayers, Samuel, 45
Sayre, Nathaniel, 115
   Patience, widow, 115
Sayres, Lydia, 40
Schackelton, Richard, 28
Schackleton, Richard, 30
Schamerhorn, John, 90
Schenck, 99
   Peter, 88
Schenk, 99, 101, 102, 103, 114, 115, 116, 117
   Abm., 105
   John, 71
   Joseph, 115
   Mr., 114
Schenk, Esqr.
   Peter, 99
Schultz, Jacob, 59, 61
   Peter, 61
Schuyler, Aaron P., 30
   Arent, 43
   Gen., 16, 17
   Jacob, 38

INDEX

John, 38
Scot, John, 69
Scudder, 1, 2, 5, 7, 8, 9, 11, 12, 13, 15, 16, 17, 18, 19, 21, 22, 26, 27, 28, 29, 30, 32, 33, 34, 35, 48, 50, 53, 54, 55, 62
   Capt., 50
   Col., 10, 18, 25, 62, 63, 66
   Major, 13
   Nathaniel, 1
   Nathaniel, Esqr., 14
   Nathl., 51
   Wm. Lt. Col., 56
Seabrook, Maj., 2
Seaburne, John, 114
Seagrave, George Augustus, 30
Seal, John, 114
Sealy, Major, 44
Seaman, Wm., 88, 107
Sears, John, 19, 20, 21, 23, 59
Sebring, Justice, 37
Seely, Col., 66, 68, 73, 74, 76, 77, 79, 86
Seeple, Peter, 36
Sego, Saml., 36
Segor, Adam, 36
Selby, Saml., 37
Sergeant, Andrew, 39
   David, 39
Serooss, Jacob, 60
Serren, Jessie, 108
Serring, Jas., 78
Serrings, Jas., 84
Serterthand, John, 98
Servess, Jacob, 61
Severn, John, 9
Shagor, Mary, 31
Shaler, Capt., 16

Timothy, Capt., 15
Shankel, Leonard, 33
Shanket, Adam, 33
Shannon, Daniel, 59
   John, 59, 108
Sharp, Anthony, 33, 35
   Anthony, Maj., 58
   George, 33, 36
   Isaac, 13
   Jacob, 33
   John, 33, 36
   Mathias, 39
   Morrice, 33
   Morris, 33
Sharpe, Henry, 46
Sharpenstein, Morrice, 34
Shatwell, Joseph, 115
Shaw, John, 30, 36
   John, Capt., 29
Shea, Joseph, 36
Shenck, John P., 72
Shepard, Catherine, 95
Shepherd, Wm., 59
Sherard, John, 91
Sherman, Thos., 11
Shever, John, 89
Shewd, Samuel, 32
Shight, Henry, 43
Shiler, Philip, 33
Shipman, Matthais, Lt. Col., 58
Shizzler, Henry, 30
Shoemaker, Gunrod, 87
   Thomas, 53
   Thos., 59
   Wm., 53
Shoope, Henry, 44
Shoot, William, Capt., 101
Shoudon, Wm., 72
Shoulder, Jacob, 87, 90, 91
Shreeve, Esqr.
   Israel, Col., 2
Shreive, Col., 88
Shreve, Col., 111
Shrewer, Col., 53
Shults, Jacob, 58

Philip, 58
Shultz, Phillip, 59
Shupe, Henry, 46
Shurley, Wm., 59
Sickle, Abraham, 39
Sickles, Zachariah, 3
Silback, Coonrad, 24
Siloy, Samuel, 36
Silpan, Conrad, 23
Simmons, Capt., 95, 100, 109
   Mr., 105
Simonson, Simon, 31, 43, 44, 45
Singleton, John, 88
Sinnickson, Mr., 115
Sip, Negor Man, 19
Sirran, Jesse, 100
Skelton, Jos., 63
   Joseph, 69
Skill, Samuel, 83
Skillman, Geradus, 107
Skinner, Cort., Mr., 54
   Genl., 57, 65
   Timothy, 30
Slack, Henry, 29
   Job, 29
Slater, Joseph, 60
   Saml., 57
Sleby, Saml., 37
Sliger, George, 35
Sliker, George, 33
   Laurence, 33
Sloan, Capt., 89
   James, 16, 17
   William, 103
Slocum, John, 15, 19
Smaley, David, 76
Smith, 57, 58, 59, 60, 61, 66, 67, 68, 69, 70, 71, 72, 73, 74, 75, 76, 77, 91, 92, 108, 109, 110, 111, 112
   Aaron, 58, 59
   Abraham, 13

INDEX

Benj., 86
Benjamin, 88
Capt., 92
Clarke, 114
Ezekiel, 63, 68, 69
Henry, 24, 33, 36
Hugh, 88
Hugh, mate, 89
Isaac, 35
Jacob, 24
James, 26, 45
Job, 31
John, 53, 58, 59, 66, 88
Joseph, 52, 53, 59, 77
Joseph, cooper, 73, 75, 85
Judge, 56
Michael, 31, 42
Mr., 66
Nathaniel, 81, 82
Nicholas, 24
Peter, 33
Peter, Dr., 90
Richard, 8
Samuel, 33, 35, 93
Tallman, 8, 12
Thomas, 13
Thos., 87
Watres, 86
Willam, 12
William, 6, 12, 13, 52, 109
William, Mrs., 69
Wm., 6, 11, 48, 73, 95, 109
Wm. P., 51, 79
Smith, Esqr.
  Daniel, 31
  William P., 57, 105
Smock, Peter, 31
Smyth, Abraham, 77, 78
  John, 78, 108
  Joseph, 78
Smyth, Esqr.
  John, 113

Sneider, Christian, 108
  Martin, 108
Snider, Christian, 59
  Elias, 59
  Martin, 59
  Peter, 53, 59
Snooke, Casper, 30
Snowden, Richard, 21
Soullard, John, 87
Soverrign, David, 36
Soyier, Jacob, 91
Sparks, Esqr.
  John, 16
Speaker, 62
  Mr., 9, 64, 65, 66, 67, 68, 69, 70, 71, 72, 81, 84, 85, 90, 91, 97, 99, 101, 102, 106, 107, 114, 115
Spencer, Mrs. Oliver, 79
  Oliver, Col., 32, 79
Spier, Abraham, 58
Spinning, Benjamin, 90, 91
  John, 90, 91
Sproul, John, 98
Sreider, James Martin, 50
St. Clair, John, 38
  Joseph, 35
Stager, John, 46
Stages, Mary, 40
Stagg, Isaac, 66, 70
  Richard, 16
Stanton, Richard, 20
Stapleton, Doctor, 15
Star, David, 74
Starke, Col., 112
Start, John, 45
Steel, John, 36
Stelle, Thompson, 25
Stephenson, John, 31
Sterling, Jas., 58
Stevens, James, 45
  John, 88
  William, 109
Stevens, Esqr.
  John, Hon., 86

Stevenson, Thomas, 59
Steward, Bickley, 1
  Edward, 84
Stewart, Edward, 89
  John, 45, 46
  Pricilla, 69
  Priscilla, 69
Stile, Senr.
  Jacob, 33
Stiles, Junr.
  Jonn., 97, 116
Still, Abel, 114
Stillwel, Obidiah, 85
Stillwell, Capt., 7
Stine, Jacob, 33, 34
  John, 33, 34
  Martin, 33
Stockton, John, 63
  Joseph, 63
Stockton, Esqr.
  Richard, 70
Stoddard, Capt., 94
Stoothoff, Cornelius, 91
Stout, Capt., 36, 37, 56, 103
  Elijah, 85
  Reeder, 57
  Samuel, Capt., 103
Stout, Esqr.
  Nathan, 9
Stoutan, Joseph, 64
Stouten, Joseph, 117
Strawbridge, George. mariner, 94
Strubel, Tedrick, 34
Stryker, Capt., 93
  Jonas, 72
  Peter, 112
Stubel, Tretrick, 33
Stukey, Daniel, 10
Sullivan, Col., 83, 84, 88
  Genl., 48
Sutton, David, Rev., 61
  Nathan, 9
  Nathen, 11
  Richard, 33

INDEX

William, 55
Suydam, Charles, 52
   George, 51
Swackhamer, Samuel, 33
Swartfeller, Matthias,
   111, 112
Sweeney, John, 94
Sweeny, John, 95
Sweeton, Andrew, 83
   john, 86
   John, 87
Swim, Vincent, 108
Symmes, 1, 2, 4, 5, 7, 8,
   9, 10, 15, 17, 18,
   19, 21, 22, 23,
   24, 27, 28, 29,
   30, 32, 33, 34,
   35
   Col., 9, 10, 25, 63
   John Cleves, 1
   Justice, 4, 5, 7
   Mr., 26, 27
Symmons, Capt., 112

T

Tallman, 52, 62, 67, 81,
   83, 85, 86, 89,
   90, 91, 102, 103,
   113, 116, 117
   Harmanns, 62
   James, 58
   James, Capt., 15
   Mr., 88
   Peter, 51, 79
   Stephen, 8
Talman, 62, 63
   Mr., 81
Tapscott, Jas., 83
Tatticker, Frederick, 30
Taylor, Ann, 99
   Edward, 64, 65, 75,
   97, 102
   Fenwick, 34
   Fenwicke, 33
   George, 64
   Jeremiah, 64
   John, 3, 38, 57

John, Major, 15
   Joseph, 99
   Mr., 66
   Robert, Dr., 35
   Wm. (son of Wm.), 11
Taylor, Esqr.
   Edward, 9, 10, 12
   john, 8
   John, 98
   Robert, 39
Taylor, Junr.
   George, 98
Teelte, Elias, 59
Teeple, John, 37
   John, tavern keeper, 37
Teeplenn, John, 36
Templeton, William, 95
Ten,
   Eyck
      Conrad, 62
Ten Eyck, Coenradt, 109
   Frederick, 68
   Fredk., 92
Teple, Peter, 69
Terhune, Gerret, 64
Thatcher, Barthlw., 35
   Bartolomew, 60
   Edmund, 29, 30
   Jas., 57
   Jonas, 58
   Joseph, 7, 9, 10
   William, 57
Thom, Henry, 51
Thomas, Abel, 97
   James, 97
   Mathias, 33
   Matthias, 36
Thompson, 15
   Isaac, 110
   John, 36, 37, 83
   Newcomb, 85
   Robert, 11
   Thomas, 4
   Thos., 50, 98
   William, 19, 107
Thomson, John, 57, 79, 81

Newcomb, 84
Thorn, Isaac, 55, 56
   Jacob, 56
Thorne, Abraham, 116
Thornhill, Wm., 38
Thorpe, Morris, 79
   Norris, 81, 83
Throckmorton, John, 19
Throckmorton, Esqr.
   Joseph, 19
Thron, Jacob, 55
Throp, William, 8
Tice, William, 11, 12
Tichenor, John, 100
Tidbit, Edward, 92
Tiers, Anraham, 16
Tifford, Gertrude, 26
Tilton, Ezekiel, 98
   John, 98
   Mrs., 98
Tincke, Conred, 105
Titus, Philip, 59
   Samuel, 84
Todd, John, 39
Tomkin, John, 86
Tomlinson, John, 81
Tont, Robert, 93
Torhune, Stephanus, 91
Totten, John, 106
Tovert, Jacob, 33
Townshend, Benjamin,
   50
   Capt., 93
   Levi, 50
Trimer, David, 33
   Jacob, 33
   Leonard, 33
   Mathias, 33
   Nicholas, 33
   William, 33
Trimmer, David, 36
   Wm., 35
Tronk, Henry, 60
Troop, John, 43, 45
   John, Lieut., 44
Troup, Esther, Mrs., 92

INDEX

John, 92
Tuthill, 16
Tucker, Capt., 81, 88
   Samuel, 84
   Wm., 85
Tucker, Junr.
   Samuel, 85
Tunison, Cornelius,
   Capt., 39
Turner, Jeremiah, 60, 70
   Nathan, 71
   William, 94
Tuthill, Justice, 26
Tuthill, Junr.
   Edmund, 37
   Ephraim, 37
Tuttle, Benjamin, 44, 46

U

Updicke, Birgoon, 72
   Lawrence, 72
   Peter, 72

V

Vago, Jacob, 98
Valentine, William, 2
Van Anglin, John, 3
Van Bloricum, Hendrick, 100
Van Borson, David, 75
Van Boskirk, John, 65, 83, 90, 94
Van Brunt, Hendrick, 83, 84
   Nicholas, 116
Van Bryck, Barnardus, 61
   Bernardus, 62
Van Brycke, Barnardus, 65
Van Buren, 43
   Dr., 109
   James, Dr., 30
Van Bursen, David, 80
Van Burson, David, 94
Van Buskirk, Andrew, 30, 42
   Daniel, 31
   John, 57, 61, 62, 80, 96
Van Buskirk, Esqr.
   John, 31
Van Busson, John, 61
Van C[N?]orden, David, 86
Van Camp, Abraham, 55
   Thos., 79
Van Cleaf, Benj., 114
   Wm., 76
Van Cleve, Benjamin, Capt., 71
Van Clief, Aaron, 11
Van Cortlandt, Philip, 8
Van Court, Elias, 93
Van Courtlandt, Col., 31, 34
   Phillip, Collo., 40
Van Courtlandt, Esqr.
   Philip, Col., 47
Van Dike, Jacob, 105, 107
Van Dyne, William, 68
Van Geison, Abraham, 94
   Gerrit, 94
Van Gieson, Abm., 83, 90
   Abraham, 80, 96
   Elizabeth, 50
   Garret, 31, 43, 62, 65
   Gerret, 96
   Gerrit, 83, 90
Van Klyne, Penelope, 113
Van Mater, John, 11, 12
   Mr., 107
Van Matter, John, 9
Van Nest, John, 64
   Justice, 107
Van Norden, Gabriel, 42, 45, 57, 61, 62, 75, 80
Van Orden, David, 77
   Gabriel, 31
   Henry, 77
   John, 39
Van Order, David, 78
   Henry, 78
Van Ripen, Simeon, 91
Van Riper, Adrain, 108
   Altia, 31
   Altie, 40
   Libitie, 40
   Thos., 100
Van Saan, Cornelius, 25, 26
   Isaac, 26
Van Saen, Cornelius, 25
   Isaac, 25
Van Sean, Isaac, 25
Van Sickle, Jacob, 39
Van Sicklen, Lambert, 37
Van Zandt, Wynant, 57
Van Zant, Mr., 63
   Winant, 63
   Wynant, 72
Vanburen, James, Dr., 43
   Jas., Dr., 42
Vanbuskirk, David, 42
   John, 45
Vanbusson, John, 57
Vancamp, Thos., 80
Vance, Samuel, 95
Vancourt, John, 99
Vanderbelt, Jacob, 57
Vanderhule, Gershom, 99
Vanderlink, Henry, 99
Vanderveer, Cornelius, 67
Vandervender, Christopher, 36
   Jacob, 36, 38
Vandike, Henry, Col., 99
   John, 107
   Lt. Col., 11, 25
Vanduyn, Wm., 91
Vandycke, Henry, Col., 113
Vandyke, Wm., 82
Vangieson, Abraham, 61
   Baraham, 57
   Garret, 41, 45, 57, 61
   Gerrit, 80
Vanguson, Abraham, 45, 46
   Cornelius, 46
   Garret, 45
   Isaac, 46

INDEX

Vanhorne, Laurance, 31
Vanmeter, Joseph, 98
Vanorden, Gabriel, 45
Vanriper, Labbitee, 31
Vansant, Gerrit, 103
Vaught, Christopher, 10
   John, 10
Ver Bryck, Bernardus, 96
   Samuel, 62, 65, 96
Verbryck, Bernardus, 80
   Samuel, 80, 94
   William, 4
Verbryske, Barnabus, 57
Verbyrck, Bernardus, 94
Vertondyck, Jacob, 65
Vervalier, Henry, 66
Vice President, Mr., 88
Vlauvelt, Jacobus, 61
Vliet, John, Major, 109
Von Mater, Benj., 107
Vooght, Christ., 60
   Christopher, 61
   John, 60
Voorhies, Abraham, 62
   John, 64
   Oakie, 60
Voorhis, Abraham, 109
   Capt., 96
Voorhise, Capt., 114
   John, 71, 105
   Oakley, 113
   Okey, 91
   Stephen, 114
Vreeland, Enoch, 78
   Isaac, 78
   Peter, 89
Vreelandt, Derrick, 31
   Enoch, 76
   Peter, 76
Vreland, Deich, 110
   Dirck, 113
Vroom, Peter D., 4

W

Waddel, Henry, Mr., 50
Waddell, Harry, 35
Waddelle, Henry, 4
Wager, Allen, 32
Walder, John, 33
Waldorf, John, 36
Walker, David, 11
   Mesheck, 43
Waller, Robert, 116
Wallington, Phebe, Mrs., 22
Waln, Mr., 110
   Richard, 35, 55, 112
   Richd., 110
Walton, Captain, 1
   Elisha, Capt., 1
Walts, George, 36
Ward, Abigail, 40
   Capt., 89
   Hannah, 24, 26
   Hannah, Mrs., 79
Wardel, Solomon, 102, 115
Wardell, John, 3
Warford, James, 60
   Moses, 60
Warner, John, 60
Warrington, Fras., 89
Wars, John, 31
Warthandicke, Jacob, 62
Washington, Gen., 3, 8, 10, 89
   General, 5, 28, 44
   Genl., 73, 74, 87, 89, 95, 101
   George, 24
   George, Genl., 80
Waterhouse, Henry, 60, 61
   Hezekiah, 60
Watson, George, 98
   Thomas, 2, 5
   Thos., 5
Watson, Esqr.
   Thomas, 2
Watts, George, 27
   Thos., 82
Wear, John, 33
Weatherby, 15
   Henry, 9
Weaver, Henry, 39
   Joseph, 7
   Joseph, Capt., 58
   Peter, 39
   William, 77
   Wm., 78
Webb, Capt., 6, 16, 17
Webster, john, 58
Weekley, Samuel, 89
Weeks, Hannah, 40
Weighman, Henry, 29
Weir, Wm., 38
Weis, Philip, 36
Weiser, Jacob, 90
Welcher, John, 16
   Thomas, 16, 41
Wells, James, 14, 49, 74, 116
   Jas., 75, 79, 91
   Mrs., 42
   Rachel, Mrs., 116
   Samuel, 26
   Saml., 42
   Samuel, 47
Welsh, David, 33
Welsh, Junr.
   William, 33
   Wm., 34
Welsh, Senr.
   William, 33
Wescott, Richard, 28
West, Uriah, 108
   Urich, 100
Westbrooke, Aaron Ross, Lieut., 28
Westervelt, Casparus, 42, 44
   Caspavas, 31
   Jacob, 66
   John, 66
   Peter, 66
Wetherbee, 22
Wetherby, 16
   Edmund, 1
   Henry, 10, 11, 12, 13
Wharton, Mr. President, 11
   President, 14

INDEX

Wharton, Esqr.
  Thos., 93
Wheeler, Elizabeth, 24, 26
White, Elea, 50
  John, 36, 37
  Robert, 63, 68, 69
  Thomas, 33, 35, 59
Whiteacre, John, 109
  Jonathan, 110
Wick, Moses, 95
  Wm., 95, 116
Widdonfield, Henry, 81
Wieks, Joanna, 31
Wilburne, Edward, 114
Wilgurst, John, 31
  William, 31
Willet, John, 102
  Thos., 38
Willets, James, 58
  James, Capt., 58
  John, 33
Willett, John, 97
Willgus, John, 32
  William, 32
William, John, mariner, 94
Williams, 20
  Abraham, 86, 89
  Daniel, 13
  Edmund, 4, 8
  Giles, 21
  John, 94
  Mary, 54
  Mrs., 43
  Nathaniel, 54
  Thomas, 18
Williams, Jr.
  John, 8
Williamson, Capt., 96
  Cornelius, 7, 9, 10
  Genl., 95
  John, 89
Williamson, Esqr.
  Mathias, 94
Willis, John, 27, 31, 66, 69, 70
Willot, Thomas, 36
Willson, Alexander, 14
  Jonn., 33
Wilsh, Senr.
  Wm., 34
Wilson, Abuson, 31
  Benjamin, 2
  Ebenezer, 33
  Jacob, 116
  Jas., 83
  Jonathan, 31
  Jos., 116
  Mr., 93
  Richard, 10, 12
  Thos., 63, 68
  Wm., 89, 100
Wilson, Senr.
  Gabriel, 29
  Robert, 31
Winckler, John, 37
Winds, Brig. Gen., 73
  Brig. Genl., 86, 110
  Brig. General, 28
  Col., 28
  Genl., 28, 84, 96, 103, 113
Wise, Jacob, 36
Wiser, Philip, 33
Wiser, Junr.
  Philip, 33
Wist, Stephen, 11
Witlock, John, 114
Wolley, Thomas, 3
Wood, 95
  Abigail, 31
  Ezekiel, 16
  Hezekiah, 3
  Jacob, 75
  Joanna, 43
  Mary, 24, 26
Woodruff, Asher, 67
  Caleb, 112
  Ezekiel, 67
Woodruff, Jr.
  Ezekiel, 43
Woodward, Anthony, 1, 10, 18, 22, 106, 113
  Anthony, aka"Little Anthony", 108
  Jesse, 5, 6, 7, 8, 10, 30, 32
  Mr., 6
  Nathaniel, 110
  Thomas, 18, 21, 22
  Thomas (son of Anthony), 10
  William, 1
Wooley, Anthony, 9
  John, 9, 31
  Wm., 83
Woolley, Benjamin, 10
Woolverton, Thos., 30
Woortman, John, 110
Wortendyck, Jacob, 57, 61, 80
Worth, Benjamin, 49, 50, 59
  Ellenor, 66
  James, 49, 59
  Saml., 63
Worts, Monice, Mr., 9
Wrench, Mathew, 69
  Matthew, 67, 70
Wright, Austern, 91
  Austin, 77
  Hannah, Mrs., 43
  John, 14
  Mrs., 43
  Richard, 83
  Samuel, 11
  William, 43
Write, Moses, 85
  Moses, Mrs., 85
Wurts, Morrice, 7
Wyants, Joshua, 73
Wynant, Dr., 92
Wynants, Benj., 74
  Benjamin, 74

Y

Yalter, John, miller, 73
Yard, Mr., 101
  Wm., 86

INDEX

Yateman, Peter, 85
Yates, Robert, 72
Yatter, John, miller, 75
York, Thos., 98
Young, David, 59
   Fredk., 33
   Hamilton, 55
   Henry, Lieut., 102
   James, 117
   Peter, 16, 33, 35, 60, 61
   Philip, 107
   Phillip, 64
   William, 33
Younglove, Ezekiel, 99
   Sarah, 99
Youngs, William, 58

Z

Zabriska, Hendrick, 70
   Jas., 43
   John, 42, 43
   Peter, 43
   Yost, 42
Zabriskie, Esqr.
   John, 31
Zane, Isaac, 87, 90, 91
Zebrisci, Jacob C., 41
   Jost, Lieut., 41
Zobrisci, Jost, 41
Zobriski, Benjamin, 91
   Henrick, 66